THE
CASE
for
TRUMP

ALSO BY VICTOR DAVIS HANSON

Warfare and Agriculture in Classical Greece

The Western Way of War

Hoplites (editor)

The Other Greeks

Fields Without Dreams

Who Killed Homer? (with John Heath)

The Wars of the Ancient Greeks

The Soul of Battle

The Land Was Everything

Bonfire of the Humanities (with John Heath and Bruce Thornton)

An Autumn of War

Carnage and Culture

Between War and Peace

Mexifornia

Ripples of Battle

A War Like No Other

The Immigration Solution (with Heather MacDonald and Steven Malanga)

Makers of Ancient Strategy (editor)

The Father of Us All

The End of Sparta: A Novel

The Savior Generals

The Second World Wars

THE
CASE
for
TRUMP

VICTOR DAVIS HANSON

BASIC BOOKS

New York

Basic Books
Hachette Book Group
1290 Avenue of the Americas, New York, NY 10104
www.basicbooks.com

Printed in the United States of America

First Edition: March 2019

Published by Basic Books, an imprint of Perseus Books, LLC, a subsidiary of Hachette
Book Group, Inc. The Basic Books name and logo is a trademark of the Hachette Book
Group.

The Hachette Speakers Bureau provides a wide range of authors for speaking events. To
find out more, go to www.hachettespeakersbureau.com or call (866) 376-6591.

The publisher is not responsible for websites (or their content) that are not owned by the
publisher.

Editorial production by Christine Marra, Marrathon Production Services. www.
marrathoneditorial.org

Book design by Jane Raese
Set in 13-point Bulmer

Library of Congress Control Number: 2018968200

ISBN 978-1-5416-7354-0 (hardcover), ISBN 978-1-5416-7353-3 (ebook)

LSC-C

10   9   8   7   6   5   4

For the "Deplorables"

CONTENTS

PART FOUR
THE ORDEAL, TRIUMPH—AND ORDEAL—
OF PRESIDENT TRUMP

PART FIVE
EPILOGUE

PREFACE

The Case for Trump explains why Donald J. Trump won the 2016 election—and why I and 62,984,827 other Americans (46 percent of the popular vote) supported him on Election Day. I also hope readers of the book will learn why Trump's critics increasingly despise rather than just oppose him. Often their venom reveals as much about themselves and their visions for the country as it does about their opposition to the actual record of governance of the mercurial Trump.

Donald Trump ran as an abject outsider. He is now our first American president without either prior political or military experience. Frustrated voters in 2016 saw that unique absence of a political résumé as a plus, not a drawback, and so elected a candidate deemed to have no chance of becoming president.

The near-septuagenarian billionaire candidate, unlike his rivals in the primaries, did not need any money, and had little requirement in the primaries to raise any from others. Name recognition was no problem. He already was famous—or rather notorious. He took risks, given that he did not care whether the coastal elite hated his guts. These realities unexpectedly proved advantages, given that much of the country instead wanted someone—perhaps almost anyone—to ride in and fix things that compromised political professionals would not dare do. With Trump, anything was now felt by his backers to be doable. His sometimes scary message was that what could not be fixed could be dismantled.

Trump challenged more than the agendas and assumptions of the political establishment. His method of campaigning and governing, indeed his very manner of speech and appearance, was an affront to the Washington political classes and media— and to the norms of political discourse and behavior. His supporters saw the hysterical outrage that Trump instilled instead as a catharsis. His uncouthness, even if it was at times antithetical to their own code of conduct, was greeted by them as a long-needed comeuppance to the doublespeak and hedging that characterized modern politics.

Trump became the old silent majority's pushback to the new, loud progressive minority's orthodoxy. His voters quite liked the idea that others loathed him. The hysterics of Trump's opponents at last disclosed to the public the real toxic venom that they had always harbored for the deplorables and irredeemables. The media and the progressive opposition never quite caught on that trading insults with Donald Trump was unwise, at least if they wished to cling to the pretense that contemporary journalists and politicians were somehow professional and civic minded.

Predictably as president, Trump said and did things that were also long overdue in the twilight of the seventy-three-year-old post-war order. Or as former secretary of state Henry Kissinger remarked in July 2018 of the fiery pot that Trump had stirred overseas, "I think Trump may be one of those figures in history who appears from time to time to mark the end of an era and to force it to give up its old pretense."

Trumpism on the campaign trail and after the election was also a political belief that the interior of the country should not be written off as an aging and irrelevant backwater. It was not its own fault that it had missed out on globalization. Nor had midwestern red and purple states become permanently politically neutered by either new demographics or their own despair at the new centers of cultural and financial power on the coasts. Instead, America's once industrial heartland was poised for a renaissance if given the chance. Voters who believed that promise could in the heartland's eleventh hour still win Trump an election.

Perhaps most importantly, Trump was not Hillary Clinton. After the primaries are over, most presidential elections are rarely choices between seasoned political pros and amateur out-siders, or good nominees versus bad ones. They are decisions about tolerable and less tolerable candidates.

Both Clinton and Trump entered the 2016 race amid scan-dal. But Clinton's miscreant behavior was viewed as quite dif-ferent. She had almost always been in the public eye, either as a first lady, a senator, and secretary of state, or a campaigner for and surrogate of her husband and a candidate herself. In other words, Hillary Clinton's life had been embedded in high-stakes politics. She, like her husband, had leveraged public of-fices to end up a multimillionaire many times over—well apart from the serial scandals of Whitewater, cattle-future specula-tions, the demonization of Bill Clinton's liaisons, the Clinton Foundation's finances, the Benghazi fiasco, the Uranium One deal, the unauthorized use of a private email server as secre-tary of state, and the hiring of Christopher Steele to compile a dossier on Donald Trump. Hillary also somehow became quite rich by monetizing the likelihood that she would be eventually the spouse of the president, or later, and far more lucratively, the president herself.

Trump's sins (e.g., multiple bankruptcies, failed product lines, endless lawsuits, creepy sexual scandals, loud public spats, crude language, and gratuitous cruelty), in contrast, were seen as those of a self-declared multibillionaire wheeler-dealer in private enterprise. His past tawdriness was regrettable and at times he had found himself in legal trouble. But Trump had not yet abused the people's trust by acting unethically while in office—even if the default reason was that he had *never* yet held elected or appointed positions. Voters in 2016 preferred an au-thentic bad boy of the private sector to the public's disingenuous good girl. Apparently, uncouth authenticity trumped insincere conventionality.

Donald Trump's agenda also arose as the antithesis to the new Democratic Party of Barack Obama. After 2008, Democrats were increasingly candid in voicing socialist bromides. And they were many, including open borders, identity politics, higher taxes, more government regulation, free college tuition, single-payer government-run health care, taxpayer-subsidized green energy, rollbacks of fossil-fuel production, and a European Union–like foreign policy. Progressives talked up these leftist visions mostly among themselves without much idea how they sounded to a majority quite unlike themselves. To be called a socialist was now a proud badge of honor, no longer to be written off as a right-wing slur. By 2018, Trump's Democratic critics were not shy about calling for the abolition of the US Immigration and Customs Enforcement and were courting openly avowed socialist candidates.

Yet these supposedly populist proposals were proving an anathema to the traditional working classes of rural America, as well as urban blue-collar industrial workers and many of the self-employed. Democrats also advanced them with a cultural disdain for the lower middle classes and rural people in general. Twenty-first-century progressivism had become increasingly pyramidal, perhaps best called "oligarchical socialism," with the extremely wealthy advocating for redistribution for the poor. Elites not subject to the ramifications of their own policies ruled from on top. The subsidized poor answered them from far below. Both barely disguised a shared disdain for the struggle of most of those in between.

The Republican traditional answer to such Democratic overreach after 2009 had resulted in historic electoral gains in state and local offices, and the recapture of the US Congress. Yet Republicans had not won a presidential vote with a 51 percent plurality since 1988. They had lost the popular vote in five out of the six preceding elections. Something clearly had gone wrong with Republican leadership at the national level. Bob Dole, the late John McCain, Mitt Romney, and other establishmentarians proved hardly effective mastheads.

The Republicans also had their own sort of unpopular dogmas in addition to uninspiring national candidates. Fair trade was seen as less important than free trade. Illegal immigration was largely ignored to ensure inexpensive unskilled labor for businesses. Constant overseas interventions were seen as the necessary wages of global leadership. Huge annual budget deficits were ignored. A powerful and rich United States could supposedly afford both trade deficits and to underwrite ossified military alliances and optional adventures. The culture and concerns of the two coasts mattered more than what was in between, as if both Democrats and Republicans would draw their talent from and serve first those on the Eastern and Western seaboards.

All these themes—who the outlier Trump was and how he behaved, the anger of the red-state interior, the unattractive alternative of Hillary Clinton, the progressive takeover of the Democratic Party, and the inept Republican response to it—frame each chapter of this book.

Yet if candidate Trump should have been elected, does president Trump warrant such confidence? Has he pursued a positive agenda, rather than just being against what the two-party establishment had been for, and has his controversial and often chaotic governance nevertheless proven effective?

At the end of his second year in office, the answer was yes. *The Case for Trump* argues that at home the economy in Trump's first six hundred days was better than at any time in the last decade. Massive deregulation, stepped-up energy production, tax cuts, increased border enforcement, and talking up the American brand produced a synergistic economic upswing, as evidenced by gross domestic product (GDP) growth, a roaring stock market, and near record unemployment. Abroad, Trump restored military deterrence, and questioned the previously unquestionable assumptions of the global status quo, both the nostrums of our friends and the ascendance of our enemies. The obdurate Never Trump Republicans of 2016 by mid-2018 had become either largely irrelevant or had begun to support the Trump agenda.

These themes frame the formal plan of this book. The argument covers the three years since Trump announced his presidential bid in July 2015 to mid-2018, as he neared the end of the second year of his presidency.

Part 1, the first three chapters of the book, explore (1) the nature of a divided America that Trump found and leveraged, (2) the signature issues by which he as a candidate successfully massaged that split, and (3) the clever use of his own person to fuel his often-divisive message.

As for those challenging Trump for the Republican nomination, part 2's three chapters review all the anemic alternatives to Trump that prepared his pathway to election. The steady move leftward of the Democratic Party made victory far easier for Trump. Democrats were no longer much interested in the plight of the white working class.

Early on, Trump also counted on the inability of out-of-touch Republicans to galvanize conservative voters. Republicans had become stereotyped as a party at the national level of persuasive abstractions and logical think-tank theories. Wall Street, the US Chamber of Commerce, and the Republican Party could not convince the lost half of America that doctrinaire agendas would do much for anyone anytime soon.

Just as importantly, Trump argued that both parties were embedded deeply within the shadow government of the "deep state." For Trump, that vague and controversial term could mean almost whatever he wished. Sometimes it was an amorphous bureaucratic beast that had taken on a life of its own to transcend politics and become parasitic. Its main aim was no longer public service, but to survive and multiply. The insidious power and reach of the IRS, of unelected law-making justices, of the intelligence agencies, of the social welfare bureaucracies, and of the regulatory agencies increasingly controlled, frightened, and sickened Americans.

So Trump blasted this "swamp" that, he claimed, had targeted his candidacy. His them-us rhetoric galvanized voters of both parties in a way not seen in the quarter century since the sloppy populism of third-party candidate Ross Perot.

In part 3, I examine Trump's three larger themes that framed his political agenda: America was no longer great; he was certainly not Hillary Clinton; and somebody in some sense "unpresidential" was sorely needed in the White House. Trump nonstop warned of American decline and he promised to make the next generation's lives better than those of their parents'. Trump's "Make America Great" theme, however, was neither rosy optimism nor gloom-and-doom declinism. Instead, it came off to half the country as "can do-ism": an innately great people had let the wrong politicians drive their country into a quagmire. But it still could be led out of the morass to reclaim rapidly its former greatness by simply swapping leaders and agendas. The problem was one of the spirit and mind, not a dearth of resources, enemies at the gates, or a failed economic or social system.

Trump also hammered on the particular unsuitability of the insider Hillary Clinton. He turned Clinton into not just another corrupt politician ("crooked Hillary") or a liberal bogeywoman. She was now also emblemized as a careerist government totem, and thus by extension the icon of what was wrong with conventional American politics.

Both as candidate and president, Trump also was judged by his critics in the media in an ahistorical vacuum, without much appreciation that prior presidents had on occasion adopted his brand of invective without commensurate criticism, given the pre-internet age and a media that was often seen in the past as an extension of the Oval Office. In addition, Trump's method and message could not be separated, either by critics or supporters. If other politicians had adopted his policies, but delivered them in the manner of Jeb Bush or Marco Rubio, then they would have likely failed to get elected, and if elected likely not carried them all out. Yet if different candidates had embraced Bush or Rubio agendas, but talked and tweeted like Trump, they would have certainly flopped even more so.

In part 4, I assess the volatile Trump presidency, which began without a honeymoon. From the morning after his victory, he met hysterical efforts to thwart his agenda and soon to abort his presidency. Unlike prior Republican presidents, Trump saw the hatred of the Left as an existential challenge. As a sometimes former liberal, perhaps Trump was shocked at the animosity he incurred, given that he had always before easily navigated among the cultural and political Left. But now, candidate and president Trump would either defeat the "fake news" press or it would surely crush him. There could be no draw, no truce, no reconciliation. No quarter was asked, none received. Trump never bought into the decorum that a president never stoops to answer cheap criticism. Rather, he insisted that he even must be petty and answer everything and always in kind, or often more crudely than his attackers.

I end part 4 with a critique of Trump's governance through his first eighteen months in office, and show how he achieved initial economic and foreign policy results not seen in a generation.

A brief epilogue speculates on the lasting effect, if any, of Trump's efforts at national renewal in general—and in particular on whether Trumpism has changed the conservative movement or the Republican Party in any lasting way.

I end with a few notes of caution. I wrote the first draft of this book in mid-2018, after about six hundred days of the Trump presidency. Given the failure of the polls in 2016 and a collective loss of confidence in their predictive accuracy, a mostly anti-Trump mainstream media, and Trump's own volatility, it is impossible to calibrate the ultimate fate of the Trump administration or even the course of events in the next week, much less the next 860 days.

One example of this Trump paradox of polling contrary to popular wisdom is illustrative. In mid-July 2018, Trump was pronounced by experts in Washington to have suffered the worst ten days of his presidency. Furor met his supposedly star-crossed Russian summit. Then there was the subsequent clearly sloppy press conference with Russian president Putin in Helsinki, Finland, that earned stinging criticism from even Republican pundits and politicians. Trump traded barbs with his now indicted former lawyer and likely government witness Michael Cohen. CNN released an example of attorney Cohen's secretly recorded old conversations with Trump about possible payments to a long-ago paramour. More media predictions about the course of Robert Mueller's nonending investigation focused on obstruction and conspiracy. Yet in the NBC/WSJ poll, Trump through it all climbed a point to a 45 percent favorability rating—with near-record approval from Republicans. Critics publicly rejoiced that Trump still did not win 50 percent approval, but privately they feared that the paradoxes and ironies that had accompanied his improbable 2016 victory were still poorly understood—and still in play.

Donald Trump's political career started in mid-2015 when he announced his presidential candidacy. Although Trump was a prior tabloid celebrity, and had voiced often conflicting views in print and on television on a wide range of issues, we learned the details of his politics and leadership mostly from three years

of campaigning and governance. Given that paucity of information, for analyses of Trump's rhetoric, agenda, and record I
draw freely on evidence and quotations from *both* his campaign
and brief presidency. That is a legitimate chronological confla-
tion of material for at least two reasons.

So far Trump has proved to be one of the rare presidents
who has attempted to do what he said he would. He has also
not acted much differently in 2017–18 than he said he would
during 2015–16. That continuum is why his critics understandably fear him, and why his hard-core supporters often seem to
relish their terror.

Only after the election did Trump's critics more boldly express their contempt for his supporters. Their disgust was unwise to vent fully when it was still crucial to win swing states.
What blue-state America really felt about Trump's voters in 2016
often fully emerged only in 2017–18, when it was a question not
of winning a close election, but of delegitimizing a presidency.

I often speak of the "Trump voter" or the "Trump base." Yet
those supporters were not necessarily synonymous with the
"Republican base" or even the "conservative base." Instead,
they were a new mishmash of older, loosely defined interests
that often were the mirror images of those of Ross Perot, the
Ronald Reagan candidacy, and the Tea Party. They could be
Democrats, Independents, or (more often) discontented Republicans. Trump could not win the presidency or maintain his
support without them, but he also could *not* succeed only with
them. They were instead the force multipliers that allowed a
Republican president to win in key states thought unwinnable.
And yet they were usually not necessarily assets transferable to
other establishment Republican candidates.

Trump is not just a political phenomenon. His person dom-
inates the news, the popular culture, and the world's attention.
About Trump, no one is neutral, no one calm. All agree that
Trump meant to do something big, either undoing the last half

century of American progressivism, or sparking a cultural and political renaissance like no other president since Franklin Delano Roosevelt, or crashing the traditional American political establishment and its norms of behavior altogether. All knew that he was no Bush, no Clinton or Obama. Americans accepted that reality from the first day they met Trump in his new role as a politician and had their impressions confirmed each day of his presidency.

Finally, I note that I have never met Donald Trump. Nor have I visited the Trump White House. I have never been offered, sought, or accepted any appointment from the Trump administration. Nor have I been in communications with members of the Trump campaign and have not sought out anyone in the administration. Living on a farm in central California can preclude inside knowledge of Washington politics, but, on the upside, it also allows some distance and thereby I hope objectivity.

I wish to thank Jennifer Hanson, Bruce Thornton, David Berkey, Megan Ring, and my literary agents Glen Hartley and Lynn Chu for offering valuable improvements to the manuscript, along with Lara Heimart, my editor at Basic Books, for both her constructive criticism and encouragement. For the past fifteen years I have enjoyed the support of and residence at the Hoover Institution of Stanford University and the encouragement of its former and present directors, John Raisian and Thomas Gilligan. I owe a special debt of gratitude for the continued direct help of Hoover overseers Martin Anderson; Lew Davies; Robert, Rebekah, and Jennifer Mercer; Roger Mertz; Jeremiah Milbank; and Victor Trione, as well as the confidence and support of Roger and Susan Hertog. Roger for over a decade has been a treasured friend who has offered me invaluable insight on a variety of issues.

Trump is a polarizing figure whose very name prompts controversy that soon turns to acrimony. My aim again in *The Case for Trump* is to explain why he ran for president, why he surprised his critics in winning the 2016 Republican primaries and general election, and why, despite media frenzy and the nonstop Twitter bombast, Trump's appointments and his record of governance have improved the economy, found a rare mean between an interventionist foreign policy and isolationism, and taken on a toxic establishment and political culture that long ago needed an accounting.

Victor Davis Hanson
Selma, California

MEET DONALD J. TRUMP

*Ordinary men usually manage public affairs better
than their more gifted fellows.*
—Thucydides, *History of the Peloponnesian War*
(spoken by Cleon, son of Cleaenetus)

On June 16, 2015, voters met sixty-nine-year-old flamboyant
billionaire, and now Republican presidential candidate,
Donald J. Trump at his own eponymous Manhattan high-rise.

The outsider offered no apologies for promising to be the
first successful presidential candidate to have no political experience. Trump came down on his escalator, ready for the beginning of a nonending war with the press and civil strife within
his party. He postured like Caesar easily crossing the forbidden
Rubicon and forcing an end to the old politics as usual.

Trump arrived with few if any campaign handlers. He soon
bragged that he preferred an unorthodox small staff to ensure
immunity from political contamination altogether. He boasted
that he would pay for his own campaign. "I'm using my own
money. I'm not using the lobbyists. I'm not using donors. I
don't care. I'm really rich."

But if the legendarily parsimonious billionaire planned to use mostly his own funds, then he was likely to run the most outspent presidential campaign in history. Sure enough, by Election Day, Hillary Clinton would raise almost half a billion dollars more than Donald Trump's roughly $600 million and still lose the Electoral College vote. Trump seemed oddly naïve about the reality that in presidential politics the rub is not so much about having lots of your own money, but rather the ability to get lots more of other people's money.

What followed was the strangest presidential candidate's announcement speech in memory. Trump's stream-of-consciousness talk went on and off—and back on—script. Reporters were stunned but also mesmerized by his lowbrow, sometimes crude tone and its content.

Politicos immediately dubbed Trump's rants political suicide. They were aghast not so much about what he said, but that he said it at all. Some pros boasted that his first campaign speech would likely be his last.

Unlike most all politicians, Trump did not hide that he was egotistical ("I beat China all the time. All the time!") and bombastic ("I will be the greatest jobs president that God ever created"). He did not care that he fibbed ("Even our nuclear arsenal doesn't work"). Much less did he worry that he was politically incorrect ("We get Bergdahl. We get a traitor. We get a no-good traitor."). No politician had spoken like that since Ross Perot or Pat Buchanan. And neither of them had come close to winning the presidency.

I listened to determine whether Trump had any persuasive arguments. He did. Lots of them, even if not all were relevant campaign issues. I did not know whether Trump companies did well in China. But I certainly had read of worrisome problems about the readiness of the American nuclear arsenal. Former national security advisor Susan Rice had misled the country about the desertion of Sergeant Bowe Bergdahl in claiming he had served "with honor and distinction." In truth, he *was* a traitor of sorts who left his fellow soldiers on the front lines in Afghanistan on June 30, 2009, and walked out to be captured by the Taliban, endangering others who would look for him.

Unlike Barack Obama's similar "I," "I," "I" repetitiveness, Trump's first-person monotony could be strangely addictive. He was capable of saying anything to anyone at any time and anywhere. Shock followed because Trump supposedly should never have said what is not to be said—or at least not to be said in the way that he said it. Yet he had a unique ability to convey a truth that was rarely spoken, even as he exaggerated details.

How could you categorize Trump? He sounded neither orthodox Republican, nor consistent with his own often liberal past. Trump did not just damn unfair trade. He slandered China. But he still did so with a strange sort of admiration for its ability so easily to swindle America. In Trump's world, commercial cheating and China were synonymous: "When was the last time anybody saw us beating, let's say, China in a trade deal? They kill us." That assertion seemed self-evident.

Economic gurus scoffed at the specter of tariffs. Yet turn to the *Wall Street Journal* and there were also daily stories of flagrant Chinese trade violations and confiscations of American technology. These sensational news accounts were often accompanied by editorials assuring readers that the ensuing nearly $350 billion annual trade deficits were no big deal. But if so, why did a cagey China seek to increase them so much? And if China violated environmental, labor, financial, copyright, patent, and commercial regulations to accrue such huge surpluses, what remedies were there for redress, given past presidential rhetoric, both harsh and appeasing, had utterly failed?

Most politicians routinely called for "comprehensive immigration reform," but without ever defining what they meant. Or rather, representatives knew all too well what they meant when they substituted the euphemism "comprehensive" for the politically unpalatable updated bracero ("arm") program of guest workers ushered in from Mexico and Central America. The soothing noun "reform" was a way of avoiding the unspeakable "amnesty."

Not Trump. He left no doubt what he intended: "When do we beat Mexico at the border? They're laughing at us, at our stupidity." In fact, at home in California's vast Central Valley I knew a lot of Mexican nationals who had laughed at American stupidity. They had explained to me how they crossed the border far more easily than I did when reentering the United States through customs—and with far less worry that there would be any consequences in lying about one's legal status.

Trump then thundered his clarifications: "I would build a great wall. And nobody builds walls better than me, believe me. And I'll build them very inexpensively. I will build a great wall on our southern border and I'll have Mexico pay for that wall."

This boast was the first foretaste of the forthcoming bizarre Trump crowd chant: "Make Mexico pay!" I remembered that, before 1993, my home was often broken into and vandalized. After I built a six-foot-tall, 550-foot block circuit, unlawful entries decreased 90 percent. Throughout history, walls work. They do today, whether they are Israel's barrier separating the West Bank or Facebook owner Mark Zuckerberg's fences around his own properties. I have never seen a Malibu estate without a wall and gate.

Trump's threat sounded crazy to reporters. But the present normal was crazy too, at least to one who lived it rather than wrote about it from a distance. Mostly Mexican nationals, some of them on public support, sent home annually about $30 billion. Would Trump imply that a 10 percent tax on remittances might pay for a $3 billion section of the wall each year?

Left unsaid was that Mexico ran up a $71 billion trade surplus with the United States. Its elites often encouraged its own citizens to break American immigration law, as a way of relieving social tensions inside Mexico and earning the Mexican government foreign exchange. As a candidate, Mexican president Andrés Manuel López Obrador *later* confirmed Trump's charges when he bragged that Mexico could send its own citizens across the border anytime it wished, and that the United States had little control over its own sovereignty ("We will defend migrants all over the American continent and the migrants of the world who, by necessity, must abandon their towns to find life in the United States; it's a human right we will defend").

Trump then doubled down more ominously: "When Mexico sends its people, they're not sending their best. They're not sending you. They're not sending you. They're sending people that have lots of problems and they're bringing those problems with [*sic*] us. They're bringing drugs. They're bringing crime. They're rapists. And some, I assume, are good people."

Journalists understandably scorned such us-them hyperbolic polarization. They still quote "rapist" to imply that Trump slandered all Mexican citizens, rather than his clumsy exaggeration of the number of violent criminals who came into the United States illegally. Yet, well aside from gangs, the IRS has estimated that illegal immigrants had used over one million false or stolen identities—including on one occasion my own.

When one finds dead game cocks and rotting fighting dogs, along with stolen stripped-down trucks in one's orchard, or Norteños gang members *in mediis rebus* stripping copper wire from irrigation pumps, or goes to the emergency room only to encounter waiting families of Bulldog gang members squared off against their Sureños rivals, Trump's rants reflected lots of Americans' realities far more accurately than did the equivocations of a Jeb Bush or Hillary Clinton. I doubt either grandee hears gunfire at night, or invests in armored rural mail strongboxes to replace what is left of their old, shredded, bullet-holed US postal–approved mail receptacles.

The Manichean Trump went on. He reduced foreign policy to rhetorical fisticuffs between them abroad and us at home. Trump confidently promised to out brawl our rivals and win the zero-sum wars they supposedly had started. As president Trump, he would later tweet the astounding heresy "When a country (USA) is losing many billions of dollars on trade with virtually every country it does business with, trade wars are good, and easy to win."

In his finale, Trump bellowed out a take on Ronald Reagan's earlier vow "to make America great again." That turnabout would supposedly happen when Trump hit back on unfair trade. He would bring manufacturing jobs back to the United States. He would secure the border and stop illegal immigration. Trump either promised to win optional wars or more likely not fight them.

In the contemporary America of no-win T-ball and moral equivalence, Trump seemed a Rip Van Winkle. He was waking up from a 1950s slumber into an unrecognizable culture that had long ago passed on his zero-sum, dog-eat-dog world view. Yet many of Trump's signature issues often polled his way. That reality made his rivals' veritable neglect of them all the stranger.

Trump's message and candidacy were not exactly novel. Middle-class populism—less government, doubt over overseas military commitments, fears of redistribution and globalization, and distrust of cultural elites—was as old as the Athenian landed revolutionaries of 411 BC, who for a brief moment overthrew the radical democracy. How Trump trashed Washington was more or less similar to the manner in which the comic dramatist Aristophanes, in right-wing populist fashion, had ridiculed Athenian gentry and its subsidized followers. In fact, most Athenian writers from the Old Oligarch to Thucydides, Plato, Xenophon, and Aristotle often dreamed of a better way of consensual government than Athenian radical democracy and its propensity to destroy—or to kill—by a 51 percent majority vote of the assembly on any given day anyone who might disagree with the supposed majority.

Trump himself played an ancient role of the crude, would-be savior who scares even those who would invite him in to solve intractable problems that their own elite leadership could not. Trump was not that much different from the off-putting tragic hero—from Homer's Achilles and Sophocles's Ajax to modern cinema's Wild Bunch and Dirty Harry.

As for Trump's dark view of American decline, his campaign slogan of renewal also was not novel. Trump's "Make America Great Again" was, in historical terms, perhaps just a continuance of a long tradition dating back to the Roman emperor Augustus, a great builder ("I found Rome a city of bricks and left it a city of marble") who promised to end—and did—eighteen years of war and a century of civil chaos, and to reestablish Roman grandeur.

Or maybe Trump sounded more like a frenzied Martin Luther ("Sin greatly, but believe still more greatly") starting the Reformation in 1517 by nailing his ninety-five condemnations of a corrupt church to the door of All Saints' Church in Wittenberg, Germany. Trump's fellow establishment Republicans were to play the roles of Luther's venal bishops and corrupt functionaries.

What was certainly clear from the first day of the campaign was that the former Democrat, and now Republican, Trump was hardly calling for George H. W. Bush's squishy "thousand points of light." He did not revive the banal "kinder and gentler nation"—the elder Bush's correction for the supposed callousness of Reaganism. Not for him was George W. Bush's "compassionate conservativism," at least as the younger Bush had intended that therapeutic phrase. There was nothing similar to Mitt Romney's blasé slogans "True strength for America's future" or "Believe in America."

Trump was unapologetic about America's past. The future, not yesterday, mattered. If anything, our leaders had been too "weak"—a Darwinian word not properly used anymore in an age of lectures about "toxic masculinity." His key adverb was "again." That is, America was once "great," and so could easily be great *again*.

Trump's use of superlatives envisioned decline as a Nietzschean matter of choice. Sinking into oblivion was not fated. The United States was not predetermined to evaporate in the way that a victorious Great Britain in 1945 was soon surpassed by a bombed-out Germany or Japan rising from the ashes. Being great meant "winning" and becoming respected by enemies and friends abroad. For Trump, it was all a simple matter of will, not means. Such thinking was an anathema to politicians. For many it gave off the scent of 1930s European dictators. They preferred promising to improve an already great America, not remaking it into something out of its better past.

The media pounced on Trump's supposed preposterous contradictions. How could he usher in an era of stability, prosperity, and good governance in a supposedly post-industrial, culturally post-modern, and post-religious America? Was not GDP boosterism at odds with green sensibilities, or the idea that China was the fated global leader?

Most Americans had never watched Trump's fourteen-year hit reality show *The Apprentice*. Nor had they ever read one of his ghostwritten "art of the deal" best-sellers. They had no idea of Trump's negotiating style, his use of exaggeration or spinning fantasies as a bargaining chip, or his embrace of verbal intimidation to confuse his adversary.

What Americans had heard in prior years about Trump derived mostly from occasional tabloid stories about his lurid personal life and his televised and often profanity-ridden spats with minor celebrities and politicians. All that was hardly a guide to determining whether his message would resonate. The immediate sniffing and clever put-downs of cable news pundits were not analyses of whether he could win, much less why he could win.

But after his opening salvos, Americans of all persuasions did sense that Trump was not going to go away — if for no other reason than a mostly liberal media would initially not let go of such a ratings bonanza. They certainly seemed to delight in the initial internecine blood sport Trump had unleashed among Republicans. Candidate Trump, as a result, would likely benefit from hundreds of millions of dollars in free publicity because he was far more entertaining than his far more experienced primary rivals, the veteran governors such as Jeb Bush, Chris Christie, and Scott Walker, or the fresh-faced senators Ted Cruz and Marco Rubio. Before Trump imploded, the networks thought he would likely incinerate the Republican Party along with him—while improving their own balance sheets.

Moreover, even in his debut as a national political candidate, Trump displayed an uncanny ability to troll and create hysteria among his media and political critics. In their anti-Trump rage, they revealed their own character flaws, instability, insecurities, and ignorance—in a manner many had not seen before. Media moguls had no idea that they were helping to birth what they would soon rue as their own Frankenstein monster, with a life force that they could soon not control and that would nearly destroy its creators.

Trump also was a far more dangerous outsider to the status quo in that he did not appear as a third-party unicorn chaser like the wonkish and underfunded Ralph Nader. He was not a conspiratorial Ross Perot (who nevertheless captured 18.9 percent of the vote in 1992 and probably cost George H. W. Bush his reelection). Indeed, Trump was an interloper who planned to hijack the Republican Party and recalibrate it as his own, a sort of virus whose DNA would take over the host.

What then followed from that June 16, 2015, opening speech was equally unprecedented. Trump in succession utterly destroyed sixteen well-qualified Republican rivals. All sixteen by media standards were more knowledgeable of the issues. All were younger. Most appeared better prepared and organized. And all lacked the ability to channel pent-up conservative anger at "them."

Respected polls such as the Princeton Election Consortium on election eve put Trump's chances of victory *at 1 percent*. In the last twenty-four hours of the campaign, the *New York Times*, tracking various pollsters' models, concluded to its reassured readers that Trump's chances of winning in such surveys were respectively 15 percent, 8 percent, 2 percent, and less than 1 percent. Clinton supporters grew irate at fellow progressive poll master Nate Silver shortly before the vote. As an apostate, Silver had dared to suggest that Trump had a 29 percent chance of winning the Electoral College.

In sum, according to conventional electoral wisdom, Trump should not even have had an outside chance of winning the presidency (he was occasionally polling 10–15 points behind Hillary Clinton in the weeks after his campaign announcement). That he did still astounds—or perhaps shocks—that so many could be so wrong about his chances. Any book on Trump must at the outset explain the conventionally inexplicable, and address a series of paradoxes.

Expert pollsters and pundits were wrong in their predictions of a Trump failed nomination, failed election, and, in its first months, failed presidency. Many warped their own institutional protocols, their training, and their professional ethos to construct what they wished to be true so that it might become true. Those who always loudly warned against "groupthink" fell willing victims to it. Those who preached about journalistic ethics and disinterested analysis proved unethical and biased, as if the purported Trump monster justified extraordinary countermeasures and exemptions from professional codes.

Trump's critics loathed him. That singular odium did not arise just from Trump's checkered personal and business past. Trump hatred was also not fully explained by his herky-jerky and cruel bombast or his absence of a proper curriculum vitae. At times, the antipathy to Trump seemed class driven. Trump's strange orange hue, his combed-over thinning and dyed yellow hair, his "yuge" tie and grating Queens accent made him especially foul tasting to the coastal elite Left.

Worse still, Trump campaigned as the anti-Obama. He threatened to undo everything done from 2009 to 2017. Obama had once promised to "fundamentally transform" the United States. But Trump was more likely to do just that by fundamentally dismantling the entire Obama transformation and easily so, given that Obama had ruled largely through amendable executive orders.

The Washington and New York conservative establishment grew to despise Trump more than his progressive enemies. Trump certainly did not talk or speak as they did. Many had argued that Trump's nonconservative past nullified his conservative present. Clearly, few Beltway Republican fixtures and talking heads were going to be getting invitations from a Trump White House. The subtext of Trump's foreign policy was to put out of business the bipartisan foreign policy establishment of New York and Washington, by the simple argument that the world they had created was now a relic, and that Afghanistan, Iraq, Libya, and Syria were not shining examples of the brilliance of American interventionism. Nor were the UN, NAFTA, and NATO immune from criticism and radical reform.

A warning: one problem in assessing Trump's popularity was always that voters were not honest about their views of him, given fears of perceived social ostracism that might follow from their candor. Americans soon saw their friends turn away when asked their favorite candidate in 2016, terrified to even utter the monosyllable "Trump."

A common joke spread that Trump supporters had been "body snatched," in reference to the classic 1956 horror film *Invasion of the Body Snatchers*: normal one moment, only to wake up as "pod people," with an alien in control of their otherwise accustomed body and appearance. Even among friends, voting for Trump was supposed to have revealed deep character flaws in a friend, heretofore unnoticed and only now come to the fore.

But there was also another force multiplier of stealth voters rarely acknowledged. Just as conservative and independent Americans hid their sympathies for Trump, so too others more liberal and centrist masked their antipathies to the transformation of a Democratic Party into a radically progressive movement. Either way, the result was the same: Trump support would be underestimated or missed by the media, sometimes by ignorance, but as often by intent.

Donald Trump may be the unlikeliest populist, but a populism of the middle class nonetheless he ran on, and populist much of his agenda has been. Why that is so is the subject of this book, which is neither a Trump biography nor an insider's chronological account of the Trump campaign and presidency.

I have no interest in proving Trump either a demon or a deity, in contrast to whether he is unique and of the moment or a precursor to something that will endure. I am a conservative on most issues, and as a fifth-generation farmer have written favorably of agrarian populism in a number of prior books and in a variety of contexts. I grew up in the same house where I now live, and in a farming Democratic household that worshipped Harry Truman and John F. Kennedy and would have voted for a yellow dog on the ballot if it had just registered Democrat.

All my siblings in 2016 either voted for Bernie Sanders or Hillary Clinton; all no doubt assumed Trump marked something ominous—and perhaps their own brother too for voting for him in the general election. My late mother as a Jerry Brown California judicial appointee would not have appreciated the Trump candidacy, or, likely, her son's vote for him in 2016 and his support for most of the Trump record since.

PART ONE

WHAT AND WHO
CREATED TRUMP?

*I don't want to sound like I'm bragging, but usually
when I talk to senators, while they may know a
policy area better than me, they generally don't
know political philosophy better than me. I got the
sense he [Barack Obama] knew both better than
me . . . I remember distinctly an image of—we were
sitting on his couches, and I was looking at his pant
leg and his perfectly creased pant, and I'm thinking,
a) he's going to be president and b) he'll be a very
good president.*

—David Brooks, August 2009

Chapter One

THE TWO AMERICAS

*The pundits, the pundits like to slice and dice our
country into red states and blue states: red states for
Republicans, blue states for Democrats. But I've got
news for them, too . . . We are one people, all of us
pledging allegiance to the stars and stripes, all of us
defending the United States of America.*

—Barack Obama, keynote address,
Democratic National Convention, July 27, 2004

The growing split in the United States was not the clichéd
"two Americas" of rich and poor without a middle class.
That was the popular but stale sloganeering made popular most
recently by multimillionaire trial lawyer, former senator, failed
presidential candidate—and scandalized—John Edwards.

The new divide instead is becoming far more encompassing,
especially since 2008. It is an ominous one of an estranged middle class and increasingly expressed in political, cultural, social,
and—most alarmingly—geographical terms. Yet even in our
age of high tech, some of the differences echo as far back as the
cultural divides that eroded the Greek city-state. Maritime, cosmopolitan, urban, and democratic Athens fought agricultural,

inward, rural, and oligarchic Sparta to the south for the soul of the Hellenic city-state, a fight that most other Greek poleis wished Sparta to win.

In the early 1970s, network television mastered glitzy computer graphics and began covering presidential races by showing color-coded maps of the United States. States that voted Democratic were originally shaded red. Republican ones appeared blue. But by the 2000 election the color schemes had switched. Perhaps the color change was due to a desire by the liberal media to countenance the traditional idea that red was an off-putting Bolshevik color, and blue a traditionalist or soothing hue.

In the 1990s, an array of issues such as the post-industrial and global economy, illegal immigration, and the Democratic monopolies of big-city mayorships split the country apart along new regional lines. There was a growing pattern in the Electoral College that had supplanted old sectarian tensions. No longer was the country cut in two by old Civil War–era North-South binaries. The nineteenth-century strains between the frontier West and the Eastern Seaboard establishment had also warped into something novel.

Instead, the new left-wing/right-wing split played out in a clustering of states, with shorelines on the seas a chief determinant. Democrats won almost all states along the two coasts and some of the shore states of the Great Lakes. Republicans controlled most of the vast expanses in between. In terms of geography, the electoral map showed a vast sea of red. Indeed, it covered nearly 80 percent of the territory of the United States. But recalibrate such maps on the basis of population, and suddenly blue balloons expanded from the coasts to blot out much of the red space. Indeed, blue-state demography smothered nearly half of the red geography.

Translated into presidential politics, the results were stunning. The United States is not an Athenian-style direct democracy of 51 percent rule, but a representative republic whose elections are determined by the Electoral College. That reality meant that the slightly greater blue popular vote, concentrated in far fewer states, might increasingly become redundant in choosing a victorious candidate. And the anomaly is just what happened in both the 2000 and 2016 elections. Those outcomes, as Trump likely knew, were because Republicans, without a national majority popular vote, tipped swing states in the Midwest by margins as close as 1–2 percent.

Trump inherited this divided America and continued, in reverse fashion, Barack Obama's earlier efforts to widen the gulf. A once "dazzling" Illinois Senate candidate, Barack Obama gave a riveting ecumenical speech at the 2004 Democratic National Convention. It is now remembered as his inaugural debut as a national political figure. But less than five years later, Obama began governing the United States as if there really were two Americas, with more an attitude of triumphalist "I won" than his earlier inclusive "hope and change." That partisanship was not unusual for a president, but one-sidedness perhaps was for someone variously described ecumenically by media stalwarts as a "god," or who, in his own words, would begin to lower the seas and cool the overheated planet.

Of course, Obama also inherited a dividing America. But he gambled his career on leveraging the split to what he felt was the winning side. Obama, as did most campaign analysts, wagered prematurely that his blue states—demographically, culturally, and politically—were the nation's preordained twenty-first-century future.

Yet for at least the next few decades, it was unlikely that Los Angeles and Boston would inevitably bury Salt Lake City and Kansas City. California's culture would not anytime soon spread to Utah and Tennessee or even to Wyoming and Georgia. Even in the age of the multicultural salad bowl, the melting pot of intermarriage and assimilation still retained the power to turn tribal groups into less ideological Americans. Or, should the assimilationist model fail, then the white working class might decide that it too should privilege its tribal identity in the fashion of other minority groups, even if that solidarity invoked eerie remembrances of the nation's pre–civil rights past.

As a result of Obama's agendas, when the two-term president left office with final majority approval, his political legacy nevertheless was a blue atoll in an ocean of red. Over his tenure, his party had lost the House. It gave up the Senate. The majority of state legislature chambers (99-69) and governorships (33-17) were now Republican. Obama had given the Republicans a good chance at winning the Electoral College in 2016, and after the elections, not since 1920 had the Republican Party emerged stronger. It may have been blasphemous to concede, but Barack Obama, for at least the first two years after his departure, had all but destroyed the traditional role of Democrats as a federal, state, and local majority party—and in its place had paved the way for a new neosocialist ascendency.

Over Obama's polarizing tenure, the critical swing states of the Midwest had mostly flipped from their more frequent blue to red, at least on the state level. With the exception of Minnesota, all midwestern states by 2018 had elected a Republican governor. And aside from Illinois, Republicans swept every midwestern state house.

In a 2018 Economist/YouGov poll, 53 percent of midwesterners voiced an unfavorable opinion of the Democratic Party. As columnist Julie Kelly argued, Obama's electoral legacy may have been a new Midwest that is insidiously becoming another red-state South that had earlier in the 1960s flipped from Democratic to Republican.

Yet few observers had grasped that behind the radical local and state realignment was a more fundamental and profound class anger at coastal elites. Centrist voters began to doubt the wisdom of globalization. They pushed back against the Democratic Party's move culturally leftward. Most equated

Democratic apparent obsessions with identity politics as a new sort of off-putting racialism. Trump had assumed from the outset that a midwestern presidential shift was long overdue.

When he announced his candidacy, Trump apparently had digested Obama's lessons and its corollaries, and then figured out antidotes to them. He gambled that the forgotten interior of America could still help him defeat its coastal counterparts, and thereby win him the whole. The counterintuitive trick was not so much to unite the country to win a 1984 Reagan-like landslide. That feat was *impossible* for twenty-first-century American political candidates, even for a landmark candidate like Obama, and inconceivable for an even more polarizing Donald Trump.

Instead, what had doomed prior Republican presidential candidates, such as nominal conservatives John McCain and Mitt Romney, was their inability to capture *all* of the red interior. When a Republican candidate at the outset writes off the electoral votes of large consistently blue states such as California (55), Illinois (20), Massachusetts (11), and New York (29), there is never much margin of error, after forfeiting 115 of the 270 votes needed for victory. Prior Republican inability to win consistently states like Michigan, Ohio, Pennsylvania, and Wisconsin was largely because national candidates either could not, or would not, energize the disenchanted white working class.

They failed especially those without college degrees, many of whom had apparently become Election Day dropouts. These disenchanted had been turned off just as much by Republican establishment rigid free-market orthodoxy, free but not fair trade, and open borders as by progressive identity politics. As it turned out, Trump would win three key swing states once deemed irrevocably blue: Michigan (by a 0.2 percent margin), Pennsylvania (0.7 percent), and Wisconsin (0.8 percent). Or in other words, Trump won the election because about eighty thousand voters in just three states swung his way.

Yet those states had been previously considered impossible victories for any Republican. A better way to look at Trump's novel success was that he did far better than any recent Republican candidate in those states. In comparison to 2012, Trump won an astounding 290,000 more votes in Pennsylvania than did Romney, 180,000 more votes in Ohio, and about 165,000 more votes in Michigan. Most importantly, Trump easily won Florida with over 450,000 more Republican votes than in 2012.

Note that the proverbial angry Trump voter was *not* the only Trump voter. Indeed, Trump would go on to win roughly 90 percent of Republicans. The loud Never Trump Republican antipathy oddly had little Election Day effect. Trump won about the same percentage of his party as did John McCain and Mitt Romney. He captured a majority of white men and women, suburban professional voters, as well as independents. Most of his voters were identical in terms of income and education to past voters for Republican candidates. Trump rallies were geared to the working class and got lots of attention. But more quietly, Republican business executives, entrepreneurs, and conservative mainstreamers still voted a straight party ticket as if Trump were a John McCain or Mitt Romney.

But the key point again was that, within that matrix, past Republican candidates like John McCain and Mitt Romney *had still lost*. It was not so much that red- and purple-state working-class voters were the only basis of Trump support (he won 66 percent of the white noncollege educated). Rather, they were by far his—and all other Republicans'—most critical component. Without their overwhelming fealty, or barring another transformative Reagan candidate, neither Trump nor any other contemporary Republican candidate will likely again find a pathway to the presidency.

Most importantly, what were the deeper causes behind the widening coastal-interior split into which Trump tapped?

In the rural-urban rift of the 1990s, deindustrialized red states had lost relative economic clout. They were likely to stay more rural. Cities like Detroit, Cleveland, and Milwaukee were considered ossifying, while Portland, Seattle, or San Diego were ascending. For a time, blue states grew and became even more urban. Again, the polarization was multifaceted, and yet predictably consistent. In classical fashion, liberal cosmopolitanism with windows on the sea warred against conservative traditionalism turned toward the land.

The coastal blue states often believed they were winning the cultural wars. Sometimes the blue mindset grew haughty, and insisted that no quarter should be given. In a widely quoted and disseminated essay in the online blog *Medium* in early 2018, progressives Peter Leyden (founder and CEO of Reinvent) and Ray Teixeira (fellow at the Center for American Progress) saw the divide as existential, permanent, and intractable. They urged liberals to take no prisoners. And they were clear about the need to defeat and eliminate rather than compromise with their enemies:

> The opportunity for compromise is then lost. This is where America is today . . . At some point, one side or the other must win—and win big. The side resisting change, usually the one most rooted in the past systems and incumbent interests, must be thoroughly defeated—not just for a political cycle or two, but for a generation or two.

The divide in which some "must be thoroughly defeated" always sharpened—due to a variety of force multipliers. One, mobile Americans and floods of newcomers—nearly 50 million foreign nationals now live in the United States—sorted out on the basis of tribe, culture, and politics, not just by old criteria such as weather, economic opportunity, family ties, and physical environment. Minorities and gays more likely have preferred the cities and liberal states. Immigrants, legal and illegal, find more generous state support, and fear immigration enforcement less, on the coasts. One-third of all American residents currently on welfare live in California, as do a quarter of the nation's illegal aliens—a state where one in four was not born in the United States, but otherwise with just 12 percent of the population.

A second force multiplier is that reds trapped in high-taxed and regulated blue states often relocated, especially in their retirement years when expense rather than income was a central concern. Blues, feeling culturally deprived in small government and less cosmopolitan red states, did too. Politics in the primaries shifted both hard left and hard right to reflect these new more monolithic state parties. Take-no-prisoners primary candidates paid fealty to their bases. Again, Trump did not create these divides. He merely found existing sectarianism politically useful, and, like President Obama, he far more adroitly leveraged it than had prior Republican nominees.

Three, again, the so-called blue-state model of social media, steep taxes, big government, social liberality, smaller families, sophisticated culture, and high incomes has become the more culturally influential. It dominates universities, foundations, entertainment, and media. Trillions of global dollars have poured into coastal Amazon, Facebook, Google, and Microsoft (resulting in a market capitalization of over $3 trillion), and to the high-tech companies that spin off, and the hipster cultures they spawn.

The great universities—the Ivy League, Cal Tech, MIT, Berkeley—are on the coasts. They hone the skills necessary to do well from globalized commerce and trade. When I dine on University Avenue in Palo Alto, the food, the ambiance, and the people's diction and dress might as well be on Mars, so foreign are they when compared to eating out in my rural hometown, three hours—and a world away—south of Fresno, California.

There is nothing quite like Hollywood, Wall Street, or Stanford in Nebraska or Kentucky. A state of 40 million residents like California draws about half its income tax revenues from roughly 150,000 tax returns. State government in Sacramento assumes that either the state's very wealthy became so by California's unique window on the high-tech globalized world, or that those with multimillion-dollar incomes can navigate around a 13.3 percent state income tax top rate. Trump, from the very beginning, saw that his budding idea of populism could be turned against hyper-rich progressives, especially their perceived hypocrisies of advocating policies whose consequences fell more heavily on others less fortunate. In other words, the influence of a minority of the population was exaggerated by its ubiquity in the popular culture and the globalized economy.

A fourth consideration in why America was dividing into two antithetical cultures was that wealth creation was growing even more unevenly distributed. The middle classes in red states had since at least 1970 suffered stagnating incomes in real wages, as compensation lagged behind increases in worker productivity, while the blue-state elite were getting richer than ever—and loudly and publicly so. This fact also posed a paradox for progressives. For example, the 1980 per capita income of Washington, DC, was only 29 percent above the average for other Americans. Yet by 2013, the city's average income had soared to 68 percent above the rest of the country's.

In California's San Francisco Bay Area, average per capita income leaped from 50 percent above the rest of the United States to an incredible 88 percent higher. That lucre was largely due to astronomical increases in the compensation of the proverbial 1 percent. Homes in California's coastal corridor sold for ten times the amount per square footage of identical counterparts just a three-hour drive away in the state's interior from Fresno to Bakersfield. New York City, the center of global investments and banking, in 1980 had enjoyed an 80 percent higher than average per capita income. Thirty-three years later, the margin had exploded to 172 percent.

The explanation, again, was not complicated. Financial and legal services, banks, insurance firms, wealth management firms, technology companies, and universities now enjoyed in theory 7.4 billion global clients for their unique services and products. The exact inverse was true for many of those in America's interior who made, sold, and grew things that now were far more easily and cheaply copied, replaced, or superseded abroad.

Globalization had flattened the hinterland as jobs and commerce were outsourced to lower-cost Asia and Latin America. And yet the disequilibrium had never been fully leveraged by politicians (unless on occasion in negative fashion by Barack Obama in his infamous "clingers" put-down of rural Pennsylvanians in 2008).

American muscular jobs and smokestack industries began disappearing as the world became more connected. They re-emerged abroad in low-wage and mostly unregulated countries. The resulting stagnation in the hinterland was almost justified by elites as an "I warned you" sort of morality—as if the supposedly backward, stubborn interior deserved its fate or at least lazily did nothing to preempt it. The former nobility of muscular labor and hard physical work transmogrified into foolish adherence to mindless drudgery.

Confident coastal affluence and chic were seen as almost pre-ordained, or at least the proper rewards for the right people. Attitude mattered: doing well or not doing well was behind much of the ideological sermonizing directed at "losers" by so-called winners. Trump saw that by championing the "forgotten man," he was not so easily caricatured as a heartless Mitt Romney or rich man Jeb Bush. Democrats would smear Trump as racist, sexist, nativist, and homophobic. But it was harder to slur him as heartless, given that the richest counties in the United States voted against him, and the poorest stuck with him, while Hillary Clinton raised hundreds of millions of dollars more from the wealthy in the 2016 campaign.

The condescending blue-state narrative was almost as if opioids and trailer houses had driven away hardware stores, 160-acre farms, and tire factories, rather than the globalized disappearance of jobs fueling the malaise of the unemployed. From the view of capitalization and profitability, traditional mining, farming, fuel, and rail companies lost clout to tech, finance, service, and information conglomerates.

In reductionist terms of spreadsheets, the world more than ever wanted what the American coasts had. But it had long ago appropriated or xeroxed America's interior's wealth, manufacturing, and industrialization. It was much easier to outsource a table grape operation to Mexico than a computer engineering firm. China can make steel pipes more easily than it can found another Harvard or Princeton. And Vietnam makes clothing far better than it designs hedge funds or computer software.

This insidious decline of the Rust Belt by 2016 was the embryo of Donald Trump's candidacy. It would remain the core of his presidential resilience. In rural central California in the 1990s, I had begun meeting poor underemployed or jobless working-class whites. They were easy to spot given their trademark "thousand-yard stare." They enjoyed few white privileges either to increase or to lose. In contrast, where I worked in Palo Alto, eyes seemed brighter, chatter was nonstop; pedestrians half ran. Life was so good that all the senses were still not enough to drink it up. Living went into hyperdrive: crosswalks in Palo Alto were a pedestrian's no-man's-land of rolling-stop BMWs and Mercedeses. Drivers in my hometown's intersections seemed to be slumbering when you walked across the street.

Still a fifth cause of the new divide were the internet and social media. Both insidiously warped and exaggerated perceptions of class and cultural tensions. Before 1990, when a white bigot shot an African American in a brawl in Memphis, or a black teenager beat up a shopper in Chicago, or an unstable leftist professor slandered the president, it was largely a minor local news story in a country of 250 million. Now such isolated events went viral on social media as if they were referenda on the entire mental health of the nation. The episodes were followed by furious comments posted by news aggregators, designed to further inflame hatred. The formula in seconds turned pathological. When a politician or celebrity read any news account on the internet that incensed him for a moment, without thinking he tweeted his first gut reaction, eager to get ahead of the mob or to signal his singular indignation. Furious condemnations followed, igniting more venomous counteraccusations.

If the once minor and local beef electronically soared to achieve magical numbers of "hits" on millions of computer screens, then the national cable news outlets picked up the "story" as if it were an existential global crisis and had confirmed cosmic ideologies. And the constructed cycle was repeated not just weekly or daily, but hourly, ensuring millions were permanently in a state of outrage across cultural and political divides.

Within hours boredom with the now old narrative set in, the sensationalism subsided—until a few hours later a new, more incendiary anecdote went national. Each of these irrelevant outrages was insignificant in isolation, but they aggregated and finally confirmed preset biases of Left against Right and Right against Left. Entire careers and a lifetime of achievement could be nullified in seconds by an ill-considered internet sneeze, which in minutes was considered a newly opened portal into a heretofore unknown but malignant soul.

Finally, when race and class were factored into the blue-red bifurcation, the political divide widened far more. African Americans increasingly began to control big-city governments. Hispanics dominated southwestern metropolises such as Los Angeles and San Jose. Meanwhile, a new profile of the single hipster, the gentrified yuppie, or the coastal urbanite arose. His disposable income fueled a revolution in upscale condos and townhouses, boutique vacationing, fine dining, and conspicuous consumption. And he did not care so much about the price of a suburban three-bedroom, two-bath home, saving money for kids' braces, or the quality of schools in the neighborhood.

Gentrification and the gospel of good taste spread. Blue states began to focus on the cultural concerns and lifestyles of the upscale, and on generous state sustenance of the poor and often minority. Privilege and success were camouflaged by a veneer of trendy progressive politics—even as regulations, zoning restrictions, no-growth policies, and high taxes decimated the middle class and created entire enclaves of coastal homeless people. If it were a choice between permanent green spaces between expansive hillside estates and sprawling housing tracts to allow the middle class the chance to buy a home, elite environmentalism won every time.

Northern California professionals with granite countertops, stainless-steel appliances, and teak floors worried in the abstract more about the homeless, the poor, and the nonwhite than did those of the lower middle class who more often lived next to the dispossessed and could scarcely pay for their own Formica, white refrigerators, and linoleum. It was understandable that those with more disposable income could afford empathy. But it was incomprehensible that those without money were somehow written off as the more callous—at least until the billionaire Trump of all people appeared to side with the lower middle classes.

For example, in the greatest blunder of the 2016 election, Hillary Clinton all but condemned "half of Trump's supporters" into what she called "the basket of deplorables."

You know, to just be grossly generalistic [sic], you could put half of Trump's supporters into what I call the basket of deplorables. Right? The racist, sexist, homophobic, xenophobic, Islamophobic—you name it. And unfortunately, there are people like that. And he has lifted them up. He has given

voice to their websites that used to only have 11,000 people—
now 11 million. He tweets and retweets their offensive hateful
mean-spirited rhetoric. Now, some of those folks—they are irredeemable, but thankfully they are not America.

But after writing off over half of the nearly 63 million who
would eventually vote against her, Clinton then patronized "the
other basket" of Trump supporters as the naïve and confused
who needed her empathy and sympathy ("Those are people
we have to understand and empathize with as well"). In other
words, just sixty days before the 2016 election, Clinton had
written off tens of millions of potential voters as either evil for
their support for Trump, or bewildered and in dire need of
reeducation. Ironically, the white working class whom Hillary
had dismissed as "not America" and "irredeemable," as well as
those deserving some sort of pity, were precisely those whom,
as a candidate in 2008, she had once sought to pander to along
racial lines (far more overtly than did Trump) in order to coun-
teract Obama's own race-based appeals.

As Clinton once upon a time put it on the primary campaign trail: "Senator Obama's support among working, hard-
working Americans, white Americans, is weakening again, and
how whites in both states who had not completed college were
supporting me. . . . There's a pattern emerging here. . . . These
are the people you have to win if you're a Democrat in sufficient
numbers to actually win the election. Everybody knows that."
Hillary Clinton won the 2008 Pennsylvania primary over Barack
Obama. But he later carried the state in two general elections on
the basis of overwhelming urban minority turnout, after which
Clinton lost Pennsylvania to Donald Trump in 2016. Moreover,
Obama in 2008 had dismissed Clinton's earlier and various appeals to the previously ignored white working class as a cheap
campaign stunt: "She's talking like she's Annie Oakley. Hillary
Clinton is out there like she's on the duck blind every Sunday.

She's packing a six-shooter. Come on, she knows better. That's some politics being played by Hillary Clinton."

In the deindustrialized heartland, in stereotypical terms, the white working-class male increasingly fell into opioid addiction and other pathologies like suicide, a shortened life span, ill health, illegitimacy, divorce, family disintegration, and a declining birth rate. For years such maladies did not spark a national crisis. It was assumed that amid such wreckage an unemployed machinist did not care about registering and turning out to vote in the manner of his better-off parents and grandparents. Self-hatred and listlessness, not multimillionaire stolid candidates like John McCain or Mitt Romney, were cited by pundits as reasons why naturally conservative voters stayed home in 2008 and 2012.

Before Trump, few politicians saw an opening in defending the forgotten working class of the interior, which may have been far larger than believed. And predictably, after the 2016 election, head-scratching experts sought to reexamine why their so-called exit polls had missed the impending Trump surge.

A Pew analysis discovered that, in fact, college-educated whites did *not* make up 36 percent of the electorate as believed. Instead, college graduates were an estimated mere 30 percent of voters. And they were certainly outnumbered by working-class whites without college degrees. Apparently, pollsters had not factored in the quite obvious fact that those like themselves with college degrees were the most likely to talk to pollsters, to fill out surveys, and in general to let their views be known. Those without BAs were the more likely to keep quiet in the shadows.

Trump's election should have changed progressive calculations, or at least burst the liberal bubble. But it did not. Hollywood was shocked and the country mystified when in March 2018 an unlikely pro-Trump, and soon to be disgraced, Roseanne Barr resurrected her long-moribund comedy show. By often sympathetically portraying white middle-class lifestyles and voicing some pro-Trump sentiments, Barr garnered record ratings for her new sitcom.

White, lower-class pathology was often known to the Left in the manner of a stiff, dissected frog, reeking of formaldehyde on a middle-school biology class desk. It had been widely publicized in Charles Murray's statistical dissection, *Losing Ground: American Social Policy, 1950–1980*, and Robert D. Putnam's *Our Kids: The American Dream in Crisis*—and in far more riveting personal terms by J. D. Vance's *Hillbilly Elegy: A Memoir of a Family and Culture in Crisis*.

But as far as government remediation went, the sinking white former middle class lacked the cultural tastes of the progressive rich. And they had long ago forfeited the empathy accorded the distant poor. Or was it sometimes worse than that? Often the white elite signaled their disgust of the "white privilege" of the disintegrating middle class as a means of exempting their own quite genuine white privilege of insider contacts, professional degrees, wealth, inheritance, and influence. Again, the anger that Trump tapped had been a long time in coming. But few politicians knew it firsthand, much less saw it as merited or even useful in the political sense.

One of the ways of calibrating just how out of touch and condescending the elite progressive had become was to zoom ahead to glimpse post-election progressive depression. In 2017, fantasies still trumped the hard lessons of recent history. This divide between self-ascribed affluent sensitive white elites and their supposed interior inferiors was embarrassingly summed up shortly before the Trump inauguration by Northern California entrepreneur Melinda Byerley. She proved to be a modern-day French minister Charles Maurice de Talleyrand-Périgord, who had *"learned nothing* and *forgotten nothing* [italics added]."

Byerley, a founder of the Silicon Valley company Timeshare CMO, became a window into the mind of the Clinton voter by an infamous, embittered Facebook posting about why miffed coastal elites hated those unlike them:

> One thing middle America could do is to realize that no educated person wants to live in a sh**hole with stupid people. Especially violent, racist, and/or misogynistic ones . . . When corporations think about where to locate call centers, factories, development centers, etc., they also have to deal with the fact that those towns have nothing going for them. No infrastructure, just a few bars and a terrible school system.

Byerley voiced the traditional progressive palliative that Trump's rise was attributable to racism and misogyny, rather than to economic discontent and a weariness that the losers of globalization were scapegoated by the winners as responsible for most of America's supposedly historical pathologies. Byerley also might have revealed progressive insular arrogance. The infrastructure of Menlo Park and Palo Alto—roads especially—is substandard. Silicon Valley's private academies are rapidly expanding to serve a high-tech elite that refuses to put its children in the area's increasingly diverse but challenged public schools.

High-crime areas of Redwood City and East Palo Alto are within biking distance of Apple, Facebook, and Google headquarters. Near them SUVs and recreation vehicles are jammed overnight along the streets, serving as de facto homes for third-tier workers who cannot afford apartment rents. I can attest that there are more bars per capita in Palo Alto than in rural Michigan small towns—and certainly more syringes, feces, rats, and hepatitis on the streets of San Francisco than on those of Indianapolis, Columbus, or Pittsburgh.

These post-election vignettes are also especially instructive about the red-blue divide. They illustrate why Trump leveraged the national schism better in electoral terms than did Hillary Clinton. Progressives were also more honest and candid about what they really thought of their red-state counterparts when there was no longer a need for election-era prudence and pretext.

So, sixteen months after the election, in March 2018, a still-bruised and sulking—but also liberated—Hillary Clinton seconded Byerley's contempt in a public speech in India. If anyone still thought that Clinton's infamous campaign smear of Trump's voters as "deplorables" and "irredeemables" was at the time a gaffe, it was only such in the sense of Michael Kinsley's cynical Washingtonian definition of the noun ("A gaffe is when a politician tells the truth—some obvious truth he isn't supposed to say"). Trashing her fellow citizens in ways that ingratiated Clinton with a foreign audience would convince no one that she had lost the election to supposed Russian collusion. Clinton in Mumbai now openly doubled down on Trump's deplorable red-state voters, to remind her own base that she had meant what she had said the prior September by castigating entire groups of supposedly illiberal and deluded voters: "So I won the places that are optimistic, diverse, dynamic, moving forward." An American's vote against Hillary Clinton, then, revealed him as depressed, monotonous, listless, and regressing.

According to the later testimony of *New York Times* reporter Amy Chozick, who had followed the Hillary Clinton 2016 campaign, Clinton supposedly sulked and whined on the evening of her defeat: "They were never going to let me be president." Chozick also reported of the embittered inner Clinton circle: "The Deplorables always got a laugh, over living-room chats in the Hamptons, at dinner parties under the stars on Martha's Vineyard, over passed hors d'oeuvres in Beverly Hills, and during sunset cocktails in Silicon Valley." Of course, Chozick disclosed the contempt *after*, not during, the election.

In September 2018, former vice president Joe Biden returned to the campaign trail on the eve of the midterm election, and doubled down on Hillary Clinton's earlier concept of deplorable Trump voters with a new sobriquet, "dregs of society": "This time they—not you—have an ally in the White House. This time they have an ally. They're a small percentage of the American people—virulent people, some of them the dregs of society." Biden's "they" in fact were *not* a small percentage of the American people, but in 2016 represented 46 percent of all Americans who voted, and they were most certainly not the "dregs" of anything.

Trump's nonstop campaign message to his supporters that they were as hated by the coastal elite as they were liked by him was no exaggeration. Yet to extract the true feelings of the Washington apparat and progressive elites, we again have to look carefully for indiscrete putdowns never meant to be aired, or to post-election angst when winning Michigan or Ohio no longer mattered.

Sometimes the elite disdain for middle America turned pathological. Apparently, Trump's critics believed that his natural supporters even smelled and smiled differently than normal Americans. Shortly before the election, FBI agent Peter Strzok—assigned to investigating the Hillary Clinton email scandal as well as Donald Trump—texted to his paramour Lisa Page his contempt for any who voted for Trump: "Just went to a southern Virginia Walmart. I could SMELL the Trump support."

In a similar vein, an unidentified FBI employee also texted to another FBI attorney, on the day after the 2016 election, his contempt for the Trump voter and middle America: "Trump's supporters are all poor to middle class, uneducated, lazy POS [pieces of sh*t]." In summer 2018, *Politico* reporter Marc Caputo tweeted of the crowd he saw at a Trump rally: "If you put everyone's mouths together in this video, you'd get a full set of teeth." He later doubled down and snarled: "Oh no! I made fun of garbage people jeering at another person as they falsely accused him of lying and flipped him off. Someone fetch a fainting couch."

Tech writer Sarah Jeong, newly appointed to the *New York Times* editorial board, earlier had tweeted of "white people" an entire series of racist putdowns: "Are white people genetically predisposed to burn faster in the sun, thus logically being only fit to live underground like groveling goblins?" "Oh man it's kind of sick how much joy I get out of being cruel to old white men." "White people marking up the internet with their opinions like dogs pissing on fire hydrants." And on and on. The *Times*, which in the past had established a zero-tolerance policy about past racist writing for its writers, excused Jeong. It argued that she had been simply, albeit sloppily, replying to internet trolls and therefore her racist tweets were no window into a racist heart.

The point of these examples is to show that highly educated elites (Caputo has a journalism degree from the University of Miami, Jeong graduated from Harvard Law School, Strzok received a master's degree from Georgetown) all engaged in crude stereotyping of a demographic, in a manner that they assumed involved no downside, but rather approbation from their peers. For decades, race and gender studies academics had argued that overtly expressed racism against whites was not racism, but had to be contextualized by prior white oppression. In the age of furor and crude slurs against Trump, their theories now went off campus and were being adjudicated by a wider constituency— and they did not seem to win agreement from the general public. The irony, of course, is that these professionals displayed far less humanity in their crude putdowns about smells and toothlessness than did the targets of their smears. It was hard to pose as the easy moral superior to Trump by matching and sometimes exceeding his purported crudity.

What is again odd about these examples of open progressive contempt for the American interior is not just how ubiquitously politicians and journalists voiced them, but also how candidly and indeed confidently they repeated notions of smelly, toothless, lazy "garbage people." In that sense, who hated Trump and what he represented also explains precisely why so many went to the polls to elect him, and why Trump's own uncouthness was in its own manner contextualized by his supporters as a long overdue pushback to the elite disdain and indeed hatred shown them. As one side loudly snickered about the stinky white Trump demographic, the other quietly voted.

Laura Moser, a Washington, DC, progressive writer and Bernie Sanders supporter, recently moved to Texas to run (unsuccessfully) for Congress. Her Democratic primary rivals soon had a field day, dredging up her past disdain for even the thought of living in Texas. Moser had preened in *Washingtonian* magazine about why living in high-priced, crime-ridden Washington was still preferable to residing as near royalty in the hinterland:

> On my pathetic writer's salary, I could live large in Paris, Texas, where my grandparents' plantation-style house recently sold for $129,000. Oh, but wait—my income would be a fraction of what it is here and I'd have very few opportunities to increase it. (Plus I'd sooner have my teeth pulled out without anesthesia, but that's a story for another day.)

She added, "Our lives are challenging and full and seldom boring, and I wouldn't trade our shabby row house on four major bus routes for a stately manor just outside of Tulsa—not for any price." Thematic was not just mockery of red-state America, but self-congratulation on one's superior virtue and cultural enlightenment, as if the one explained the other.

Another aim of collating both these pre- and post-election dismissals of half of America is to again remind that Trumpism was fundamentally a reaction, *not* a catalyst. Given the vehemence shown to "hardscrabble" America, the only mystery about Trump's candidacy is that it took so long in coming. My former colleague at *National Review*, the conservative social critic Kevin Williamson, once created a storm when he more or less dared to suggest that mobility—moving away—was about the only antidote to innate white lower-class pathologies:

> The truth about these dysfunctional, downscale communities is that they deserve to die. Economically, they are negative assets. Morally, they are indefensible . . .
>
> The white American underclass is in thrall to a vicious, selfish culture whose main products are misery and used heroin needles. Donald Trump's speeches make them feel good. So does OxyContin. What they need isn't analgesics, literal or political. They need real opportunity, which means that they need real change, which means that they need U-Haul.

I too grew up, and still live, outside a small town in California's Central Valley. For a century (1880–1980) it was a prosperous multiethnic and multiracial community of working- and middle-class families. Of a cohort of about 250 graduating seniors in 1971, only about 10 or so of us went away to four-year colleges. Most found no need to leave Selma. Labor was needed at home, given a wide variety of high-paying jobs among the area's various fabrication and manufacturing industries—or taking over their parents' vibrant family farms, or working shifts in unionized canneries and food-processing plants.

By 1990, almost all of those plants had closed. By 2000, most farms had been sold off and the land consolidated under corporate auspices. By 2010, high unemployment was chronic, drug addiction was endemic, crime commonplace. In 1970, we did not have keys for our outside doors; in 2018, I have six guard dogs.

Thousands of illegal immigrants, mostly from the state of Oaxaca two thousand miles away in southern Mexico, had often replaced the departed. Many new arrivals came illegally. Most from Mexico did not speak English. Some conversed in an indigenous language quite different from Spanish. And most did not have high school diplomas. Many could not read and a few signed their name in the local bank with an *X* or *Z* or some such notation. They worked hard for subsistence wages when they could find them, as well as off-the-books odd jobs—even as social welfare services in some form subsidized about half the town's population. Among the busier stores in town was a Western Union office from where thousands in local dollars were sent each month home to Oaxaca. The more successful of the illegal immigrants found higher-paying jobs in construction and midlevel farm management, even as they usually saw no pressing need to apply to become citizens.

Selma is now a bedroom community of Fresno, with a population nearing twenty-five thousand. Yet the per capita income still remains a bit over $12,000 a year. A third of all youth under eighteen live below the poverty line. Selma's remaining native poorer whites, ethnics, and second- and third-generation Mexican Americans, who would not or could not leave, are not culpable for the vast transformations in the city's economic, social, and cultural landscape. Those changes were mostly a result of the laxity of immigration enforcement and importation of inexpensive labor, globalized trade policy, and the vertical integration of agriculture. Their once prosperous and stable community did not really deserve to erode. They were and are certainly not lazy or stupid people, and they had sought all sorts of remedies to redress their plights and save their town. Yet, even today, the new Selma is hardly a negative asset. That Trump was more sympathetic to the consequences of these multifaceted global forces of erosion than was Hillary Clinton did not just win him critical swing state voters. It also made it more difficult to tar him as a heartless Mitt Romney caricature.

Decline is always a chicken-and-the-egg paradox. But there is less evidence that suddenly around 1980, the population of the red-state interior abruptly ceased to function and turned slothful, thus driving away employers, than the overwhelming data that the industrial and manufacturing foundations of the US economy were utterly changed by global shifts and disruptions not seen since the Industrial Revolution—and thus beyond the ability of working-class communities to absorb. Trump's own mercurial fortunes, even if self-induced, often had hinged on global recessions and transformations. Fairly or not, such commercial vulnerability had given him insight into the disasters faced by others.

Trump may have demagogued such progressive arrogance and bias. But it was certainly not hard to do so, since the media and politicians so easily condemned themselves, especially after the election when they had no longer much need to keep up their guard. For example, blue disdain for red America seemed to permeate almost all the political controversies of the age. It certainly characterized some of the polemics over House Intelligence Committee chairman Rep. Devin Nunes's (R-CA) investigation of allegedly improper use of the FISA (Foreign Intelligence Surveillance Act) courts and FBI wrongdoing in association with former FBI director James Comey. Nunes grew up on a dairy farm (not far from my own farm). Worse still in the eyes of the elite, he majored in agricultural business at Cal Poly, San Luis Obispo.

Translated, that meant he de facto must be over his head in Washington. Coastal critics focused on Nunes as the proverbial rustic dunce. *Roll Call*'s David Hawkings tsked, tsked: "The match between his backstory and his prominence seems wholly incongruous and helps underscore the perception that Nunes is cavalierly playing at a very high-stakes game while in way over his head."

MSNBC analyst Elise Jordan equated farming with inability: "Why are Republicans trusting Devin Nunes to be their oracle of truth? A former dairy farmer who House Intel staffers refer to as 'Secret Agent Man,' because he has no idea what's going on."

Jordan apparently assumed the intelligence and savvy required to run a small farming operation did not equate to those of a cable TV talking head. Peter Lance of the *Huffington Post* sniffed, "There's certainly nothing in his résumé that would have qualified him for the post."

Similar was the later coastal-class disdain shown Trump White House press secretary Sarah Huckabee Sanders. Her progressive sins were many, as a mother of three, devout Christian, Oklahoman, and daughter of former governor and conservative presidential candidate Mike Huckabee. Critics variously targeted her looks, her religion, her accent, and her bearing in a way that few had criticized prior press secretaries. Actor Jim Carrey tweeted a monstrous cartoon of her, with the caption "This is the portrait of a so-called Christian whose only purpose in life is to lie for the wicked. Monstrous!"

Earlier, *Los Angeles Times* columnist David Horsey had mocked Sanders's appearance, scoffing that she "looks more like a slightly chunky soccer mom who organizes snacks for the kids' games . . . Rather than the fake eyelashes and formal dresses she puts on for news briefings, Sanders seems as if she'd be more comfortable in sweats and running shoes." In June 2018, a small restaurant in Lexington, Virginia, made national news by refusing to serve customers Sarah Sanders and her family.

New York Times columnist Frank Bruni echoed the coastal contempt for the Oklahoman Sanders: "To listen to her pronounce 'priorities' is akin to hearing the air seep out of a flat tire, and she leaves half of the consonants on the curb." At the April 2018 White House Correspondents' Dinner, a mostly liberal and often smug media was treated to slurs of Sanders by hip comedian Michelle Wolf. She focused on the press secretary's appearance and Arkansas background: "I actually really like Sarah. I think she's very resourceful. But she burns facts and then she uses that ash to create a perfect smokey eye . . . Maybe she's born with it, maybe it's lies. It's probably lies."

Actor Peter Fonda advocated a more violent fate for the Arkansas native: "SS (Sarah Sanders) is a lying g*sh [an obscene term for the female genitalia], too. And 'g*sh' is much worse than c*nt. Maybe we should take her children away and deport her to Arkansas, and giving [sic] her children to Stephen Goebbels Miller for safe keeping."

Coastal elites rarely seemed to stop, reflect, and ask themselves by what particular standard they were dismissing those of the interior, much less whether their contempt was only fueling ever greater countercontempt. After all, neither Carrey, Horsey, nor Bruni had ever caricatured Barack Obama, a graduate of Harvard Law School, after he kept pronouncing corpsmen with a hard p, as if soldiers were zombies, or seemed to think that the Maldives were the Spanish version of the Falklands. Again, these are not extraneous examples, but post-election reflections of why Trump's message so resonated with those who saw a condemnatory urban elite as hardly deserving of the notion of elite.

Yet how would Trump recapture these proverbial blue-dog Democrats, the old Reaganite working class, or the Tea Partyers?

Except for a few razor-close Republican wins in Phoenix, Oklahoma City, and Fort Worth—and a bigger victory in Mormon Salt Lake City—no major American city voted for Mitt Romney in the 2012 presidential election. In supposedly solid red states, urban areas nonetheless still voted solidly Democratic. Austin, Dallas, Houston, and San Antonio went blue in 2012. Twenty-seven out the nation's thirty major cities voted Democratic in 2012.

Two electoral assumptions followed from such one-sidedness. One, the urban liberal coastal states were already lost to Trump, as they mostly had been for prior Republicans for the last thirty years. Two, to win most of the purple swing states, Trump would then need to rack up such large majorities in the hinterlands that the lopsided Democratic tallies in a Cleveland and Columbus, Philadelphia and Pittsburgh, or Ann Arbor and Detroit could not compensate.

Trump understood that many of the deplorables, despite their clear contempt from liberals, also despised white establishment Republican elites even more than they did the identity-politics Democrats. Right before the 2012 election, I was given a ninety-mile ride through southern Michigan by a retired autoworker. I listened mute for nearly two hours as the sixty-year-old driver railed at and damned aspects of Obama's first presidential term, from Obamacare to record numbers on food stamps. As I started to get out of the van, I tried to leave amicably by offering him mild encouragement: "Well, I guess you'll have your chance to send him a message in a few weeks by voting for Romney."

The driver's face immediately screwed up. He bristled. "Romney? Romney? Hell, no! I'll hold my nose and vote for Obama. Or maybe not vote at all! Geez, Romney came to Michigan wearing his wing tips with starched jeans!"

In the following chapters, we will examine the particular messages and the unique style of the messenger that Trump crafted to win Michigan and Ohio. But in a more general sense, Trump by his speech, his bearing, and his perceived remedies had to win over those like my retired unionist, anti-Romney, rural Michigan shuttle driver. The off-putting billionaire Trump had to convey that the blue coasts and their party despised the interior—had contempt for this driver's culture, his values, his very people. As it turned out, that challenge, quite apart from Trump's histrionics, proved not a particularly difficult thing to do, given the hubris of his opponents in broadcasting their disregard and their propensities for damning those who supported Trump even more than Trump himself.

Both the Obama campaign and the Trump candidacy relied on revving up their respective bases to vote along both class and in some sense racial lines as well. Scorn for red-state America, of course, had been a subtext of Obama's 2008 election messaging. But the political opportunity for pushback was insufficiently capitalized upon by the inept McCain campaign, despite the presence of rural Alaskan, twangy Sarah Palin. She proved vivacious and probably upped the ticket's polls. But she was inexperienced, poorly prepared, often sandbagged by McCain aides, and was soon buried beneath an avalanche of media contempt within a hostile cultural landscape. Nonetheless, there had been plenty of working-class openings had McCain only wished to exploit them.

During the 2008 campaign, Obama himself had occasionally reverted to the "white men" tropes earlier found in his autobiography *Dreams from My Father* ("Still, there was something about him that made me wary. A little too sure of himself, maybe. And white . . ."). In Obama's much heralded March 2008 speech ("A More Perfect Union")—an apology for long-held intimacy with the Reverend Jeremiah Wright—the future president drew a moral equivalence between the racist firebrand Wright and his own white grandmother. She had scrimped to send Obama to prep school. But such sacrifice seemed to have won only conceited indifference for her efforts: "I can no more disown him [Wright] than I can my white grandmother."

When later he was called out for equating Wright's racism with his supposedly clueless grandmother's fears of being alone on a street with young African American males (in the manner that progressives such as Jesse Jackson, Mark Cuban, and Lena Dunham have similarly confessed such fears), Obama further dismissed her with the now infamous slur: "She is a typical white person."

Millions of soon to be Trump voters remembered that contempt for years afterward. It may be now blasphemous to concede that much of the current division in the country was deliberately whipped up by Obama. Often in mellifluous tones and with near academic authority, he accentuated racial and cultural differences. And his purpose was to galvanize a new blue-state coalition that would institutionalize his own successful trajectory to victory.

After losing the Pennsylvania primary of 2008, a contrite Obama had further caricatured the white working class as near zombies of a xenophobic and racist sort who had not supported his candidacy: "And it's not surprising, then they get bitter, they cling to guns or religion or antipathy to people who aren't like them or anti-immigrant sentiment or anti-trade sentiment as a way to explain their frustrations."

The anthropologist Obama may or may not have meant that most whites have racist tendencies. But he certainly implied that most all white rural Pennsylvanians did. Yet due to record urban registration and voting, and lackadaisical rural turnout, he easily beat, by an over 10 percent margin, a hapless John McCain in Pennsylvania in 2008. Most likely, thousands of the "clingers" stayed home. They concluded that it was not worth their effort to vote for a perceived elitist Republican even over an insulting liberal Democrat. Or perhaps their critics were right that they had disengaged altogether from civic participation.

By Obama's second term, the press mostly had ignored what had become monotonous caricatures of the supposed Neanderthal white heartland. During his September 2016 Laos trip, Obama again blasted Americans as veritable racists with his favorite adjective/adverb "typical/typically": "Typically, when people feel stressed, they turn on others who don't look like them."

Obama neither spoke a foreign language nor seemed to be informed about other countries and continents (e.g., he had earlier stated that his home state Hawaii was in Asia, and that Austrians spoke a language called Austrian). Yet in that same speech in Laos, Obama voiced another theme that would be later repeated even by Republican elites: American stagnation, insularity, and lack of sophistication were due to arrogance and laziness: "If you're in the United States, sometimes you can feel lazy, and think we're so big we don't have to really know anything about other people." Most voters in Michigan, however, knew that Hawaii was an American Pacific Island state, and that Austrians no more spoke Austrian than Americans did American.

In sum, the mainstream press never caught on that Obama had done some of the foundational work for an us-them backlash that would become so useful for someone like a Trump. Talk radio, conservative cable news, and the internet had pounded Obama mercilessly not because, as alleged, of his race, but for his progressive politics and perceived snark and snobbery.

Obama's stereotyping had lots of help. His eight years often emboldened an imitative cohort of blue-/red-state dividers. In this pre-Trump, new age of racial polarization, few proved quite as crude as Minnesota governor Mark Dayton. In 2015, he lashed out at any Minnesotans who questioned the wisdom of allowing into his state mostly unvetted refugees from Somalia, a few with demonstrable Islamist ties: "If you are that intolerant, if you are that much of a racist or a bigot, then find another state. Find a state where the minority population is 1 percent or whatever." Then Dayton zeroed in with contempt for the white working class: "Our economy cannot expand based on white, B+, Minnesota-born citizens. We don't have enough."

What exactly defined B+ citizens? And what were the criteria of Dayton's A to F human scale? And did most Minnesotans not make Dayton's B+ cut in a way Somalis did?

A weird normal before 2015 had kept encouraging such pejorative pre-Trump generalization. Usually taboo sexist and class attacks freely focused upon and demonized Sarah Palin. She had become a sort of Rorschach test symbol of contempt for the rural and poor white working class. Late-night comedian David Letterman joked of the statutory rape of her fourteen-year-old daughter Willow: "One awkward moment for Sarah Palin at the Yankee game—during the seventh inning, her daughter was knocked up by Alex Rodriguez." Essayist Andrew Sullivan kept peddling a fabulist's "truther" conspiracy theory that Sarah Palin had once faked her own pregnancy with another child, her disabled son Trig, apparently to hide the fact that Trig was really the illegitimate child of her daughter Bristol, who was apparently hidden away during her respective pregnancy.

The popular cartoon of a culpable white person persisted as an unsympathetic figure deserving of scripted condemnation. As Letterman and Sullivan anticipated, there was only an upside in saying just that. Or as the popular African American essayist Ta-Nehisi Coates phrased his racial disdain in supposedly high-brow fashion: "When people who are not black are interested in what I do, frankly, I'm always surprised . . . I don't know if it's my low expectations for white people or what."

The formerly centrist Republican Colin Powell resonated the new feeling of elite contempt that was peaking in 2016. From the trove of his hacked emails of 2016, he seemed eager to play his own race card by caricaturing "poor white folks," while blasting Trump as a pariah—all the while name-dropping the Hamptons and Bohemian Grove, and whining that Hillary Clinton's jacked-up campus lecture fees imperiled his own. Each publicized slur in and of itself was quickly forgotten. But in aggregate these thematic putdowns cemented an image of liberal disdain for the heartland and only stocked Trump's arsenal of retaliation.

The popular side of Coates's hard bigotry of low expectations was something akin to the rapper—and Obama favorite and White House guest—Kendrick Lamar's hit album cover. A mutilated corpse of a white judge (replete with x'd-out zombie eyes) lies at the foot of young African Americans toasting his demise on the White House lawn. In early 2018, an emeritus President Obama, no longer worried about reelection, resonated

Lamar's themes through selection of his official portrait painter, Kehinde Wiley.

Wiley is an identity-politics conceptual artist who emphasizes his own black and gay identity as essential to his work. He previously had courted controversy on two occasions for recalibrating well-known paintings from the past, reworking the scenes of violence in interracial fashion. In these two paintings, a black woman, sword in one hand, is holding up the severed head of a white woman she has just decapitated. Or as Kehinde Wiley once described his black-on-white beheadings to the *New York Times Magazine,* "It's sort of a play on the 'kill whitey' thing." Had Trump later engaged such an official painter, who in the past had said the same racist things about nonwhites, he would have been branded as bigot himself.

In even more bizarre fashion, well after the 2016 election—when the practical and political wages of elite contempt for the white and red-state working classes should have been a clear electoral warning—some Never Trump Republicans in disgust with Trump only doubled down. Liberated from being blamed for a Trump defeat that never happened, they now unwittingly confirmed the very undercurrents that had elected Trump president in the first place and might again. Even more importantly, the now undisguised contempt from the elite conservative Never Trumpers reminded the country that the bias was not so much political as cultural and regional. They hated Trump not just for his own pathologies, but for his resonance with half the country they considered even more disgusting.

New York Times resident conservative David Brooks, in a column about so-called white and economically backward America, simply could not suppress his disdain:

> These rural places are often 95 percent white . . . Are these counties marked by high social cohesion, economic dynamism, surging wages and healthy family values? No. Quite the

opposite. They are often marked by economic stagnation, social isolation, family breakdown and high opioid addiction. . . .
It is a blunt fact of life that, these days, immigrants show more
of these virtues than the native-born.

Note how Brooks deliberately conflated illegal and legal immigration by his use of the inclusive and generic "immigrants,"
as if working-class objections to entering the country illegally
were synonymous to nativist dislike of legal immigrants as well.
Somehow Brooks had discounted all other factors that lead to
a particular American county's prosperity. He certainly ignored
natural resources, good government, location, climate, and surrounding geography. Instead, he adjudicated the relative material success of a locale on the basis of racial or native-born
representation.

In the Central Valley of California, nativists and chauvinists
often make mirror-image arguments to Brooks's own—and to
prove the very opposite point. They cite far greater per capita
incomes in small towns like Exeter and Kingsburg. Both have
far higher so-called native white populations and far lower illegal immigrant numbers than do nearby mostly Latino and
impoverished Orange Cove and Parlier. The latter towns are
characterized by far higher crime and worse schools. In sum,
blue pundits were making stereotyped arguments that they
would decry as racist or reductive if applied to minorities.

In an off-the-cuff aside during a taped panel discussion at a
Washington think tank, another Never Trump Republican establishmentarian, Bill Kristol of the *Weekly Standard*, could be
even more candid in the aftermath of the election in his derision
for the thinly disguised stereotypical Trump voter:

Look, to be totally honest, if things are so bad as you say with
the white working class, don't you want to get new Americans in? . . . You can make a case that America has been great

because every—I think John Adams said this—basically if you are in free society, a capitalist society, after two or three generations of hard work, everyone becomes kind of decadent, lazy, spoiled—whatever.

Here Obama's early stereotype of a lazy American popped up again, albeit with less restraint in tying slothfulness most prominently to what was referred to by others as the "POS" or "garbage" white working class. It would be easy to say such dismissive comments were haphazard or the rants of a few pundits in New York or Washington. But, in fact, scorn for the white middle class, before and after the election, was widespread among many elites, and it ignited a Trump backlash.

The so-called Calexit leader Shankar Singam, in a television appearance to promote the secession of California from the Union, took up Mark Dayton's theme of replacing Americans with better people, in the context of the flight of the middle class from California. Only that way would their welcomed departure make room for a wave of superior immigrants. Singam boasted that, in fact, the United States "should be grateful for us": "If everyone in the middle class is leaving, that's actually a good thing. We need these spots opened up for the new wave of immigrants to come up. It's what we do."

Erstwhile Republican and Never Trumper Max Boot elaborated on that theme of swapping out populations in June 2018, by dreaming that the United States could deport American citizens who were Republican Trump supporters and essentially replace them with Latin American "newcomers" of uncertain legal status: "If only we could keep the hard-working Latin American newcomers and deport the contemptible Republican cowards—that would truly enhance America's greatness."

After the election, deporting deplorables was supposedly a facetious trope to underscore the irony of deporting illegal aliens. Or so *New York Times* columnist Bret Stephens seemed to imply when he wrote: "So-called real Americans are screwing up America. Maybe they should leave, so that we can replace them with new and better ones: newcomers who are more appreciative of what the United States has to offer, more ambitious for themselves and their children, and more willing to sacrifice for the future. In other words, just the kind of people we used to be—when 'we' had just come off the boat." But after claiming that he was being ironic, Stephens concluded his column by confirming that he wasn't really: "We're a country of immigrants—by and for them, too. Americans who don't get it should get out." His argument was little more than that complaining that illegal immigration undermines the rule of law qualifies the complainer for voluntary deportation.

Note that the supposed pathologies of native-born Americans were assumed to be mostly those of the white middle class. They were not the sins additionally, and sometimes more frequently, of the inner city and of the barrios. Again, the nobility of immigrants was also emphasized by conflating illegal immigration with often merit-based legal immigration.

For a movement that denied its antipathy for Trump and was fueled by a class-based contempt for his supporters, it was remarkable how frequently critics resorted to a "deport them" anger at Trump voters—who, after all, were US citizens and had a perfect right to worry over the deliberate subversion of federal immigration law, accompanied by virtual open borders, and the influx of well over 11 million illegal aliens. The point is not to pile example upon example of silly elitism, but to convey how deeply a coastal culture despised its own antithesis, a disgust that transcended and predated Trump himself.

While it is easy to find such quotations of elite disdain among analysts, politicians, and pundits, it is more difficult to document the counterpunches from the reviled. Some did write about the perils of such contempt. But more often the pushback was instead aired through daily talk radio, transitory social media, or furious online commentaries to news articles and was discounted. The media missed the growing backlash, discounted it, or added to it.

What was common both to McCain's and Clinton's aborted 2008 efforts at populism—and their shared 2016 about-face derision for Trump who pulled it off far better than they—was inauthenticity. Trump could be uncouth and crude. He may have been chameleon-like throughout his long business career. But in 2016 he came across as genuinely concerned about the proverbial "clingers," "deplorables," and "crazies." The voters sensed that empathy. They assumed that in 2024 a post-election Donald J. Trump, wherever he was, would not, like McCain and Clinton in 2016, bite the very populist hand that he once had begged to feed him.

In 2016, Manhattanite Donald Trump, with mansions in West Palm Beach and Beverly Hills, was quite eager to mine the red-blue divide in a way that primary opponents and more genuine popular heartland politicians such as Wisconsin governor Scott Walker or Ohio governor John Kasich either would—or could—not. The Left had created a sense of deterrence. Appeals to the white working class were blasted as tantamount to racism, in a way that liberal identity politics were not. And most conservative politicians simply did not wish to invite progressive invective.

Trump had no such reluctance to court the struggling midwestern working class. What most national candidates envisioned as a liability or at least a taboo, Trump saw as an advantage and opening. In an insightful stroke of marketing, Trump could put on a $10,000 suit and shoes, and still appear more the garish blowhard leaving a bowling alley. His Queens accent, his transparent effort to stay youthful with tanning beds, hair dye, and facial surgery, his ample girth and fast-food tastes came across as one with the same uncontrollable habits and appetites of the forgotten man. The more the Eastern Seaboard wealthy disparaged him, the more his cred in Youngstown or York grew. He certainly looked more the part of purple state swing voter than did the far less conspicuously wealthy Mitt Romney, Barack Obama, or Hillary Clinton.

J. D. Vance, author of *Hillbilly Elegy* and an initial and fierce critic of Trump ("Trump instead offers a political high, a promise to 'Make America Great Again' without a single good idea regarding how"), astutely explained Trump's strange billionaire populism:

> Many in the US and abroad marvel that a showy billionaire could inspire such allegiance among relatively poor voters. Yet in style and tone, Trump reminds blue-collar workers of themselves. Gone are the poll-tested and consultant-approved political lines, replaced with a backslapping swashbuckler unafraid of saying what's on his mind. The elites of DC and NY see an offensive madman, blowing through decades of political convention with his every word. His voters, on the other hand, see a man who's refreshingly relatable, who talks about politics and policy as if he were sitting around the dinner table.

Was that paradox the key to the Trump enigma: an ability to make his poorer and more middle-class rivals seem abject snobs and inauthentic snarks, as if populism was a state of mind and attitude rather than preordained by class? After all, Senator Bernie Sanders ran as a neosocialist populist in the 2016 Democratic primary. He campaigned in rumpled clothes with a Brooklyn, rather than Trump's Queens, accent. He railed against crushing student loans and a corrupt elite establishment, even as his former college-president wife was under an FBI probe for bank fraud.

The supposedly callous, spoiled, egotistical, and privileged Trump early in his campaign began using the first-plural personal pronoun "our" for the heartland's supposed losers. Such endearment—entirely ignored by the media—would likely not have occurred to either Romney or Clinton (or for that matter the more genuine red-state populists Walker or Kasich). Suddenly the nation heard of "*our* miners," "*our* farmers," "*our* vets," and "*our* workers." Whether genuine or fabricated, "our" was a far smarter trope than Hillary Clinton's 2016 campaign write-off of an entire industry and disdain for "those folks" or Romney's "those people."

During the campaign, Hillary Clinton's "deplorable" tic, despite her best efforts, could not be restrained. No sooner had she arrived in West Virginia, and she was in some sense calling for the veritable destruction of the entire state's economy.

> So, for example, I'm the only candidate who has a policy about how to bring economic opportunity using clean renewable energy as the key into coal country. Because we're going to put a lot of coal miners and coal companies out of business.

Did Clinton believe that she could prove Trump divisive by promising to put "a lot of coal miners out of business"? How could a sane candidate call for a compassionate energy policy while going to West Virginia and promising to end the livelihoods of tens of thousands?

Again, it was not difficult to see who and what had created Trump. He had seen a critical preexisting and vast swath of potential voters in proverbial swing states who were angry over their accelerating decline. They were resentful over the disdain shown them by elites, especially the likes of Barack Obama and Hillary Clinton. And they were irate at the winners of globalization who had somehow blamed them for being the global economy's losers.

During the Obama years a whirlwind of social changes had come from on high, either by court decisions, deep-state fiat, or executive orders—gay marriage, women in combat units, transgendered bathrooms, open borders, and amnesty—with little time for the country to digest them or congressional representatives to debate such issues as a matter of laws.

Trump supporters also believed that a good job was the font of a good life. It was the wellspring alone from which followed a stable two-parent family, home ownership, and a sense of confidence and pride. Without it, everything went into reverse. As the astute political scientist Henry Olsen put it of the failure of both parties to fathom the Trump appeal:

> It's no accident that the very people who flocked to Donald Trump turned their backs on the Romney-Ryan ticket ... The Left tends to fail by looking at the problem as merely material. To them, increased government subsidies and enforced minimum wage hikes solve the problem. But neither solution confers the pride that comes from a job, nor does either solution address the system that places these people under a continual competition that they simply cannot win. They are palliatives that ease the suffering of the body but ignore the suffering of the soul.

Where Trump's Republican rivals, Barack Obama, and Hillary Clinton had all seen a spent political force, Trump embraced the forgotten as potentially the most important voters in the nation, a sort of dormant volcano that needed a gritty Vulcan to awake it. In Trump's reckoning, it was as if a clerk in southern Ohio or a machinist in Pennsylvania—if he or she would just come back out to vote—was worth a thousand voters in San Francisco or New York under the rules of the Electoral College. The latter's blue states were never going to flip red, and thus their voters were redundant and symbolic rather than pivotal and real.

Trump himself had flipped globalization on its head: the masters of the universe in the coastal states of New York and

California, at least when it came to the Electoral College, were the real losers whose superfluous votes were marginalized. What Trump sorely needed to complete his wake up of the somnolent working-class dragon and win the blue-red divide were concrete agendas, a sort of updated "Contract with America" that had won Republicans the House in 1994. Trump required campaign themes that would galvanize his base and eventually win over even centrist Republicans, Independents, and stray Democrats. And soon he found wedge issues mostly neglected—or perhaps even unknown—by both parties.

Chapter Two

TRUMPISM

A civil war is going to break out inside the
Republican Party along the old trench lines of the
Goldwater-Rockefeller wars of the 1960s, a war for
the heart and soul and future of the party.
—Patrick J. Buchanan, *Where the Right Went Wrong*

To leverage the cultural and class divide, to win the Republican primaries and to fuel a general election bid, Trump zoomed in on a number of signature issues. All of them at various times had been the haphazard property of earlier right-wing and, on occasion, left-wing populists. But from the moment that Trump announced his candidacy, he monotonously hammered these concerns—as if they were uniquely novel and his own throughout the campaign, the presidential transition, and his first two years in office.

Even more unusual, what Trump ran on in 2015–16, he almost immediately sought to implement as president in 2017–18. That consistency rallied his base. It also astonished his critics, who privately had consoled themselves after his victory along the lines of "at least Trump cannot be serious."

But he was. And he made that clear with a number of agendas.

Candidate and then president Trump faulted Bush's Republicans as much as Obama's Democrats for optional, costly, and inconsequential wars, from Iraq to Libya. For Trump, the objection was not that intervening abroad was necessarily immoral. Rather, such interventions were allegedly fought for ungrateful others, at the expense of Americans at home, especially the working classes. In political terms, Trump decided to run against much of the current Washington bipartisan foreign policy establishment and the previous three administrations that had intervened in Afghanistan, Iraq, and Libya.

When Trump serially complained, "We don't win wars anymore," he did not mean just that the United States should be more muscular in finishing conflicts. Specifically, America should fight more reactively than preemptively, but only where America can realistically win. "Well, I'll tell you what, I don't mind fighting," Trump conceded in February 2016, "but you have got to win and number one, we don't win wars, we just fight, we just fight. It's like a big—like you're vomiting, just fight, fight, fight."

For Trump, "I don't mind fighting" apparently meant that he could "bomb the sh*t out of ISIS" (and then leave). But staying in or even trying to get out of Afghanistan would be more like "vomiting." For Trump, the eventual geostrategic stakes were less important than onetime Oakland Raiders owner Al Davis's truism, "Just win, baby."

Apparently, Trump cynically understood war and grand strategy as rather analogous to the nature of the business world. What people profess is really predicated on perceptions of success and resulting esteem: win a war and the why and how it started are less important. Lose a war and suddenly blame ensues over who dreamed up such a debacle. The Greek historian Thucydides in a more general sense said the same thing over twenty-four hundred years ago, when he distinguished the pretext (*prophasis*) from the true cause (*aitia*). Trump had an uncanny ability to prune away *prophases* and get to the heart of what people thought rather than what they professed. Trump, the TV star and entrepreneur, also placed a high value on ratings and money. In such a commercial value system, wars were deals, or, rather too frequently, bad deals that could quickly prove too unpopular and costly to be worth the intended results.

Yet only fighting winnable wars for strategically logical aims is more easily promised than done. Once in office, Trump himself would renege on some of his campaign promises to leave Afghanistan. "We made a terrible mistake getting involved there in the first place," Trump admitted in October 2015. "We had real brilliant thinkers that didn't know what the hell they were doing. And it's a mess. It's a mess . . . And at this point, you probably have to [stay] because that thing will collapse about two seconds after they leave."

During his first month in office, Trump was still channeling these campaign themes to White House visiting executives: "We've spent $6 trillion in the Middle East. We've got nothing. We've got nothing. We never even kept a small, even a tiny oil well. Not one little oil well. I said, 'Keep the oil.'"

As president, Trump would soon learn that the United States had seven hundred military facilities around the world and treaty responsibilities with allies whose autonomy depended on American bombers, soldiers, and warships. The dilemma, then, would be how to deter Syria from using chemical weapons against children, to send a message to Syria's Russian abettors to cease their sponsorship of Syrian president Bashar al-Assad, and to signal to enemies like North Korea and Iran that the United States was unpredictable—all the while not getting involved in an optional and possibly costly overseas misadventure in the Middle East.

So there were risks and contradictions in Trump's loud maverick foreign policy posture, shared largely only by Senator

Rand Paul among his primary rivals. To explain his Jacksonian nationalism—a defiant readiness to retaliate overwhelmingly against aggressors, but not to start optional wars—Trump seemed always to return to the Iraq War (2003-8). It was his symbol of the entire flawed doctrine of neoconservative elective nation building. In contrast, during the 2016 Republican campaign most Republican candidates had felt it wise to keep mum about Iraq. Not Trump: he sensed an opening and pounced.

Trump apparently guessed that his rival Republican senators and governors were somewhat embarrassed that thirteen years ago they had supported the removal of Saddam Hussein. But on the other hand, as violence in Iraq had spiked in 2004-6, many erstwhile supporters had long ago squared their circles of support by blaming the Bush administration's incompetent implementation of the occupation and reconstruction. Their new fallback position was analogous to "*My* brilliant three-week removal of Saddam Hussein—*your* loused-up four-year aftermath."

In part, General David Petraeus's 2006-8 surge of troops into Iraq had also quieted the anti-war fervor by mid-2008. When Obama took office in January 2009, more American soldiers were daily dying of accidents worldwide than due to hostile enemy action in Iraq. Iraq and what it portended, then, were supposedly no longer the contentious issues they had been in the 2004 election.

In part, a new Republican consensus had also spread that Iraq had finally "worked." In 2010, even Vice President Joe Biden had preened, "I am very optimistic about—about Iraq. I mean, this could be one of the great achievements of this administration." Obama himself had proclaimed the nation to be a "sovereign, stable and self-reliant Iraq, with a representative government." That success was his justification for pulling out all US peacekeepers at the beginning of his reelection campaign at the end of 2011.

When Iraq then quickly fell apart in 2012, the Republican boilerplate complaint was that Obama had undermined a secure and stable country, and thereby empowered ISIS (written off by Obama as "Jayvees" or amateur terrorists of no real import) to fill the vacuum. To get an idea of something similar to the ensuing chaos, imagine if President Eisenhower in 1956 had yanked all US troops out of the Korean demilitarized zone to fulfill a campaign promise to end "Truman's war"—and then assumed Seoul could have survived both its nearby North Korean and regional communist enemies.

Was it smart, then, for candidate Donald J. Trump to beat a dead horse, in blasting every aspect of the war? Indeed, by mid-2015 Trump was daily faulting George W. Bush for the way he got into Iraq ("lies" about weapons of mass destruction) more than he was chastising Obama for the way he got out. Apparently, the outsider Trump saw Iraq as emblematic of subsequent Republican and Democratic post-war interventionist stupidity—as if Obama and Secretary of State Hillary Clinton had pursued their own mini-Iraqs in the misadventure in Benghazi, Libya, and the decade-and-a-half continuous and inconsequential slog in Afghanistan. Again, Trump the businessman thought they were all "bad deals," whose benefits never justified the costs.

There were a few other dangers in Trump's digging up Iraq, given his own contradictory and often disingenuous past positions. Despite his heated denials, Trump had once initially supported the Iraq War. When radio disc jockey Howard Stern asked him in 2003 whether the United States should invade Iraq, Trump responded, "Yeah, I guess so. I wish the first time it was done correctly." When the post-Saddam violence escalated, Trump grew furious at the stalemate. He renounced and then clumsily denied his early support (as did most), and began castigating Bush to the point that he said the president had deserved impeachment. His calls were not so different from those of leftists such as the left-wing filmmaker Michael Moore or the anti-war activist Cindy Sheehan.

Would Jacksonians in rural Pennsylvania and Ohio wish to hear that Iraq a decade later was a complete waste of blood and treasure? "Let me tell you something," Trump told an interviewer in 2016. "I'll tell you it very simply. It may have been the worst decision—going into Iraq may have been the worst decision anybody has made; any president has made in the history of this country. That's how bad it is, okay?"

In political terms, as a conservative populist, Trump was beginning to sound to the Republican establishment a lot like Pat Buchanan's neoisolationist bid against George H. W. Bush in 1992. In truth, Trump's message was not so much different from Buchanan's, but the times most certainly were. Avoiding optional interventions was now far more resonant in an age of open borders, a rising China, and record national debt. The more Trump went after Iraq, the more it apparently became easier for him to question more broadly the costs of *all* of America's commitments abroad, from NATO to the UN to the Israeli-Palestinian "peace process."

The challenge here was that the charge of isolationism only cemented the slur against Trump that he was reminiscent of Charles Lindbergh and his support of the America First Committee (founded in September 1940). Lindbergh had sullied his folk hero status and at best had once remained silent as Hitler and Mussolini extinguished European democracies, and at worst charged that interventions abroad were the work of international Jewry, British monarchists, and other sundry conspirators.

The challenge for Trump politically was to find a way to leverage the controversy over Iraq and nation building, as well as general overseas commitments, in terms of domestic self-interest. He hinted that much of his anger at interventionism was bad cop–good cop deal making—only by questioning the very need for NATO could Trump force European members (who were geographically closer to perceived enemies than was the United States) to honor their pledges. Only by increasing their anemic defense budgets could the European people earn help from their distant American counterparts.

Indeed, by 2018 a few formerly tightfisted NATO members were at least upping their commitments. Trump took credit for the increase in contributions and bragged about a newly empowered alliance ("I took such heat, when I said NATO was obsolete. It's obsolete because it wasn't taking care of terror. I took a lot of heat for two days. And then they started saying Trump is right.").

The more America kept clear of quagmires and misadventures like Syria, Libya, and Afghanistan, Trump argued, the more it might marshal its resources to blast away at ISIS, or stand up to Iran, North Korea, and China—or spend the money at home. Note again Trump's foreign policy style: threaten and bluster would convey his seriousness or even crisis, seriousness and crisis would prompt overdue reform, and finally reform would make America and its allies stronger. The downsides of an accidental military conflict or permanently estranged allies were worth the risk.

Trump told Middle America that he wanted lots more missiles, tanks, planes, and nukes, more money for soldiers and veterans—even forces in space—but only if the money would not be wasted on ungrateful Iraqis, Afghans, or Libyans, even as Americans were hurting at home. In the beginning, Trump's message had weakened hawkish primary rivals like Marco Rubio and Ted Cruz by connecting wasted blood and treasure with stagnation, if not depression, in the heartland. Later as president, Trump honed his policies as nationalist rather than isolationist, muscular rather than weak, and enhancing Western security by loudly addressing rather than quietly ignoring problems.

Trump's talk of punitive bombing and big defense budgets distanced him from neoisolationists like Senator Rand Paul, who often proved a Trump critic on matters of foreign policy. For balance, Trump frequently on the stump blasted Hillary Clinton on her past support for the Iraq War and her more recent responsibility for and later indifference about the disaster in Libya, in which the ambassador Chris Stevens was murdered, one of only six US ambassadors killed in the post-war era. Earlier, in October 2011, Clinton had let out a creepy laugh about the Libyan finale of Muammar Gaddafi's brutal street murder: "We came, we saw, he died." Within weeks, as violence arose after Gaddafi's fall, no one in the Obama administration any longer claimed the Libyan intervention as a success. Clinton was becoming an easy foreign policy target.

Trump's style was flawed in at least one regard. Whereas he assumed that his art-of-the-deal brinksmanship would be appreciated for the results it obtained, his negotiating partners would not always concur. They resented being strong-armed for even legitimate and long-overdue concessions. They blamed Trump for both embarrassing them and creating, in diplomatic doublespeak, an "unhealthy atmosphere" or "misfortunate climate" between otherwise "friends and allies." The paradox of the art-of-the-deal paradigm was that it was intended in business for mostly one-off negotiations in which Trump's advantage often left lingering acrimony, which was irrelevant if the two parties of an agreement then usually permanently parted ways. But the techniques of bluster and overreach left diplomatic bitterness if the relationship and rivalry were ongoing and demanded near constant and continual negotiations over the years. In other words, either it would take a long time for resentful NATO allies to get used to the idea of meeting their military spending promises or soon they would catch on to Trump's art-of-the-deal transparent threats, and simply ignore them.

How then to describe Trump's agenda abroad?

In April 2016, candidate Trump had earlier tried to answer just that lingering question with a comprehensive strategic speech. He faulted past administrations' policies and promised to replace "randomness with purpose, ideology with strategy, and chaos with peace." The central theme was that a new US foreign policy should be calibrated on the interests of American citizens, at least in the transparent short term. "Under a Trump administration, no American citizen will ever again feel that their needs come second to the citizens of foreign countries," Trump repeated constantly.

Fine. But, again, what did such an announcement mean in the real world of NATO, providing a nuclear umbrella for Japan, South Korea, and most of Europe, as well as keeping Israelis, Taiwanese, the Kurds, and a host of other vulnerable people safe from their rapacious neighbors? In other words, what would Trump do with the inherited, costly, and messy obligations that more or less make the post-war world work most of the time—if the Iranians blocked the Straits of Hormuz, the North Koreans shot more missiles into Japanese airspace, or Vladimir Putin annexed Estonia?

Apparently, candidate Trump in his address had promised that he would protect allies, if attacked, but not seek optional interventions that might in theory lead to some nebulous long-term US advantage: "I will never send our finest into battle unless necessary, and I mean absolutely necessary, and will only do so if we have a plan for victory with a capital V." Again, Trump mostly omitted any mention of how to win the United States' seventeen-year-long role in Afghanistan, the small but ongoing US ground support operations in genocidal Syria, and close cooperation with Saudi Arabia against the Shiite Houthis in Yemen. Apparently, Trump figured that to demand cessations of these operations that others had started would call upon him the wrath of hawkish Republicans and fuel charges of isolationism (if not make him look weak), and that so few troops were dying in these interventions that few Americans even grasped the depth of US involvement.

In addition to his formal address on foreign policy, Trump during the campaign had outlined five problems with current Obama US foreign agendas: (1) "Our resources are overextended"; (2) "Our allies are not paying their fair share"; (3) "Our friends are beginning to think they can't depend on us"; (4) "Our rivals no longer respect us"; (5) "America no longer has a clear understanding of our foreign policy goals." Trump then followed with purported remedies, mostly sharing the theme of diverting expenditures from abroad to home.

Critics on the campaign trail immediately labeled Trump a destroyer of the bipartisan American-led post-war order, a chorus that delighted Trump in setting him apart from what were not particularly popular policies. Later, Washington foreign policy doyen Richard Haass would write a blistering attack ("Liberal World Order, R.I.P.," *Project Syndicate,* March 21, 2018) on President Trump's foreign policy, strangely predicated on supposedly stupid landmark decisions like leaving the Paris climate accord or demanding radical changes in the Iran deal and NAFTA. A whole genre of such critical articles would soon follow, written by the Washington foreign policy establishment and damning Trump for his renunciations of a number of former US commitments, such as adherence to the International Criminal Court or aid to Palestinian "refugees."

Haass, however, did not factor in his analyses either the nature of Trump's art-of-the-deal negotiating style or the reality that all such agreements were not always in America's interest—and may not necessarily have been designed to be. For example, after leaving the Paris climate accord, the United States did better in reducing carbon emissions than had almost all its European critics. What followed the pull-out from the Iran deal were foiled Iranian-planned terrorist operations in Europe, popular Iranian protests against the theocracy at home, and zero incidents of Iranian hazing and confrontations with American warships in the Persian Gulf.

Much of Trump's hyperbole was due to his now familiar tactic of bargaining, angling, and cajoling for better deals. Some of his ideas were a genuine desire not to repeat an Afghanistan, Iraq, or Libyan intervention. Other bromides were deliberately couched in ways to provoke and send his rivals and the establishment into hysteria (as, for example, apparently Haass in March 2018)—and to ensure nonstop free media coverage for the controversial Trump deal making. Most of Trump's speech, however, actually critiqued past defense cuts. It promised to restore the loss of US deterrence. It offered new stalwart support for friends, with no more outreach to enemies and rivals (such as Cuba, Iran, or Venezuela).

Later, President Trump's national security team was to unify all these loose campaign pledges and package them into a coherent idea of "principled realism." That was a term that superseded hot-button adjectives like "muscular" and "Jacksonian." But principled realism still suggested that America would only act when it could effect change that was in its own or its alliances' interests—and only when the conditions were such that it would and could win at a cost worth the effort.

In practical terms, the Trump National Security Strategy document, first drafted under National Security Advisor General H. R. McMaster, would come to mean bombing ISIS, facing down North Korea to denuclearize, decertifying the Iran deal, growing closer to spurned allies like Egypt and the Gulf monarchies, warning China of its illegal creation of Spratly Islands bases, leveraging NATO to meet its members' defense commitments, and unapologetically providing Israel more spiritual and material support.

President Trump's secretary of defense, General James Mattis, national security advisors H. R. McMaster and his successor, John Bolton, ex-secretary of state Rex Tillerson, UN ambassador Nikki Haley, and CIA director Michael Pompeo (who replaced Tillerson at State) were not part of the Trump campaign when he gave his comprehensive April 2016 speech. But their appointments and the record of Trump's first two years more or less later threaded the needle of being tough on the international scene without being needlessly provocative or interventionist.

In other words, Trump neither embarked on a presidential "apology tour" of reciting past American sins to foreign hosts while abroad, nor sent nocturnal cash in side deals to Iran— and did not undertake a needless bombing campaign analogous to the 2011 attack on Libya. The addition of both the hawkish Pompeo and Bolton in early 2018 allowed Trump to switch from his prior "bad cop" role of threatening fire and fury and scarcely being restrained by his more sober and judicious advisors. Not now. Trump would talk more like the "good cop" who warned foreign leaders that he might have to rein in some of his team like Bolton and Pompeo, who wanted stronger reactions to perceived foreign aggressive acts.

For the purposes of winning the 2016 election, Trump would not speak loudly, as Obama allegedly did ("I don't bluff"), only to carry a small stick by not enforcing prior deadlines concerning nuclear proliferation with Iran or redlines with Syria. Nor would he, in stereotypical Jimmy Carter fashion, predictably speak softly and carry a small stick (e.g., "Being confident of our own future, we are now free of that inordinate fear of Communism").

He would not even, as President Teddy Roosevelt had originally advised, speak softly and carry a big stick.

In the end, Trump would both talk loudly and recklessly— *and* carry a big stick (and later boast about promising to "bomb the sh*t" out of ISIS and then more or less doing just that). When Trump derided North Korea's supposedly unhinged Kim Jong-un as "Little Rocket Man" or "short and fat," critics screamed that he was playing a childish game of insults with an unstable nuclear power now capable of hitting Portland or San Diego. They did not quite realize that most of the world was predicated on childish minds insulting one another or that past predictable strategic restraint was often far more dangerous than unpredictability.

Eventually, Kim agreed at least to restart talks about North Korean denuclearization after months of stepped-up trade embargoes, and likely in fear that Trump appeared as capable of anything as did Kim.

Trump's second signature agenda was recalibrating trade and indeed the entire American approach to globalization and the international post-war order. As in foreign policy, Trump sought to pose as a disrupter of the status quo. He nearly welcomed charges that he was reckless, ignorant, and dangerous, given that the onus was on his critics to defend institutions and organizations—NATO, the UN, the EU, NAFTA—that were long in need of reform.

According to the author of *The Art of the Deal* and *Think Like a Billionaire*, both Republican and Democratic free-traders had been easily snookered. Under the ruse of free rather than fair trade, they were supposedly humiliated in unfair trade pacts, mostly by China ("We can't continue to allow China to rape our country, and that's what we're doing"). Naïfs, according to Trump, supposedly had bartered away American self-interest at the expense of the working class to appease the theories of globalist elites and their foreign counterparts. Even Barack Obama back in 2008 had maligned George W. Bush as "unpatriotic" for running up budget deficits and increasing the national debt by charging the red ink on "a credit card from the Bank of China in the name of our children."

Trump was not an ideologue as much as a nationalist. He did not much worry about trade wars (indeed as president he provocatively tweeted, "trade wars are good"); indeed, to obtain trade concessions he was willing to start them to match his rhetoric with action. After all, what means were there to achieve free and fair trade without the threats of tariffs? Wise diplomats on the eve of crises certainly did not rule out the use of force.

Trump was not necessarily invested in the rules of the World Trade Organization. Nor did he calibrate the long-term effects of limiting entry of foreign goods upon consumer prices. Instead, he assumed that those countries that dumped subsidized goods on the market, demanded technology transfers from American companies that did business on their home soil, cheated on agreements, or had grown accustomed to asymmetrical trade did so because it was in their perceived own self-interest. Yet these were unsustainable global protocols should every other country follow China's chauvinistic example.

By mid-2018, Trump was threatening to impose tariffs not just on China, but on Canada, Mexico, and EU countries—or indeed on almost any nation that ran up a large trade surplus with the United States. Privately, his advisors had hinted that such blustering was "art of the deal" finagling and would result eventually in some sort of agreements at least better for American workers than the present asymmetry. Trump's critics, however, charged that the resulting ill will with allies was not worth the marginal benefits of reduced trade deficits—and made Wall Street near permanently nervous.

Prior to Trump's candidacy, economists sometimes scoffed at such concern over trade imbalances as adolescent chauvinism, as if balancing the books—not jobs, GDP, and prices—mattered. They reassured Americans that trade deficits, even a nearly $400 billion annual imbalance with China, kept consumer prices at home low, and forced American companies to face cheap imports by staying competitive, lean, and mean. And that foreign trade subsidies and dumping eventually would implode any nation abroad foolish enough to become dependent on unsustainable subsidized exporting.

The Washington foreign policy establishment usually added in that even if trade red ink was injurious, it was a small price to pay for the maintenance of the American post-war order. By assuming such deficit burdens, they argued, the United States had avoided World War III, won the Cold War, spread democracy, and created an international commercial system based on laws and kept safe by the US military. And, of course, the American establishment insisted that a powerful United States—at least the regions of it that they knew and habituated—could easily afford to ignore foreign unfair trade or commercial cheating.

When Trump in March 2018 promised to slap tariffs on imported steel and aluminum, Gary Cohn, Trump's free-trader director of the National Economic Council and chief economic advisor, abruptly resigned. But, then again, Cohn was a sort of bipartisan poster person for the advantages of expanding globalized trade regardless of US deficits. His resignation probably did not hurt Trump with his base support.

Trump was not much interested in apologies for his promised restrictions and threats of tariffs. Much less did he care about arguments that targeted tariffs only added to the cost of goods elsewhere in the economy. He kept singling out Mexico, Canada, China, Japan, a few other Asian tigers, and the European Union, again in a weird sort of admiration for their self-interested conniving. Trump concluded that they put their own workers' interests first and for a reason. If deficits were so good, or at least of no importance, then why did America's competitors seek to avoid them? "We close up factories and Mexico opens factories. What the hell are we doing? Folks, it's not going to happen anymore."

Trump simply saw China hardly liberalizing its political system due to its unfair trade advantages and huge trade surpluses— the long-held canard of the bipartisan political establishment that affluence begets liberality. Rather, an empowered Beijing was becoming even more autocratic and played more the outlaw that did not abide by copyright, patent, or anti-dumping international accords. For Trump, Beijing interpreted US patience and forbearance as naïveté to be privately mocked or weakness to be exploited, but certainly not magnanimity to be reciprocated in kind. Perhaps even some of Trump's critics agreed. But privately they confessed that the time to have stopped China's aggressions was long past. Now to belatedly question trade surpluses in any context was a heresy and would earn one the slur of being a protectionist or an enemy of the global commercial order.

Conventional wisdom, then, dictated that any remedial efforts to force China to abide by its promises would result in a full-scale trade war. China's approach to trade was analogous to Germany's stance toward military preparedness and aggression in the late 1930s. Both ascendant autocracies counted on the patience and appeasement of supposedly spent and tired liberal democracies to grant concessions, given their own willingness to raise the alternative of global unrest and upheaval.

Yet by mid-2018, even as op-eds and cable news pundits predicted a global trade war and a crashing economy, both the European Union and China signaled a readiness to talk about some of the trade imbalances incurred with the United States, and the vast account surpluses that both China and Germany accrued that had warped world commerce. By autumn 2018, China was struggling with a weakening currency, an unsteady stock market, slowing growth, and anxieties that such tell-tale signs were a result of just a few newly enacted US tariffs.

Trump's deal-making style was as consistently transparent as it was perennially damned as never before seen recklessness. He carefully selected egregious asymmetries in supposedly reciprocal trade. Then he stormed and blustered about trade wars and tariffs to come. And then he finished up by proudly bragging of subsequent "winning" at home, while he praised his erstwhile rivals for their inevitable concessions. The more Trump followed the same old script, and found undeniable though modest successes, the more his critics damned his behavior as beyond the pale and dangerous to the human race.

Even during the 2016 campaign, candidate Trump had reverted back to John F. Kennedy–style jawboning and hectoring of private corporations. He threatened them with trade and tax penalties if they outsourced, offshored, or shipped plants abroad. But he did so always in the context of how many jobs he would save by bucking globalist orthodoxy. As president, he assumed—and so did his supporters—that if he successfully bullied companies into staying put or coming home, amused CEOs would soon change their tune—especially with tax-cut and deregulation incentives. And he usually proved right.

Workers would finally have their comeuppance against their bosses, but in a nationalist and conservative, not revolutionary unionist, sense. Remember, for the reductionist the key to Trump's success was jobs. Good jobs were what ultimately made women and men independent, happy, and productive. Without them, government grew, crime increased, and families disintegrated. Oddly, few Republicans other than Trump talked of the unemployment rate in terms of human cost, as if percentage points did not represent millions of out-of-work Americans.

Trump's jawboning of companies had begun to pay off a bit after the election. By December 2016, just weeks after Trump's election, several corporations were reconsidering their moves abroad even as foreign companies promised to build new plants in the United States. Apparently, they feared that Trump was erratic and mercurial enough to do what few other presidents would have even considered—real trade wars, high tariffs, and nonstop public humiliation. Apple alone promised to pay an additional $38 billion in repatriation taxes in 2018 on profit it had made abroad, after the passing of the new tax reform law. Given that the new repatriation tax rate at 15.5 percent was less than half the old rate of 35 percent, some economists believed that over $1 trillion stashed overseas would return to the United States.

One common theme connected all of Trump's general economic policies, as well as his particular views on trade and globalization: the curative idea of rapid economic growth and, again, millions of new, well-paying jobs. To believe that radical economic improvement was still possible was to agree that Americans were previously unnaturally shackled, mistakenly depressed, or shamefully misdirected. So liberate them. Make them feel good about working, becoming prosperous, and enjoying their largess. And they may shock the world with their productivity and inquisitiveness.

For Trump—salesman, businessman, and sybarite—give a man more money and respect, and all the "-isms" and "-ologies," from race and gender to class and position, simply recede. In a larger sense, Trump offered the folk wisdom of common sense against the wonkish dictum that trade issues were too nuanced and complex to become the stuff of campaign rallies or mainstream coffee-shop talk. If and when the inner city began to see "Help Wanted" and "Now Hiring" signs advertising jobs from desperate employers, then race would become incidental, not essential to anyone's character.

Yet the crux was to what degree would Trump's populist talk of tariffs and protectionism restrict the free flow of capital and end up slowing down rather than liberating US domestic growth. After all, to get results threats were necessary. And for threats to work they had to be backed up with real tariffs—and the specter of global trade walls.

There was an inherent and internal contradiction in Trump's—or any other free-market populist's—trade agenda when it came to economic growth and promoting more jobs: if deregulation, tax cuts, energy exploration, and less government intrusion into the economy freed entrepreneurs to make more efficient and savvy decisions than did bureaucrats, why then would clumsy and obtuse federal regulators, who were eager to slap tariffs on imported steel and aluminum, know any better than the market what aided a self-correcting US economy?

Certainly, labor shortages brought on by strong growth had gradually resulted in rising wages. As an example, a California Chick-fil-A franchise owner announced in June 2018 that he was paying fast-food employees a record $17 an hour. By September, real wages had gone up 2.9 percent over the prior twelve months. Indeed, rising wages had begun to render the stale discussions of new mandatory minimum-wage laws irrelevant. Why, then, would Trump's new tax, energy, and regulatory policies not do the same with government solutions to imports and exports, and render tariffs and sanctions obsolete?

The unfairness of globalization marked yet another Trump issue that galvanized his campaign and soon became an administration trademark. A bipartisan Washington had long embraced unfettered globalization that had eroded elements within the US economy and ostensibly subordinated Americans to mostly multinational and international (and sometimes hostile) organizations.

Trump characteristically framed the issues as another zero-sum game. City slickers in New York and Washington had loaded the dice against those in Iowa and North Carolina. The way Trump saw it, the former got rich, the latter got screwed: "Globalization has made the financial elite who donate to politicians very, very wealthy . . . but it has left millions of our workers with nothing but poverty and heartache."

It was easy to tune out such classic populist demagoguery. But it was far more difficult to calibrate whether optional interventions and disadvantageous trade agreements were in the interests of the old American Rust Belt. Did anyone deny that China as a matter of policy violated copyright laws, infringed patents and trademarks, demanded technology transfers from US firms doing business in China, engaged in systematic economic espionage, and targeted US industries through the dumping of subsidized Chinese products on the world market? What exactly was the rationale that tolerated such cheating?

In terms of the 2016–17 controversies over foreign "collusion" and meddling in elections, China's espionage apparatus long ago had made a much weaker Russia's covert activity seem sophomoric. In 2018 alone, the CIA disclosed that one of its top operatives in China, Jerry Chun Shing Lee, had long ago been turned by the Chinese. Lee had likely revealed the identities of CIA personnel inside China, leading to their arrests, executions, and the veritable end of all US espionage monitoring efforts inside China. It was also belatedly disclosed as well that the chauffeur of Senator Dianne Feinstein (D-CA)—at a time when she was chair of the Senate Judiciary Committee; a high-ranking member of the Senate Intelligence Committee; and her husband, global financier Richard Blum, was conducting significant business with the Chinese—had been a spy for China for twenty years.

The deep state's answer to all these concerns was little more than a smug "so what?" Translated, this had meant that certain sectors of the US economy were to remain permanent casualties of Chinese trade mercantilism. That was the price of supposedly bringing China into the "family of nations," enriching and normalizing it, and thereby creating a larger version of Japan ($69 billion annual trade surplus with the US) or South Korea ($23 billion), as well as institutionalizing norms of global "free" trade.

In March 2018, over thirteen months into the Trump presidency, essayist Walter Russell Mead summed up well Trump's agenda in the *Wall Street Journal*, in the midst of near national hysteria over his imposition of tariffs on Chinese and other countries' exports of aluminum and steel:

> For Mr. Trump, free trade and democracy promotion are part of the globalist agenda that he has opposed for many years and believes the American public no longer supports. He also believes he can win the trade fight and that the Republican base will support him against the establishment. He believes that other nations depend so heavily on the U.S. market that he can win enough concessions to vindicate his stance.

Trump was not alone in his finger-pointing. He channeled into a far wider cosmic discontent with globalization, at least in the Western world that increasingly felt it had subsidized non-Westerners' entry into the West. So Trump was no outlier American cowboy, given the British departure from the EU, the European furor at Angela Merkel's Germany over green-lighting illegal immigration, the rise of populist movements in eastern and southern Europe and Scandinavia, and the popular disgust with global elites at the UN, the EU, the World Bank, and International Monetary Fund who seemed indifferent to complaints about the trade disparities, illegal immigration, and anti-Western policies they so often embraced.

When candidate and president Trump hammered the European Union, NAFTA, the Paris climate accord, the Trans-Pacific Partnership, and the UN, elites publicly railed at his supposed demagoguery, while silent majorities quietly assented. It was almost as if any transnational alphabetic body with the noun "accord," "association," "organization," "partnership," or "union" earned Trump's disdain as a globalist construct—anti-American, and unfair to swing-state voters.

But it was over illegal immigration (another Trump landmark concern) that he first and most effectively came to prominence. Nonstop, Trump went after open borders and unchecked illegal immigration that had allegedly ossified American workers' wages, spiked crime, undermined the melting pot, and posed national security threats. "Our message to the world," Trump thundered, "will be this: You cannot obtain legal status or become a citizen of the United States by illegally entering our country . . . People will know you can't just smuggle in, hunker down and wait to be legalized. Those days are over . . . We will build a great wall along the southern border." Trump added, "And Mexico will pay for the wall—100 percent. They don't know it yet, but they're going to pay for the wall."

When Trump prematurely announced "those days are over" he had not yet fully measured the quiet support for open borders within his own party, primarily the interest of construction companies, the hospitality industry, agribusiness, and social services in having continued access to hard-working, low-cost workers from abroad. Talking tough on illegal immigration—enforcing existing immigration law, building a wall on the southern border, and deporting sizable numbers of illegal aliens—soon earned 360-degree opposition from liberals and conservatives. Aside from the Left, Trump's Republican primary rivals were more or less committed to "comprehensive immigration reform." For many, all that was a nice way of saying "amnesty." Some, like primary rival Jeb Bush (who called illegal immigration "an act of love"), were unapologetic open-borders proponents. They were content to let the labor market, not existing law, adjudicate border crossings.

Trump, however, quickly saw that aside from the merits of the issue, cracking down on illegal immigration fed into his larger campaign narratives of an out-of-touch elite, a fossilized and incompetent establishment, and adherence to theories that hurt average folks. "America First" also could mean spending money on America's poor, not Mexico's or South America's—something that might privately appeal as well to some minority voters.

American immigration law had to remain sovereign and superior to international pieties and practices. For Trump, Mexico—the beneficiary of $30 billion in annual US remittances, and eager for a permanent safety valve that mitigated social tensions—could no more be allowed to dictate American demography than China could trade policy.

The common denominator to Trump's attacks on trade and globalization had been the loss of good-paying US jobs, especially in the hinterland. By clamping down on illegal laborers, Trump could boast that the pool of entry-level workers had shrunk in the first year of his presidency just as the economy would take off.

Again, desperate employers would then have no choice but to hire US workers, regardless of their past prejudices or reluctances. Trump's logic that good times demanded fewer alien laborers and marked the opportune moment to maximize the leverage of American labor was the exact opposite of Republican orthodoxy. The Washington party establishment usually postulated that booms meant a desperate need for laborers— foreign, guest, legal, or illegal.

It would be more difficult for the Left to fault Trump as a racist, xenophobe, or nativist when he could profess a desire to ensure that African American, Mexican American, and poor white workers all gained leverage over their bosses to increase their wages. Indeed, by December 2017, after two quarters of strong economic growth, a spate of self-deportations, and radical slowing in illegal immigration, Trump could claim that the Bureau of Labor Statistics had reported a 6.8 percent unemployment rate for black workers, which dipped to 5.9 percent by summer 2018. That was the lowest rate in the forty-five years that the data has been compiled. Over 200,000 blacks had joined the labor force. More importantly, by June 2018 the gap between black and overall unemployment (3.8 percent) had also narrowed to another record 2.1 percent. And by September 2018 the Labor Department was reporting that workers' wages in the prior year had increased almost 3 percent, as unemployment continued to stay below 4 percent.

Latino unemployment was likewise near record lows. Trump's daughter Ivanka tweeted of the news, "The Hispanic unemployment rate dropped to 4.7 percent—the LOWEST in the history of the United States. This Administration and @realDonaldTrump are working hard to create opportunities for all Americans . . . and we are just getting started!" By April

2018, applications for unemployment benefits had reached their lowest levels in forty years.

Talk of finishing the border wall was also proof of Trump's boasts to increase US security. A Hoover Dam–like project of such massive construction supposedly channeled his own developer and builder pedigree, and hijacked complaints of the last decade from both liberals and conservatives alike that "we don't build anything anymore." Ostensibly, getting tough on illegal immigration was a regional issue of the American Southwest. In reality, it only reinforced Trump's entire agenda of full employment for US citizens, and was equally aimed at angry voters in Ohio and Pennsylvania. When yet another caravan of Central Americans threatened to crash the southern border in October 2018, Trump said it was his "fault," but only "because I have created such an incredible economy and I have created so many jobs, I have made this country so great that everybody wants to come in!"

Prior and rather pathetic Republican efforts to go soft on immigration were predicated on outdated stereotypes about "family values." Spanish-speaking immigrants from Mexico and Latin America, if amnestied, supposedly would vote as if they were third-generation middle-class Cuban Republicans, even as open borders allowed hundreds of thousands of new arrivals to enter the United States illegally from Mexico and Central America.

Trump, however, thought that such thinking was a chimera birthed by the US Chamber of Commerce and the editorials in the *Wall Street Journal,* both often pro-corporate megaphones that openly advocated importing plentiful, cheap manual labor. Far more likely, amnestied illegal aliens and their American-born children would join progressive ranks, given past generous federal and state assistance and subsidies. Moreover, half of all immigrants came from the far southern states and most impoverished areas of Mexico. Most arrived without a high school diploma or English, and thus were likely to show reciprocity at the polls for Democratic-sponsored immigration laxity and ensuing entitlements.

Ironically, the only way to turn Oaxaca's masses into middle-class voters, akin to conservative Cuban immigrants, would be to close the borders and allow in diverse and legal immigrants on a meritocratic basis. Only then could the formidable powers of intermarriage, assimilation, and integration persuade illegal aliens inside the United States to emulate prior patterns of assimilation as, for example, of the Italian Catholic diaspora. Today an Italian surname, whether Giuliani or Cuomo, hardly proves a reliable guide of voter preference. That fact is also largely because half a million Italians over the decades did not enter the United States en masse illegally and perpetually.

Illegal immigration had become no longer a matter of a few thousand immigrants crossing the southern border or overstaying visas, often in search of low-paying jobs that Americans purportedly would not do. Nor was it even a dilemma about what to do with a static resident alien population "without papers." Instead, the issue became a referendum on the future of US elections, the trajectory of the Democratic Party, and the idea of melting-pot traditionalism versus salad-bowl identity politics. In a CBS/YouGov poll of spring 2018, a majority of Americans who had experienced firsthand illegal immigration felt that illegal aliens had made their own communities worse off, including a plurality of black Americans.

Trump also understood how the issue accentuated his mass-versus-elite themes. Those who supported illegal immigration usually patronized foreign nationals as servants (nannies, cooks, gardeners, baby-sitters), rather than knew them as neighbors, fellow PTA members, or guests at their teenagers' sleepover parties. As a general rule, the staunchest supporters of illegal immigration were the most likely not to put their kids in schools with the children of Mexican citizens and not to live side by side with recent arrivals from Oaxaca.

Politically, no longer did Bill and Hillary Clinton or Senator Chuck Schumer offer speeches opposing open borders as they once had in the 1990s. It was mostly forgotten that until the twenty-first century, the Democratic Party had stridently opposed illegal immigration out of the usual traditional concerns for wages, unions, and the poor, not to mention long-held xenophobia and racism. These "liberal" positions had been reinforced all through the 1960s and 1970s by United Farm Workers president Cesar Chavez. In exasperation at the Teamster Union's importation of low-wage undocumented workers, he started his 1974 "Illegals Campaign" to stop unlawful entry. Chavez's cousin Manuel and union enforcers camped at the Mexican border to form a "wet line" of union enforcers to force back "scabs" into Mexico.

How odd that Trump was resurrecting now fossilized Democratic talking points and policies. Allowing cheap labor to enter the United States, in large numbers and illegally, in old Democrats' minds drove down entry-level wages. It weakened the efforts of unions. It overtaxed social services for their own poor constituents and was manipulated by conniving employers to circumvent using American workers. Even Barack Obama, an old laborite community activist, as late as 2008 had campaigned on enforcing immigration law. During his first four years as president, Obama had reiterated (twenty-two times, to be exact) to mostly Latino pressure groups why he could not provide them with blanket amnesties and open borders: "I am president, I am not king. I can't do these things just by myself."

What had changed the politics by the time of the 2016 Trump campaign and made immigration his signature wedge issue? In a phrase: both the radically altered demography of important states and, more importantly, of the Electoral College itself, and the gradual diminution in importance of both farm labor and Cesar Chavez's United Farm Workers.

While open-borders supporters still talked about "11 million undocumented residents," that reference had ossified over a decade. It certainly no longer bore any relation to reality. In truth, yearly influxes of illegal immigrants may have easily exceeded half a million entries a year. The pool of unlawfully residing aliens in 2016 may have been likely somewhere between 15 to 20 million foreign nationals. A recent Yale University study suggested that the real number could be nearer 22 million.

Ronald Reagan's 1986 signing of the Simpson-Mazzoli Act had given amnesties to millions of residents while pulling enforcement off the border and its environs. Due to long-standing so-called anchor baby court interpretations of immigration law, millions more instant US citizens were born to the undocumented residing on American soil. They naturally shared their parents' fears and resentments. And now they had come of voting age in the American Southwest. Chain migration—the proverbial "chains" of foreign nationals who were allowed legally to immigrate to America because both citizens and lawful permanent residents can sponsor entry of their own nonnuclear family members from foreign countries—likewise spiked numbers of illegal immigrants.

Formerly red and purple states, even without lax voting laws that did not always confirm citizenship status at the polls, were beginning to turn blue. As an example of the demographic effect of illegal immigration upon the Electoral College, California, Nevada, New Mexico, and Colorado had all been won by Republican George H. W. Bush in 1988. The then conventional wisdom was that these states were favored destinations for conservative, affluent retirees and were still influenced by the Oklahoma and Arkansas Dust Bowl diasporas of the 1930s and 1940s.

Yet by 2000, his son George W. Bush had lost both California and New Mexico. In 2008, Barack Obama captured all four states. Democrats have not relinquished one of them since. The demographics were advancing geometrically, not arithmetically—especially given the flight from these states of middle-class conservatives in search of low- or no-tax alternative states without steep entitlement costs and poor schools. California, even after its initial mass exoduses, was still averaging about 150,000 more yearly departures than arrivals.

Under the growing identity politics of "diversity" themes during the Obama presidency, there were less emphases on the old affirmative-action binaries of white and black, or even white and black/brown. Instead, a new, less well-defined idea of "people of color" emerged. The idea soon aggregated almost anyone—from Caucasian Punjabi Americans and Arab Americans, to Chinese Americans and Hmong Americans—into a new nonwhite political construct. A collective grievance grew against the now perceived shrinking and soon to be politically irrelevant white majority.

In terms of illegal immigration, the new identity politics calibrations meant that traditional rivalries between blacks and Hispanics or Hispanics and Asians supposedly were consumed by a common and shared grievance against a declining majority. Ethnic leaders more likely redirected their complaints against the culture of "white privilege" and "white supremacy." Jesse Jackson's old improbable and mostly rhetorical "Rainbow Coalition" was at last materializing in the age of Obama.

The Left further muddied the waters by sometimes lumping all illegal aliens collectively with the plight of "Dreamers," those brought illegally by their parents as children to the United States. The Dreamers had been exempted from immigration enforcement under Obama's DACA (Deferred Action for Childhood Arrival) executive order of 2012. Progressives wished to convey an impression that thousands of college students and soldiers were in danger of being hauled off campuses and bases, and then shipped to a Mexico they hardly knew.

In truth, accurate data was hard to come by. In most studies, only 5 percent of DACA enrollees (the average age in 2016 was about twenty-five) had graduated from college. Somewhere between 20 and 40 percent of the cohort had dropped out of high school. Few knew how many were recipients of state assistance. Only about one in a thousand of DACA's participants had joined the military.

By summer and autumn 2018, Central American families were storming the border, seeking political asylum on grounds that they were political rather than economic refugees. In reaction, and to enforce border security, Trump followed the letter of immigration law, a policy that sometimes led to the separation of asylum-seeking parents from their children.

Such disruptions created a storm of media protest. It was conveniently forgotten that in 2014 both Barack Obama ("Do not send your children to the borders. If they do make it, they'll get sent back.") and Hillary Clinton had warned parents that deportation still faced any who sought to crash the border under the ploy of using children for their agendas. Hillary had warned in no uncertain terms: "We have to send a clear message, just because your child gets across the border, that doesn't mean the child gets to stay. So, we don't want to send a message that is contrary to our laws or will encourage more children to make that dangerous journey."

The Right worried that beneath the humanitarian professions of the Left were cold, hard demographic calculations. And they had their own stereotypes of illegal aliens. Trump had used them frequently in his blasting of some illegal immigrants as "bad hombres," who were often unemployed, convicted of crimes, not in school, and on welfare. Because the pool of illegal aliens was so large and data either politicized or impossible to obtain, both sides could be simultaneously likely correct: millions of illegal aliens were productive American citizens and yet a few million were not working or had criminal convictions or were on public assistance or had just arrived on the scent of amnesty.

The left-wing base forbade the idea of deportation; the right-wing counterpart tabooed any notion of amnesty. Euphemism muddied the waters. "Illegal alien" transmogrified to "illegal immigrant" to "undocumented immigrant" to "undocumented migrant," ending with "migrant"—the final progressive Orwellian linguistic recalibration that people simply went both ways across the border and legality and sovereignty were not factors.

Trump, however, saw immigration differently. He appreciated that the issue of flipping blue states red was not so cut and dried, in a fashion that few Republicans had heretofore grasped. Latinos mostly settled in the American Southwest. But whereas California, Colorado, Nevada, and New Mexico would likely not again become Republican, so too Texas and Arizona would not easily become new blue states.

The net effect of most Latinos residing in states that were already transformed to blue and not prone to flip tended in the future to mitigate the issue politically. Liberals often missed that paradox. But not Donald Trump. For all his braggadocio about winning everywhere all the time, Trump apparently sensed that he was always going to lose California, easily win Texas, and survive the loss of Colorado, Nevada, and New Mexico—but only if he captured the swing states in the Midwest where there were fewer Latinos but lots of voters disturbed mostly over the idea rather than the reality of illegal immigration.

The Trump base did not like selective enforcement of federal laws to benefit foreigners in a manner that was never extended to itself. It resented the notion that "sanctuary cities" could declare themselves exempt from enforcement of federal law (in a way Indianapolis or Youngstown could not simply ignore federal handgun registration or the Endangered Species Act requirements).

Moreover, for every local story of a Dreamer who graduated from Harvard that went viral on national media, there was just as commonly a tragedy in the news such as the shooting death of

Kate Steinle in San Francisco by a five-time deported illegal alien with a record of seven felony convictions—and free on bond; or Mollie Tibbetts, a twenty-year-old Iowa college student murdered by an illegal alien using a false identity. The difference, however, was one of reportage: the national media showcased the successes of illegal aliens as characteristic of their ethnic, cultural, and political profiles. They often ignored criminality by illegal aliens and usually sought to downplay or hide the offenders' backgrounds, on the theory that the truth would only further negative stereotypes and lead to "hatred," or such news of crimes would be "manipulated" to advance illiberal agendas.

Trump, of course, himself had offended Mexican Americans with his rants from the first day of his campaign, and a later allegedly pejorative reference to US district judge Gonzalo Curiel ("of Mexican heritage") who was assigned to a civil suit against ethically challenged Trump University. Outrage followed over Trump's correct but naïve identification of Curiel's heritage as "Mexican" (in the sense that there was no commensurate outcry about identifying Swedish Americans as "Swedes" or using "the Irish" for Irish Americans).

Worse followed from Trump's charge that "he is a member of a club or society, very strongly pro-Mexican, which is all fine." As often was the case, Trump was certainly clumsy in his phraseology, likely wrong about the idea of innate racial or cultural bias on the part of Judge Curiel against Trump, and probably had the weaker case in the civil suit. But on the other hand, Curiel had indeed belonged to a "club" or "society": the California La Raza Lawyers Association. In the even-steven Trump world, an Anglo judge who had sought membership in a linguistically equivalent chapter of "The Race Lawyers Association" certainly would have faced charges of bias, especially in a case involving a highly controversial public figure.

More strangely, before his campaign Trump had been all over the illegal immigration map. In 2011, he had sounded like

the later anti-Trumpers in an interview with Fox News's Bill
O'Reilly: "You know, it's hard to generalize, but you're going
to have to look at the individual people, see how they've done,
see how productive they've been, see what their references are,
and then make a decision . . . but you know, you have some great
productive people that came in."

Indeed, in 2012 Trump had chastised losing Republican
nominee Mitt Romney for his unrealistic notion of "self-deportation" ("He [Romney] had a crazy policy of self-deportation,
which was maniacal. It sounded as bad as it was, and he lost all
of the Latino vote. He lost the Asian vote. He lost everybody
who is inspired to come into this country.").

Self-deportation was an idea that once immigration law was
strictly enforced, there was no need for massive active deportations. Instead, illegal immigrants insidiously would begin to fil-
ter back across the border, in fear otherwise that eventually they
would come into contact with authorities and be summarily deported anyway. That policy actually became the Trump de facto
position in 2017–18, in the absence of new immigration legislation. Self-deportation by 2018 may have contributed in part to
radical decreases in perceived illegal immigrant residents, a feat
for which Trump took credit.

In short, how could Trump construct an immigration position that would fire up his base, remain consistent with his other
agendas, not spark hysteria following deportations of some of
the 15–20 million illegal aliens, and yet enforce existing laws to
make the border secure with the added guarantee of a wall?

In the fashion of the classical Athenian *polypragmôn* ("the
busy body"), candidate Trump attacked everyone else in the Republican primary debates on the issue as self-interested on some
aspect of illegal immigration. Mexico selfishly exported immigrants for its own economic and national interest. Democrats
selfishly wanted voters. Ethnic chauvinists selfishly dreamed of a
collective La Raza underclass in need of privileged spokespeople

such as themselves. Republicans selfishly wanted cheap labor. Liberals selfishly wanted to feel good in the eyes of the world and to expand the administrative and redistributive state.

And Trump? If everyone else was selfish, then he alone posed as selfless. He wanted immigration statutes enforced just as everyone did all laws. He, like everyone, wanted to separate the "bad" illegal alien chaff of criminals and welfare chiselers from the "good" wheat of hard-working immigrants in need of a green card. He wanted US workers to be freed from unfair foreign competition and receive, or leverage, good-paying jobs. He, as did all, wanted "diverse" legal immigration that would ensure the law-abiding and skilled or professional applicant from Nigeria or Vietnam an equal shot at the American dream. He, like most, wanted a return of the melting pot that was possible only with legal and measured immigration. And he did not want Mexico callously exporting its poor and in exchange importing $30 billion in remittances, while posing as Trump's moral superior.

Most unusually, Trump believed that there was a huge economic benefit to ending illegal immigration, despite the curtailment of cheap labor. Entry workers' wages would purportedly rise. Billions of dollars in remittances sent home to Mexico would decline. Social services would save substantial sums in decreasing entitlements. The system would become more efficient with fewer impoverished illegal immigrants, in terms of reduced identity theft, less need for interpreters and bilingual messaging, and more rapid assimilation and integration.

Ultimately, despite his bouts of invective and sloppy administration in the detention of illegal aliens, Trump had both the more logical argument and the better politics—given that sovereignty, legality, citizenship, and diversity were hard to argue with. Illegal immigration was certainly one contributing reason why he won the nomination and went on to defeat Hillary Clinton in the Electoral College.

In particular, Trump's war with Mexico over the border wall was especially good politics, given that the Mexican government had an uncanny ability of gratuitously provoking the American people. In spring 2018, it had allowed a caravan of over one thousand Central American nationals to pass through its environs as they headed northward to crash the US border. Mexico did little to hide its delight at American nervousness over the specter of another mass influx.

Mexican pundits eagerly pointed to the rise of left-wing Mexican presidential candidate and soon to be president Andrés Manuel López Obrador, who ran on an anti-Trump platform—and a sense of entitlement that Mexico should adjudicate American immigration policy. Obrador should be a warning to the United States, Mexican pundits insisted, of the wages of America's supposedly hostile acts of deporting criminal illegal aliens and attempting to fortify the border.

But, once again, a crafty Trump saw that such overt hostility would only win him further support at home. What exactly would the Obrador movement do to punish an uncooperative United States? Build its own wall to keep Americans out, refuse the transference of an annual $30 billion in remittances, reduce a $71 billion trade surplus with the United States, force its own Mexican citizens to stay put, unilaterally revoke NAFTA, or expel US companies? To all that, the Trump voter would likely have answered, "Promises, promises." By autumn 2018, Obrador had concluded a recalibration of NAFTA with Trump that was more symmetrical, and he was claiming that he would help to curtail at the Mexican southern border future caravans of Central Americans seeking to crash the US border.

Aside from his realist foreign policy, trade and globalization resets, and illegal immigration policy, Trump championed lots of ancillary, mostly boilerplate Republican initiatives—most prominently, energy development, deregulation, school choice, and full utilization of US land and resources. Indeed, by March

2018 the conservative Heritage Foundation had concluded that
the Trump administration, in little over a year of governance,
had already implemented two-thirds of its 334 agenda items.
It noted in comparison that at this point in his administration
conservative godhead Ronald Reagan had finalized only 49 percent of Heritage's conservative blueprint. That was a stunning
rubric. It undermined most of the case of the Never Trump Republicans that Trump's agendas on the economy, social issues,
foreign policy, and immigration would either prove incoherent
or liberal.

In February 2018, at the annual CPAC (Conservative Political Action Conference) meeting in Washington, Trump could
rightly boast that the Republican primary fears that he was a
closet moderate or "Rino" (Republican in name only) were now
proven false by a year of events: "Remember when I first started
running? Because I wasn't a politician, fortunately, but do you
remember I started running and people said, are you sure he's a
conservative? I think I proved I'm a conservative."

Among his other initiatives, Trump promised to and did
green-light gas, oil, and pipeline development. He would revive
"beautiful, clean coal." He favored only strict constructionist
judges, pro-life, pro–Second Amendment, and pro-tax cuts.
Trump's first Supreme Court pick, Neil Gorsuch, proved not
just a conservative constructionist, but a brilliant legal scholar
and fierce advocate in the Antonin Scalia mode—a far cry from
the progressive John Paul Stevens or David Souter nomina-
tions of past and supposedly far more reliable and circumspect
Republican presidents. His second nominee, federal appellate
justice Brett Kavanaugh, was likewise young, conservative, and
targeted by Trump's liberal legal critics. He would endure a
bruising and often brutal confirmation hearing, the longest in
the history of such senatorial nominee audits, before joining the
court. In response, Trump hinted that he would likely in the near
future enjoy a third conservative Supreme Court nomination,

ensuring that the court could be recalibrated as a 6-3 conservative majority.

Yet on what he thought were marginal or needlessly provocative issues, Trump was either not interested in, or had no problem with, unsustainable Social Security growth, gay marriage, transgendered bathrooms, or affirmative action. Again, it was his stance on war, trade and jobs, globalization, and illegal immigration that set Trump apart from almost all candidates in 2016—or for that matter in any other past election.

We have seen in the first chapter how and why a divided red-blue country had a rendezvous with an equally divisive candidate like Trump. In response, Trump found the right campaign issues to craft a pathway to victory. Yet why did not someone else—a veteran politician with more experience, and supposedly more sober and judicious temperament, more staff, more money, and more knowledge—preempt or soon supplant Trump's issues?

Could not a Marco Rubio have been elected on a Trump agenda, or a Ted Cruz skillfully absorbed Trumpism?

Or was Trumpism inseparable from Trump?

Chapter Three

"MODERN DAY PRESIDENTIAL"

I saw that Philip himself, with whom our conflict
lay, for the sake of empire and absolute power had
had his eye knocked out, his collar-bone broken, his
hand and his leg maimed, and was ready to resign
any part of his body that Fortune chose to take from
him, provided that with what remained he might
live in honor and glory.
—Demosthenes, *On the Crown*

We have seen that Trump fixated on a preexisting and re-
ceptive swing-state constituency. Then he crafted the
right issues both to fire it up and yet also to transcend it. There
is, however, still something missing in the decipherment of the
Trump enigma. It is unlikely that *any* other politician could have
followed the winning Trump formula (or would have proven as
president so chaotically conservative had he been elected).

In other words, Trump the person—warts and all, vulgar, uncouth, divisive, and yet often empathetic and concerned, despite

or because of his storied past—must explain much of his rise to power. Trump the person, then, transcended his issues. How and why Trump overshadowed his ideas and won the Republican nomination and election is the subject of this chapter.

Apparently, a third of the voters saw him as something analogous to chemotherapy, which after all is used to combat something far worse than itself. Such toxicity was felt to be needed to kill the cancer (i.e., the politics and bureaucracy of the proverbial deep state), even as the dosage might nearly kill the patient (the Trump voter) during the taxing therapy (the 24/7 media obsession with all things Trump). Trump supporters certainly did not want another palliative of McCain or Romney aspirin. And they no longer believed that a more conservative-sounding version of House Speaker Paul Ryan would be a successful substitute for the current Paul Ryan.

As we have also seen in the prior two chapters, one reason why candidate and now president Trump was not abandoned by his supporters when he often said outrageous things was precisely because they felt he was retaliatory, not preemptory. Trump, to their mind, was launched as a long-overdue ballistic missile against those who had been showering the working class with crude and often racist attacks. Trump was their long-overdue nemesis to the hubristic stereotyping of those in the media, the government, Silicon Valley, and politics, such as Melinda Byerley, Marc Caputo, Sarah Jeong, Peter Strzok—and Hillary Clinton.

Trump upon announcing his candidacy almost immediately had led all the other sixteen Republican primary presidential candidates. In a June 30, 2015, Quinnipiac University national poll, front-runner Trump garnered 20 percent support among Republican voters, even as he trailed Democratic contender Hillary Clinton by at least twelve points. Trump also registered the highest negatives: thirty percent of polled Republicans claimed that they would never support him (nearly 90 percent of Republican voters would eventually vote for him). Progressive pundits immediately celebrated the implications: Trump would win the nomination, but surely destroy the Republican Party in the general election. Most assumed that he was another right-wing Barry Goldwater or progressive George McGovern—bragging about his loyal wild-eyed base while oblivious that its eccentricities or even creepiness turned off a majority of Americans.

Yet Trump's immediate and unshakeable core support still grew. His rise was not only because his squabbling rivals fragmented the anti-Trump vote, but also, at least initially, because Trump enjoyed instant name recognition from four decades of Manhattan tabloid publicity. Also, as mentioned, Trump had for some fourteen seasons hosted *The Apprentice* (as well as later *Celebrity Apprentice*).

The reality TV show enhanced the mythography of Trump the dealmaker and mercurial boss. Each week he fired the incompetent. He rewarded the supposedly more hard-working, talented, and thus deserving—instantaneously, without appeal, filibusters, motions, votes, or bureaucratic consensus. For a country sick of Washington gridlock and stasis, the idea of a firer in chief seemed intriguing. In an age when Barack Obama had often voted "present" as an Illinois state legislator, and as president issued redlines, step-over lines, and deadlines that he would not enforce, decisiveness in and of itself had its appeal.

The Apprentice's audience over a decade and a half ranged from 20 to 30 million viewers. That number eerily translated into Trump's initial percentage of the aggregate Republican primary votes. Or to put it another way: the 28.1 million viewers of the finale to season one (2003–4) of *The Apprentice* represented 17.76 percent of the registered number of voters in the 2016 election. For a divided country that was growing tired of both Democrats and Republicans, especially their inability or unwillingness to make the tough decisions on the Iraq, Afghanistan, or Libyan wars and the economy, *The Apprentice* veteran offered escapist solutions. A tough, trash-talking but also purportedly canny man beneath his crusty veneer would rid Washington of its do-nothings, poseurs, and mediocrities—just the way he did each week on TV.

Moreover, candidate Trump, despite his invective and the media hatred he incurred, had an undeniable sort of charisma, humor, and presence. His skills and screen savvy were honed over years of repartee, improvisation, and sizing up hundreds of wannabe Trump contestants. His retaliatory invective was supposed to be antithetical to the dignity of a presidential race—and later the presidency. But he cynically sensed there was increasingly little dignity anymore in running even for the highest office.

What initially frustrated Republican base voters wanted any-way was not more "dignity" in their presidential candidates. They wanted more winning, and then more action in the White House. Trump calibrated the tempo of his talk, even his appear-ance and mannerisms, to the show's weekly ratings. So many in America came to know Trump from his television show, not the lurid stories of the Manhattan gossip columnists. And they would vote for a controversial showman who supposedly pushed the envelope but would not quite ignite it.

Through his reality show, Trump learned, perhaps better than any politician, what would sell and what wouldn't. He concluded that the audience (a.k.a. live voters) were not turned off by his garishness, crudity, or even malice. Indeed, they tuned in to see what outrageous remark he would make next. But they would quickly switch channels at inauthenticity and split-the-difference monotony. Out of that multiyear conun-drum of keeping the loyal audience watching, Trump refined his Manhattan real estate street smarts. He developed an ani-mal cunning not seen since the quick wit of Ronald Reagan, the smarminess of Bill Clinton, or the insight of Franklin Roosevelt. Trump's slyness stayed with him as president. And it continued to be dismissed by the media.

The idea of ratings was transferred to polls. Viewers became voters. Ratings had always been canonical for Trump. Ratings led to profits, and profitability was an unbiased sign of success. For most of his presidency, Trump praised or attacked on the basis of whether his targets had won or lost audiences. His critics completely forgot that. Trump was not so much vindictive as adaptable. He would bring into his fold former enemies like primary rivals Texas governor Rick Perry and Kentucky senator Rand Paul and Senate majority leader Mitch McConnell—*if they were perceived to be useful.* Current perceived advantage always trumped old personal grudges and vendettas.

Trump even judged enemies by their success or failure in pressing home their attacks on him. Take the later example of one of Trump's most notorious attackers, the vulgar comedian Michelle Wolf, who more or less ruined the 2018 White House Correspondents' Dinner by smearing his press secretary Sarah Huckabee Sanders on the basis of her appearance and Arkansas background. Yet Trump mocked her largely for not reading her audience and therefore bombing: "White House Correspondents' Dinner was a very big, boring bust . . . the so-called comedian really 'bombed.'"

Trump may have acted and sounded crudely, but beneath his uncouth veneer was an uncanny assessment of the politics of his invective. Critics repelled by Trump's boorishness, of course, must disagree. They insist that his mouth reflected his character, and character is destiny. Thus, even an effective would-be commander in chief cannot maintain appeal to the masses if his speech and comportment are unpresidential.

But who or what exactly by 2016, the country was asking, was the ultimate arbiter of what qualifies as unpresidential?

Can one be both presidential and ineffective, or unpresidential and persuasive? Mellifluously revving up supporters with calls to "punish our enemies," "get in their face," and "take a gun to a knife fight" was certainly no more presidential than adolescently tweeting "Cryin' Chuck Schumer" and "Little Rocket Man" Kim Jong-un. In a subsequent chapter, we will discuss more fully the relationship between the Trump message and Trump the messenger, but the idea that Trump was something obscenely novel in the long history of American presidential politics is simply not a sustainable proposition. If he were just predictably crude, he would never have found success on television or politics.

Trump certainly had an aura that even other celebrities lacked. When former two-term California governor and megastar Arnold Schwarzenegger took over Trump's *Apprentice* host slot in 2015, the once-hit series abruptly imploded. Schwarzenegger may have had a larger screen presence than Trump. He had far more political experience. He was probably better known than Trump had been in 2004–5 when the series started. Schwarzenegger's *Terminator* movie franchise made him nearly as wealthy as Trump. Arnold was certainly less toxic and more endearing than Trump. But he was unexpectedly one-dimensional. Arnold was seen as politically squishy, and also less effective in banter, less outrageous, and less uninhibited—and flopped.

Few critics ever analyzed why Trump's appearance and comportment resonated with his base and intrigued neutrals who otherwise might have been repelled by his agenda and personal history. American men in their sixties and seventies often do strange things to retain their youth and vibrancy. They can dye their hair, tan their skin, remove their wrinkles, or substitute loud clothes for a declining physique. Trump did all that and more. He appeared loutish to the Beltway establishment. But unlike aging Hollywood celebrities, he became more rather than less resonant and empathetic to the middle class for the strained effort, as if proof that even aging billionaires were patched together creaky everymen and insecure humans after all. Trump did not put on Beltway politicians' customary flannel shirts and jeans at state fairs or farm shows, but showed up out of place but nonetheless unadulterated and authentic with his trademark baggy suit and loud, long tie.

Most Americans in 2015–16 also did not quite know, and did not care, where Trump's odd accent came from. But they grasped that it was certainly not Washingtonian. He was not screechy in the manner of Hillary Clinton, or affected as in the cadences of Barack Obama, or nasal in the fashion of Ted Cruz, or robotic like Marco Rubio.

Trump's grammar and diction were also not schizophrenic like those of suburban politicians of the Clinton or Obama sort. Trump never faked a black patois when speaking to minorities or tried on corny homespun drawls when campaigning in bowling alleys or state fairs. Trump sounded lowbrow all the time to all the people. Thereby, he came across as transparent and regular, as if a Georgia farmer would rather hear a Queens accent than Hillary Clinton struggle with "y'all."

It is difficult to tell to what degree some of Trump's outrageousness was scripted. As a student of popular culture, he might have known that viewers of the 1980 comedy hit film *Caddyshack* overwhelmingly rooted for the obnoxious and crude—and transparent—party crasher Al Czervik (Rodney Dangerfield). In the now cult movie, Czervik was far more empathetic than his well-groomed archnemesis and habitually outraged Judge Elihu Smails (Ted Knight), the smarmy keeper of country club protocols and standards. In some sense, Trump and Clinton replayed those respective roles in the 2016 election.

Trump's appearance and diction played some part in his appeal to red-state and purple-state middle-class voters. Both empowered Trump's message, at least as calibrated by his base supporters. By nature, they were contrarians and again enjoyed the outrage of the perceived establishment that Trump ignited.

Yet it was not just how Trump spoke or appeared, but what he said that became a force multiplier of his message. George W. Bush had been cruelly caricatured for his malapropisms and mispronunciations. Almost daily a hostile media ridiculed his vocabulary of "misunderestimate," "strategery," and "nucular," supposed proof to the New York–Washington establishment of a moronic pseudo–Ivy League Texas transplant.

But Bush was laughed at largely by comparisons to acceptable political pronunciation. The coastal corridor assumed that the Yale- and Harvard-educated Bush really wished to—but could not—speak their own proper politicalese. Trump, in contrast, did not just violate Beltway cannons of grammar, syntax, and vocabulary. He simply blew them up altogether and could have cared less.

After a year or so of public exposure, all politicians become repetitive (how many times did Barack Obama refer to that stale bending "arc of history" or yet again scold the nation with his boilerplate "that's not who we are"?). Yet Trump's unprecedented tedium was not so much tired ideas and phrases, but focused on a stock campaign vocabulary of about five hundred words. A few (mostly superlative) adjectives sufficed: "awesome," "beautiful," "fantastic," "great," "huge," "incredible," "sad," "stupid," "terrible," "big-league," and "zero," along with stock adverbs such as "tremendously." There were familiar nouns and emphatics: "believe me," "millions and billions," or "moron." "Winning" and "winners" were to be emulated; "losing" and "losers" signaled a "disgrace."

Everything and everyone Trump fought was a "disaster." Was Trump then monotonous? Of course. Did it matter? Perhaps not, at least in the short term.

Repetition reemphasized basic messages delivered in a few syllables. Moreover, Trump could offer strange riffs of endearment. What other politician, in his sober and judicious mind, would ever think up the provocative "beautiful clean coal" or a "beautiful wall" on the southern border?

Trump had never read Demosthenes or Cicero. But either by ear or instinct he employed oxymorons, consonance, alliteration, ellipsis, and anaphora. Of course, he certainly was not the prepared speaker of the caliber of John F. Kennedy, Ronald Reagan, or polished teleprompter reader Barack Obama—but perhaps more entertaining in ad hoc repartee than Obama, and as good as JFK, Bill Clinton, or Reagan.

Critics understandably have seen Trump as analogous to classical demagogues, perhaps like the Athenian rabble-rouser Cleon, the bête noire of the aristocrat Thucydides's masterful history. He might also be compared by his enemies to the thuggish Roman populist Catiline in Sallust's monograph that chronicles Catiline's attempted coup and uprising. But to ancient historians, the speeches of both Cleon and Catiline are nonetheless models of rhetorical power and directness. Those who cannot speak to a crowd cannot become demagogues.

Still, the bad-boy Trump more often overshadowed in the media the good Trump. From the very beginning, Trump deliberately seemed to enjoy being accusatory, even defamatory, both to set himself off from his traditional-speaking and -acting primary rivals, and as a way of capturing hundreds of millions of dollars in free television coverage. He felt that he had to go on the offensive all the time to achieve a sense of deterrence (it was messy to launch an attack on Trump, so better left untried). Otherwise, he would spend the entire campaign and later presidency defending his often lurid past, even if that meant an endless cycle of distractions, petty spats, and off-message time wasting.

In the primaries, when anchors and hosts interviewed a knowledgeable Governor Bobby Jindal, or a charismatic Senator Marco Rubio, or a reliable Jeb Bush, their viewers knew what to expect—facts, figures, platitudes, temporizing, and split-the-difference generalities—and turned the channel. When the networks put the Trump show on the screen, viewers snapped to attention: he could say anything and in the strangest—and often cruelest—manner. Because charges of Trump's past womanizing or business failures could not always be defended either as irrelevant for a president or untrue, he usually went on the offensive in "you do it too" fashion that made attackers think twice whether their own sins might be as great as Trump's—and might no longer remain occult.

What Trump shouted from day one by intent was blared on the internet from the conservative Drudge Report headline to liberal Google News. His latest invective aired both on right-wing talk radio and left-wing NPR. It was not just Fox News that he hogged. CNN and MSNBC both despised Trump, and showcased him over Hillary Clinton. A cash-strapped and dead-last-in-cable-news-ratings CNN discovered that in 2016 it had made an extra $100 million by inadvertently coronating the ringmaster Trump. In response, Trump asked CNN to give its presidential debate profits to veterans.

Former CBS chief Les Moonves bragged of his network's own Trump obsessions: "The money's rolling in, and this is fun"—"fun" predicated on the idea that a buffoonish candidate Trump, with a brief shelf life, was preposterous and thus won ratings. But once Trump was nominated in July 2016, his defeated rivals looked back bitterly—as the Clinton campaign for a time rejoiced—that over the prior year Trump had been the recipient of an estimated $1 billion in free media attention. In some sense Trump had saved both CNN and MSNBC. He gave both a reason to exist, even if that purpose was the venting of unadulterated venom.

Of course, once Trump was president, Clinton whined that the media had played into Trump's connivances. In her postmortem, *What Happened*, Clinton complained bitterly that political journalists "can't bear to face their own role in helping elect Trump." Forgotten was the fact that her primary team once rejoiced that the media had helped to create a certain losing Trump candidacy. And Clinton herself had attacked all sorts of critics, but in a fashion that was neither as entertaining nor effective as Trump's venom.

Watching Trump certainly seemed to draw out viewers' morbid curiosity—the guilty desire to inch closer to the scene of a car wreck, or to seem outraged even as one stood fixated at brawlers in a barroom. But most important, a large minority of the country empathized with the bad-apple Trump. It believed that whatever he dished out to the media again was long overdue. Trump's popularity was a de facto acknowledgment that his media critics were even more unpopular. A November 2017 Quinnipiac poll showed that 58 percent of those surveyed objected to media coverage of Trump; only 38 percent voiced approval.

The revered veteran, prisoner of war, hero, senator, former presidential candidate, and national icon, the late John McCain, was Trump's first and most infamous personal target. "He's not a war hero," Trump crudely scoffed in July 2015. "He's a war hero because he was captured." Then he elaborated, "I like people that weren't captured." Worse, Trump had dismissed McCain at the Family Leadership Summit, a gathering of about three thousand religious, socially conservative, and pro-defense activists. Trump had earlier called McCain a "dummy" for finishing at the near bottom of his class (894) at the Naval Academy (in a graduating class of 899), without much appreciation that lots of American heroes like Grant and Patton had not done especially well at West Point.

Trump's primary rivals smelled blood and eagerly piled on to blast Trump's crudity. Former Texas governor and Trump's future energy secretary Rick Perry dismissed Trump as "unfit" and said he should "immediately withdraw" from the race. Former Florida governor Jeb Bush trashed Trump for his "slanderous attacks." Wisconsin governor Scott Walker, campaigning in western Iowa, denounced Trump's remarks while praising McCain as "undoubtedly an American hero." Senator Marco Rubio of Florida sniffed, "America's POWs deserve much better than to have their service questioned by the offensive rantings of Donald Trump."

Did Trump apologize? Not at all.

Trump, who won a questionable draft deferment from service in the Vietnam-era military, next renewed the attack by invading McCain's home territory of military affairs: "John McCain has not done enough for the veterans. The veterans in this country are suffering. The veterans in this country are treated as third-class citizens. John McCain talks a lot, but he doesn't do anything."

Trump assumed that at least some voters, albeit privately, no longer tuned in to the undeniably heroic stories of McCain's past captivity in a North Vietnamese prison. He felt that the forty-year shelf life of self-referencing such sacrifices had been reached. In the end, what was at the heart of the Trump-McCain squabble?

Perhaps the root cause was that in 2008 McCain had sought and won Trump's strong endorsement of his failed candidacy, and then had not repaid the favor in 2016. Loyalty and reciprocity were always Trump's first ethical commandments. More immediately, however, just days before Trump had attacked McCain at the Family Leadership Summit, McCain had torn into Trump voters and smeared them as "crazies"—no doubt on the expectation that the media would find nothing wrong with such disparagement. Trump's smears were usually reactive, not preemptory.

Trump replied to criticism of Senator Elizabeth Warren with a reminder of her false careerist claims of being Native American by dubbing her "Pocahontas." More furor followed. The larger feud involving Trump, McCain, and Warren continued after the 2016 election, when in November 2017 McCain snapped that "Pocahontas" was "an insult to Native American veterans' sacrifice. Our nation owes a debt of gratitude to the Navajo Code Talkers, whose bravery, skill and tenacity helped secure our decisive victory over tyranny and oppression during WWII."

Again, in the back-and-forth, Trump supporters assumed that a sanctimonious Warren had made up the yarn, successfully sought to use the false ethnic cachet for careerist advantage, and now was peremptorily outraged to hide her own embarrassment at being caught in such a con. Trump's critics had no idea that the more they loudly objected to Trump's supposedly politically incorrect use of "Pocahontas," all the more they brought attention to Warren's myth. And which, after all, was the greater sin, crudely drawing attention to Warren's fabrication, or fabricating an ancestry for careerist gain? The farce finally ended in October 2018, when an exasperated Warren embarrassingly publicized her own DNA tests to claim, quite implausibly, that a now documented, but less than one-percent, Native American heritage had corroborated her insistence that she was a minority. Trump certainly had an uncanny ability to so irritate his critics that in furor they embraced self-destructive behavior.

Trump in lower fashion went on to accuse Ted Cruz's father of consorting with communist supporters of Lee Harvey Oswald, referencing a disputed and hazy sixty-year-old photo. As the last primaries neared, Trump had reverted to his pre-politician brawling self when he sparred with a familiar foe, the fading television celebrity Rosie O'Donnell, with the usual crude insults of "fat" and "slob."

In the first primary debate, Fox anchor Megyn Kelly went after Trump for his long record of insults and purported systematically rude treatment of women ("You've called women you don't like 'fat pigs,' 'dogs,' 'slobs' and 'disgusting animals'"). Trump did not deny the allegations, but confirmed and focused them with "Only Rosie O'Donnell." In his post-debate elaboration, Trump claimed that Kelly was hysterical, with "blood coming out of her wherever," a slur rightly considered misogynist and gross. Kelly soon left Fox News and recited a scary bullying "year of Trump," which, if true, would have radically enhanced her own market value as a luminary in the pantheon of anti-Trump media celebrities.

The later "fat man" attacks on Kim Jong-un or the write-off of Canadian prime minister Justin Trudeau as "weak" were simple continuations of Trump's winning campaign method—and might likewise be efficacious when president, at least if episodic rather than chronic. Trump's crudity initially won him media attention on the press's theory that such a ratings getter like Trump in the short term would again prove lucrative, eventually become monotonous and be easily dropped, and most surely could never be president.

The list of Trump's campaign retaliatory comebacks always grew. In 2016, Trump had all but called Ben Carson (his future housing secretary) a quack surgeon. He suggested that the talented Carly Fiorina was homely ("Look at that face! Would anyone vote for that? Can you imagine that, the face of our next president?") in the similar manner that years earlier he had replied to Arianna Huffington ("Arianna Huffington is unattractive, both inside and out. I fully understand why her former husband left her for a man—he made a good decision."). Most Trump voters hoped that such invective would cease when Trump was president. It did not, and no one quite knew the full political fallout from an often slash-and-burn president, especially when Trump's ratings stayed the same or slightly rose the blunter he became.

By 2017, Trump was suggesting that his own secretary of state, Rex Tillerson (who reportedly called Trump a moron), had a lower IQ than he did: "But if he did that, I guess we'll have to compare IQ tests. And I can tell you who is going to win." His long-suffering attorney general, Jeff Sessions, was ridiculed also for being "weak" for his likely ill-considered outsourcing of the appointment of special counsel Robert Mueller to former Obama Department of Justice attorney Rod Rosenstein, who continued in his job under Trump. Indeed, for nearly two years Trump in callous fashion gratuitously bullied his own attorney general, ostensibly in hopes that Sessions would resign for the sin of recusing himself, a lapse that had led to the Mueller investigation.

Considered most outrageous was candidate and president Trump's Homeric use of adjectival epithets. Primary rivals were understandably the first to become targets. So much for Marco Rubio, who became "Little Marco." Jeb Bush was reduced to "Low-energy Jeb," and Ben Carson "lower energy than Bush." Ted Cruz was tagged as "Lyin' Ted Cruz." Opposition minority leader Senator Charles Schumer, who often teared up in speeches, went after Trump and so was quickly rebranded as "Cryin' Chuck."

When neosocialist Bernie Sanders attacked Trump as crude, he was hit with "Crazy Bernie," a nickname that resonated given the often unkempt appearance of Sanders and his unapologetic socialist agenda. Hillary Clinton, mired in scandal and rumor herself, was seared for a year with the sobriquet "Crooked Hillary." Trump critic and former senator Al Franken was little more than "Al Frankenstein." Later when former Trump intimate and advisor Stephen Bannon was reported to have mocked the Trump White House, Trump struck back at the often rumpled Bannon with "Sloppy Steve." Even Barack Obama did not escape Trump's name-tagging. By early 2018, as stories grew of Obama administration FBI and DOJ excesses, the ex-president was nicknamed "Cheatin' Obama."

Trump nemesis and fired FBI director James Comey, who had leaked to the press confidential conversations with Trump, soon was dubbed "Leakin' James Comey." More exchanges reached the surreal when Comey went after Trump's marriage, looks, and hands, with Trump firing back that Leakin' Comey was a "slime ball."

No modern president so consistently had resorted to name-calling. The country did not know quite what to make of all the presidential slurs. On the one hand, earlier presidents had certainly been crude and occasionally vicious. But usually their smears were either offered in private or only episodically in public. On the other hand, Trump picked his targets carefully. His epithets even more carefully: no one, for example, could deny that Comey leaked. And the public was tiring

of Comey's boy-scout sanctimonious sermons, as more information emerged about his own unethical behavior: helping to
mislead a FISA court with deliberately incomplete information,
denying that the Steele dossier was the chief evidence produced
for a FISA court warrant, warning the president of gossip about
him, but not disclosing that it came from an FBI informant and
Hillary Clinton–employed Christopher Steele, and leaking to
the press confidential, and in one case likely classified, memos
of private conversations with the president.

Still, what was the ultimate effect of Trump's puerile polemics?

Initially during the election cycle, they were twofold and
contradictory. For the general public, the name-calling registered negatively. Trump's personal ratings throughout 2015
and early 2016 slumped—and in a few polls have never for long
topped even 50 percent during his presidency. His favorables
sometimes sunk to below 40 percent (and would dip even further after the election as his tweeting spiked in the transition).
Throughout late 2015 and 2016, in trial runs with Hillary Clinton—herself undergoing serial bad publicity from her various
email scandals and slugfest primaries with rival Senator Bernie
Sanders—Trump often polled anywhere from 5 to 15 percentage
points behind.

By May 4, 2016, at the point when Trump's last primary opponent had dropped out of the Republican race, 60 percent
of all GOP primary voters had voted *against* Trump. Trump
would almost never win 50 percent of any state primary vote.
The combined votes of Ted Cruz and Marco Rubio outpaced
Trump's vote in twenty-five of the first thirty-five contests. In
fact, in all the primary elections, only Indiana had voted for
Trump with a majority. In the end, a remarkable 10 percent of
general election voters polled that they had an unfavorable impression of Trump and yet voted for him. The cause of voter
discontent was usually attributed to Trump's ad hominem style
and serial vulgarity.

But Trump's venom also had another, odder effect—one of energizing his base and perhaps even intriguing independents and conservative Democrats. As Trump described his loyal supporters (and was crucified by the press for so doing), "I could stand in the middle of Fifth Avenue and shoot somebody and I wouldn't lose voters." Trump knew that *within limits* he could say and do almost anything and not lose his 30–35 percentage points core support—as long as he did not renege on his promises to address illegal immigration, trade, jobs, and foreign policy, and did not slur and slander his own conservative supporters.

But, again, it was not only the Trump voter who contextualized candidate and then president Trump's often vicious putdowns and tweets. For even those beyond his base, a sort of nihilism was occasionally the reaction to Trump's latest transgressions, perhaps best captured by the biblical image of a furious Samson pulling down the rotten temple of the Philistines—on top of himself.

In other words, in addition to capitalizing on the red-state/blue-state divide with nontraditional messaging and issues, Trump himself became an everyman slayer of establishment dragons—often with weapons that were as gross as the targeted scaly monsters themselves. The media in its outrage, the Republican establishment in its horror, and the Democratic opposition in its delight all missed critical subtexts to Trump's supposedly one-dimensional broadsides. On second reflection, these subtleties may also explain why Trump during his presidency not only got away with his bouts of childish name-calling, but also profited from them.

One, Trump's slurs never ceased, but eventually they did become somewhat less chronic, as he finished his first year as president. These hiatuses were not due to Trump's introspection or regret. But rather in a Darwinian way—by design or not—they had finally created a Neanderthal sense of deterrence.

Politicians and journalists, from former vice president Joe Biden to CNN's Jim Acosta, realized that to get into a name-calling slog with Trump meant as many wounds as hits. So fewer did. Critics did not wish to end up in the sand against the bruised gladiator Trump.

The astute columnist Salena Zito, Pittsburgh *Tribune-Review* and later *New York Post* columnist, had famously also warned the press of Trump's nine lives that always revived after serial media obituaries: "The press takes him literally, but not seriously; his supporters take him seriously, but not literally." In other words, the press fixated on Trump's gaffes and missed the larger message of his rhetoric—an effort at resurrecting the forgotten working class.

The Trump base ignored his chronic and often self-induced feuds and instead concentrated on his single-minded efforts to bring them economic justice. Trump supporters would have abandoned him in droves had he become a press favorite and moved to the traditional Republican center. A more gentlemanly Vice President Mike Pence or wonkish Senate Majority Leader Mitch McConnell who never had tweeted a bad word about anyone would also never have won the presidency in 2016.

Two, Trump was more often reactive than preemptive. Or, as Trump bragged, he was merely "a counter puncher." In most cases, Trump hit back rather than gratuitously starting his feuds—and the press never caught on that sequence still mattered to many of the public. Take a sampling of Trump's most ignoble tweets and adolescent outbursts, from attacks on Senator Bob Corker's height, referencing his own secretary of state Rex Tillerson's IQ, the crude description of blood oozing from a supposedly irate Megyn Kelly, or deprecating the capture and imprisonment of war hero John McCain. The common denominator is more than just puerility and cruelty, but also *retaliation*.

All had first attacked Trump and sometimes equally viciously. Corker had claimed that Trump's White House was chaos, a reality show, and in danger of prompting World War III—a virtual charge that Trump was nuts. Anonymous sources accused Tillerson of calling Trump a moron or, at least, implying it. The secretary did not explicitly deny the charge, although he deplored the media landscape in which such accusations were made and spread. Kelly hijacked her own debate question and turned it into a scripted rant about Trump's alleged misogyny. As mentioned earlier, McCain arrogantly wrote off Trump's supporters as "crazies"—a forgotten precursor to Hillary Clinton's "deplorables." Apparently, half of America believed that there is still something to the old adolescent plea "He started it, I finished it."

Three, it was suicidal for anyone to jump into Trump's ring (who literally had participated in a professional WrestleMania bout in a World Wrestling Entertainment's "Battle of the Billionaires" event). Given the scandals, rumors, and innuendo that had swirled around Trump for a half century, voters would believe anything about him, and therefore in a sense nothing.

Trump got up each morning and expected to be defamed and reviled. His less calloused adversaries in the media and politics did not. The former reacted to hits steely-eyed and eager for revenge, the latter shocked and eager to call it all off. This was true of 2015 primary rivals, Hillary Clinton in 2016, and even Iranian and North Korean strongmen in 2017–18.

For Trump, lurid stories about the porn star Stormy Daniels or his former consigliore turned accuser Michael Cohen or the "secret tapes" of fired aide Omarosa were just a usual day's fare. But for a Mitt Romney or Paul Ryan such seedy or suspicious characters would have been shattering to their own moral sense of self and their ethical connections with voters. Kim Jong-un expected to slur Western leaders; he never expected any of them to smear him in kind.

It is hard to calibrate exactly why many of Trump's targets fared poorly after their encounters with Trump, given the latter's usual greater viciousness. But there was a sort of mummy's curse that followed his former adversaries long after the fact, as if the instigator of the dispute would eventually not end well.

Or did Trump deliberately engage with those already perceived waning in public support? After her role as edgy debate moderator, Megyn Kelly would cash in and hop to NBC, where she was greeted, often viciously, as an overrated prima donna with anemic ratings that did not justify her astronomical salary. Trump adversaries like Senators Bob Corker and Jeff Flake would announce retirements in expectation of either primary or general election defeats.

Four, ennui set in that favored Trump. President Trump's ad hominem attacks no longer were always headline news. In a strange reversal of conventional wisdom, presidential candidate, presidential nominee, and president himself Trump could be excused as "just being Trump," while the supposedly legacy media of Edward R. Murrow and Walter Cronkite was reduced to unprofessional tabloid sensationalism. By spring 2018, Trump in a few polls occasionally neared 50 percent favorable ratings, while his archnemesis, CNN, had lost 30 percent of its prime-time viewers, and ranked dead last in cable news surveys.

The public expected the host of *The Apprentice* to go low. They had never expected the late war hero John McCain as early as July 2015 to initiate the lowness by writing off thousands of concerned voters as "crazies" (he had previously dismissed newly elected senators Rand Paul and Ted Cruz as "wacko birds"), while in the shadows trafficking in the scurrilous Fusion GPS dossier. McCain later doubled down on his gambit by admitting that he had no idea whether anything in the dossier was true—and yet snapped at his critics, "Anyone who doesn't like it can go to hell."

Five, and most controversially, there was some unspoken dark truth in some of Trump's ripostes, however uncouth and unmentionable. Once Trump called attention to these realities that an Elizabeth Warren really did concoct an ethnic identity or CNN had aired false stories, his pejorative nicknames tended not to go away so easily. Nor did his crude putdowns. General George S. Patton once shocked soldiers and civilians by callously stating, "I don't want to hear of any soldier under my command being captured unless he has been hit. Even if you are . . . I want you to remember that no bastard ever won a war by dying for his country." Trump may have clumsily lifted his own McCain putdown from George C. Scott's opening Patton speech that was only slightly altered and abbreviated in the 1970 film classic *Patton*—unaware that Patton's candor usually earned him as much odium from contemporaries as it did admiration from subsequent generations, in part because it cruelly revealed a truth about human nature.

Later, when President Trump crudely labeled—in a private and supposedly off-the-record but quickly leaked conversation—countries such as Haiti a sh*t hole, outrage followed. His supporters challenged critics to make the argument that Haiti was not a mess, or that other presidents' private, but likely occasionally off-putting, White House conversations and activities were any less outrageous. After all, the press did not grow as hysterical when the public learned that First Lady Nancy Reagan had helped to schedule presidential speeches and decisions according to her astrologer's calendar of unfortunate and fortunate days, or when it was leaked that Hillary Clinton as First Lady conducted séance-like conversations with the spirit of Eleanor Roosevelt.

Once again, as characteristic of the reactions to Trump's crudity, the debate devolved into something along the Manichean lines of "Is honest vulgarity worse than euphemistic misrepresentation?"—without the third option of a quiet opting out of rudely stating the obvious. Trump supporters charged that the old order was corrupt and needed a broadside. His critics assumed its refinement was merited and well earned, but could sustain only so many volleys of vulgarity.

Trump felt that he was not necessarily speaking more crudely than past presidents whose conversations were not so often publicized. Their bad behavior had been ignored or covered up by a compliant or biased media. And they had operated in an environment of sympathetic television grandees and journalistic gatekeepers, not the no-law-in-the-arena landscapes of electronic social media and Twitter.

That debate over presidential propriety is still not resolved and will be discussed in a subsequent chapter, but it continues as the subtext to the entire controversy over Trump's boorishness: Is vulgarity either hardly new for a president, or is its singular *frequency* in the case of Trump unprecedented? Does it detract from his message or increase its effectiveness?

Or rather, is Trump all that shocking in a 2018 America, when anti-Semite and racist Louis Farrakhan was lauded by US congressmen and attended the August 2018 Aretha Franklin funeral, sitting close to ex-president Clinton. Or when the former director of the FBI deliberately leaked confidential memos of presidential conversations to the press to advance a political agenda while stooping to trash the president's hands and tan? *All* twenty-first-century norms in every field and endeavor were being constantly recalibrated.

Sixth, and most importantly, Trump's tweets and press announcements certainly drove his enemies into a media frenzy. Commentators claimed that Trump now lived rent free in the very heads of his journalist opponents, or that he teased out their preexisting biases and snobbery to the point of absurdity. Rather than apologize for his nonstop tweeting, Trump in July 2017, after yet another Twitter rant about MSNBC, goaded the media even more: "My use of social media is not Presidential— it's MODERN DAY PRESIDENTIAL. Make America Great Again!"

Journalists neurotically obsessed over all imaginable interpretations of every Trump sentence, often to the point of becoming far more unhinged than was the object of their vituperation. That seemed to be in part Trump's aim. As a candidate, he had casually declared in July 2016 that he wished that the supposedly satanic Vladimir Putin, accused of contracting out Russian hackers to raise hell in the 2016 election, might help find Hillary Clinton's thirty thousand missing emails ("Russia, if you're listening, I hope you're able to find the 30,000 emails that are missing"). Trump knew all at once that he earned liberal outrage. He amused his base. He won another few hours of headline news. He reminded his critics that he did not really care about their charges that he was a supposed beneficiary of Russian collusion. And he emphasized Hillary's laxity that in theory might well have sent classified information into the hands of Vladimir Putin.

The same was true when President Trump called Putin after the dictator won his March 2018 rigged presidential election ("We had a very good call, and I suspect that we'll probably be meeting in the not-too-distant future to discuss the arms race, which is getting out of control"). It was almost as if Trump was signaling that he not only would not be shy of mentioning Russia while under special counsel Robert Mueller's yearlong hunt for proof of collusion, but would even deliberately dare his critics to suggest that such age-old realist foreign policy initiatives were somehow proof of his guilt. After all, before Pearl Harbor, the Roosevelt administration had approved Lend-Lease shipments to a beleaguered Soviet Union reeling from German attacks, despite Soviet dictator Joseph Stalin's prior genocidal policies that had killed millions of innocent Russians. Richard Nixon had sought out China's Mao, the greatest mass murderer of the twentieth century. Henry Kissinger as Nixon's secretary of state had flattered Soviets to play them against the Chinese. Barack Obama courted both Fidel Castro and the Iranian theocrats (and praised more than faulted both), who likely had matched or exceeded Putin in the slaughter of their own citizens.

Because Trump almost never apologized, never explained, and never contextualized, he often perplexed his own staff. As a result, the ambiguity about Trump was only heightened: was Trump just a clumsy buffoon who said the first thing that came into his one-dimensional mind, or was he a multidimensional strategic thinker who liked to bait and goad elites, as a sort of mockery for others to enjoy?

No one quite knew. Apparently, that too was his point. When Trump misspelled press "coverage" as press "covfefe" in a tweet (likely due to sloppy typing on a smartphone or pad), journalists argued over its hidden meaning. Trump soon goaded them on in their inanity, tweeting back, "Who can figure out the true meaning of 'covfefe'??? Enjoy!" Thanks to an outraged media, presidential clumsiness and sloppiness were almost seen as some sort of complex conspiracy or encoded messaging.

In the end, Trump's chemotherapy was a paradox. It enhanced his message while it alienated Independents. It was inseparable from Trump's message that it both undermined and enhanced. It gave Trump authenticity as it proved his crudity. Again, the voters would ultimately decide whether Trump slurs were proof of admirable authenticity or rank toxicity.

Still, Trump did not exist in a political vacuum. While he capitalized on a restless electorate with resonant issues and an initially welcomed over-the-top persona and style, there were still lots of alternatives to Trump. If he was so noxious, why did not others less venomous impede Trump?

Something clearly was wrong with both the Democratic and Republican Parties, as well as with the so-called deep state. Both the political classes and the permanent bureaucracy previously had proved unable to offer remedies to the very maladies that Trump supposedly had exploited.

PART TWO

AN ESTABLISHMENT WITHOUT ANSWERS

UNDERSHAFT: *Oh, just what he wants to do. He knows nothing; and he thinks he knows everything. That points clearly to a political career. Get him a private secretaryship to someone who can get him an Under Secretaryship; and then leave him alone. He will find his natural and proper place in the end on the Treasury bench.*
—George Bernard Shaw, *Major Barbara*

Chapter Four

DEMOCRATIC TRIBALISM

There exists also in the human heart a depraved taste for
equality, which impels the weak to attempt to lower the
powerful to their own level, and reduces men to prefer
equality in slavery to inequality with freedom.
        —Alexis de Tocqueville, *Democracy in America*

In 2016, Hillary Clinton spent a record $250 million in negative
advertising against Donald Trump to paint him as a sexual
predator, a colluder with Vladimir Putin, a tax cheat, a dishonest developer, a bigot, an alt-right racist, a xenophobe, a dark
populist, a neofascist, a Machiavellian manipulator, a nut who
might blow up the world—or alternatively a buffoon, a joke, a
mess, and a slob. Hillary's main message was "I am not the ogre
Trump!"

Yet running just against a presidential candidate's person,
rather than his ideas, his agendas, and his party, has not usually worked in recent American history. Walter Mondale was a
charismatic, progressive, well-informed former senator and vice
president when he ran in 1984 against incumbent Ronald Reagan. Yet Mondale offered only a vague liberal agenda. Instead, he

defined his campaign mostly as against Reagan, the supposedly heartless rich man's lackey and ill-informed bumbler abroad.

When the economy grew at over an annualized rate of 7 percent from November 1983 to November 1984, the trope of Reagan as dunce or corporate shill evaporated. Mondale had little alternative vision. He lost in the seventh-greatest landslide in American history.

Republican Senate majority leader and former vice-presidential candidate Bob Dole had no real compelling message in 1996. In contrast, incumbent President Clinton had recently triangulated between Left and Right. He entertained some conservative ideas as he got the economy back on track and picked up blue-collar voters. Third-party candidate Ross Perot again siphoned off some conservative votes. Dole was demolished.

Democratic nominee Senator John Kerry should have been able to defeat an incumbent, but not particularly popular, George W. Bush in 2004. But he had no comprehensive alternate agenda. "Bush lied, thousands died" was not enough reason to vote out a sitting president in a time of war.

Ditto the same fate of John McCain and Mitt Romney. Both ran mostly as the anti-Obamas, unsure whether they themselves were to be mavericks or establishment Republicans. Despite a sluggish economy, the Obamacare misadventure, and suspicions over Obama's radical past and possible future, neither Republican challenger was able to construct a preferable alternative scenario.

In 2016, first in the Republican primary then again in the general election, being the non-Trump did neither senators Ted Cruz nor Marco Rubio much good. Candidates, of course, willingly do not wish to repeat such past failed campaign strategies. So when they still err and persist in campaigning only in ad hominem fashion, it is likely by default and due to a lack of an idea.

Such was the status of both anti-Trump Democratic and Republican orthodoxy in 2016—and may well be again in 2020. We have already seen why Trump arose, and how his agenda and person brought him to power. But Trump was also a beneficiary of the tired ideas of both ossified political parties and, indeed, of weariness with the administrative state itself. Republicans and Democrats were certainly not Trump, but they could hardly claim to be much of anything else.

In 2008, Barack Obama had wisely campaigned as a near centrist, but once elected then governed progressively while empowering the hard Left, which then took the party further to the extremes. He got elected by mostly ignoring his rival, Senator John McCain, by more or less suggesting that the onetime maverick was now too old and too blinkered to be aware of a changing America. He ran instead initially on lame-duck President Bush's Iraq War. Obama told the country it was too costly and had started on false claims that Saddam Hussein had active arsenals of weapons of mass destruction.

Given that the war by 2008 was mostly quiet, by default Obama next harped on George W. Bush's financial recklessness that had led, he insisted, to the September 2008 financial collapse. Indeed, Bush in just two terms had doubled the national debt (actually a 70 percent increase when adjusted for inflation), supposedly with a "Bank of China" credit card.

So Obama posed as a near-centrist Democrat candidate. He opposed gay marriage ("I believe that marriage is the union between a man and a woman. Now, for me as a Christian—for me—for me as a Christian, it is also a sacred union. God's in the mix."). Raising the issue of transgender restrooms in 2008 would have been absurd.

Obama also campaigned in 2008 against open borders and illegal immigration. Indeed, he promised all sorts of southern barriers: "I will secure the borders first, and I will have the border states' governors certify that those borders are secured." Obama had insisted that if illegal immigrants wanted "a green card, they would have to pay a fine." Obama added that they would have to not have engaged in any criminal activity. In addition, he insisted that they would have to learn English. Finally, they would have "to go to the back of the line so that they did not get citizenship before those persons who had come here legally."

A conservative Republican could not have said it better.

Until his sweeping reelection-cycle executive order DACA amnesty of June 15, 2012, on more than twenty occasions Obama also had claimed that exempting so-called Dreamers by presidential fiat was likely not only unconstitutional, but also the sort of abuse of power more characteristic of an authoritarian.

On matters of race, candidate Obama said he was a liberal, not a radical. He distanced himself from the candid chauvinism of his own past two books, and prior associations with the Reverend Jeremiah Wright, his personal pastor in Chicago and the inspiration for the title of his second memoir, *The Audacity of Hope*. Obama kept a prior photo-op meeting with Louis Farrakhan under wraps and occasionally lectured inner-city youths on the need for self-discipline and self-reliance.

In other words, Obama in his 2008 campaign posed for a time as a veritable old-time Democratic liberal in the fashion of Bill Clinton in 1992 and 1996, even as he winked and nodded to the left of Hillary Clinton. During Obama's second term, the nation became familiar with new ideas such as "trigger warnings," "safe spaces," and "white privilege," but in 2008 they were still mostly confined to the fringe academic domain of identity politics and racial and ethnic enclaves. Voters had little idea that 2008 candidate Obama would as 2009 president Obama soon editorialize about ongoing criminal cases involving matters of race such as the Henry Louis Gates psychodramatic arrest, and later the Trayvon Martin lethal fight with George Zimmerman, or the riots in Ferguson, Missouri, and Baltimore following police shootings of black criminal suspects.

Obama's seemingly successful campaign strategy, in classical American political style, was to downplay, and only when elected to embrace, progressive ideas. According to the *National Journal*, Senator Obama's 2007 voting record had proven the most progressive in the US Senate (Hillary Clinton's was sixteenth). But again no one would ever have known that from the 2008 dexterously run campaign. The hard Left would make allowances for the façade—and anyway, it had nowhere to go if it didn't. Obama realized that to get elected and then to govern progressively, he could never campaign progressively and tip his leftish hand to voters. That subterfuge worked twice, in 2008 and 2012, but it ultimately helped to nearly destroy the Democratic Party by 2016 and left it with few messages to counter Trump.

Voters in 2008 remained angry for months at the bailout of banks and sickened by their sinking retirement accounts, and would warm to the idea of the first African American president. Obama assumed that African Americans and perhaps other minorities would register and vote in record numbers without any required hard-Left messaging. In most of these assumptions, Obama was proven absolutely correct. He defeated John McCain by a 192 electoral vote margin while capturing 52.9 percent of the popular vote. No Republican candidate had achieved such a popular margin since George H. W. Bush's 1988 53.4 percent victory, two decades earlier.

By April 2009, President Obama enjoyed a sixty-vote supermajority in the Senate and a huge seventy-six-vote majority in the House. He was free to pass almost any legislation he wished. Imagining a 2017 Trump as president would have been impossible in the Obama euphoria. As he entered office, Obama calculated that he would avoid public outcry and not force through immediate stricter gun control, DACA amnesties, a revisit of the global mandates to reduce carbon emissions, and more liberal abortion laws. He would save progressive efforts for later executive orders and his second term. For a moment, in the style of Bill Clinton, Obama had signaled that he would keep the center and expand the base. Again, had he just done so, Donald Trump would likely never have become president.

But soon Obama reinterpreted his election and his congressional strength as a progressive mandate and began governing and moving his party accordingly. By March 2010, Obama had rammed through Obamacare on a strictly partisan vote. Clinton's third-way Democratic Party was out. Identity politics and progressive redistribution were soon in.

Foreign policy was recalibrated as an apologetic America "leading from behind" in concert with its European allies. For the Republicans, the return of Obama to his partisan senatorial record was a godsend. It ended any chance that the Democrats would create some sort of formidable bipartisan workers' movement, in the fashion of old Truman, Humphrey, Kennedy, and Clinton Democrats.

No matter: in existential terms, Obama thought he had solved for good the Democrats' prior progressive dilemmas. The liberal social agenda had largely been enacted by the 1970s, such as minimum wage laws, unemployment insurance, affirmative action, and generous Social Security disability and retirement insurance. During the Reagan Revolution the public had wondered what further redistributive social programs were needed. The government was trillions of dollars in debt. Entitlements without massive reforms and new taxes were becoming unsustainable. Technological breakthroughs had allowed the average citizen to have access to private appurtenances and appliances reserved for the very wealthy just a few years earlier.

Obama addressed all those paradoxes by assuming the goal of a radical equality of result in most spheres of human experience—an end achievable only by a humane, all-powerful, and intrusive government. Legally protected equality of opportunity was deemed not enough in a supposedly historically racist, sexist, homophobic, nativist, and xenophobic society. Instead, a mandated equality of result and outcome by a caring and powerful state was needed to keep redressing past sins of racism and bigotry. But first, such progressive dogmas had to appeal to a majority of Americans, if they were not to be merely transient footnotes to Obama's own popularity. By "appeal" I mean that most Americans would be persuaded to give up elements of their freedom to ensure state-defined equality.

So for all the stealth and misleading advertising, the next-generation progressive agenda would still eventually have to be forced upon voters who were not the immediate beneficiaries. Smelling victory in late October 2008, Obama had let down his guard in a glimpse of a different politics to come at a campaign stop in Columbus, Missouri: "Now, Mizzou, I just have two words for you tonight: five days. Five days. After decades of broken politics in Washington, and eight years of failed policies from George W. Bush, and twenty-one months of a campaign that's taken us from the rocky coast of Maine to the sunshine of California, we are five days away from fundamentally transforming the United States of America."

Obama certainly did try to transform America in such fundamental fashion. Somehow, someway, the Democrats under Barack Obama, for a fleeting moment in 2008, had captured both houses of Congress, the presidency, and perhaps the power to determine the makeup of the Supreme Court for a generation. And yet, as a result of that euphoric move to the left, by 2017 there was instead in power a Republican-controlled Congress, Supreme Court, and state legislatures and governorships. What went wrong?

Obama had not so much transformed the United States as radically diminished the Democratic Party through hundreds of new regulations on businesses, higher taxes, government-run health care, defense cuts, expanded entitlements, soaring budget deficits, substantial increases in the size of government, and frequent sermons about America's problematic history. The larger themes of the new signature progressivism were identity politics, radical environmentalism, and redistributionism. In terms of rhetoric, Democrats had targeted red-state, middle-class citizens as gun-loving, carbon-spewing, and racially illiberal obstructionists. It was considered a sin to call Obama a socialist, but by 2018 his legacy may have been that many Democratic congressional candidates were openly running as socialists and proud of the label.

In the end, Obama's progressivism never had really reflected genuine grassroots radicalization among American voters. It was birthed instead by the collective liberal euphoria of the outlier year of 2008, in which an unpopular war, a struggling lame-duck president, a young, charismatic nontraditional Democratic nominee, and an economic meltdown had tarnished the Republican brand. In 2018, ex-president Obama himself reportedly sighed of the Trump victory, "Sometimes I wonder whether I was ten or twenty years too early," implying that the United States had not quite evolved enough by 2016 to have appreciated the gift of the singular Obama presidency and its heroic efforts to recalibrate America as a neosocialist state.

Still, as a result of a lucky alignment of the stars, progressives had proclaimed Obama as a messiah of what they then called "a permanent Democratic majority." Or as *Newsweek*'s Evan Thomas put it in a 2009 television appearance, "In a way, Obama's standing above the country, above—above the world. He's sort of God."

Again, few in the media appreciated that even Obama's initial popularity and two presidential victories were not due to some new neosocialist majority or his divine character, but because he had run initially as something he did not wish to be—and was a beneficiary of the unique conditions of the 2008 campaign season. Obama would be reelected in 2012 on the strength of incumbency, his ability once again to temporarily campaign as a liberal (who empathized personal freedoms within existing norms) rather than as a progressive (who seeks fundamental changes by radically altering tradition, laws, and customs). He was, of course, helped by the continuing innate inability of the establishment Republican Party to field a viable and competitive candidate—but not by a tidal wave of support for progressive socialism.

By 2015, when Donald Trump entered the presidential race, the country had long ago headed in a direction unimaginable in 2008. Formerly arcane academic theories of racially disparate impact and proportional representation were superimposed on policy, from the Environmental Protection Agency (EPA) to federal court nominees. Borders were more or less open. By 2016, it was inaccurate to say that sanctuary cities defied federal immigration law, because federal Immigration and Customs Enforcement agents were themselves not enforcing the laws as written.

When Obamacare supporters in 2013 wanted to push greater participation in the Affordable Care Act, they created the strange "Pajama Boy" ad, featuring an urban hipster in retro glasses, clad in plaid onesie pajamas. In childlike fashion, Pajama Boy held a cup of hot chocolate and wore a smug expression. "Wear pajamas," the ad read. "Drink hot chocolate. Talk about getting health insurance." Such messaging did not go down well in rural Pennsylvania or southern Ohio. Critics speculated whether the image was a deliberate liberal caricature of a bored metrosexual designed to get the goat of conservatives. But Pajama Boy's smirk and his message of arrested development and dependence, even if a con, offered a damning portrayal of what millions of urbanites now saw as cool: getting up late, staying undressed, and sipping childhood drinks. America's Marlboro Man he wasn't. Twenty years earlier, most Democrats would have laughed at or felt embarrassed by the ad.

In an example of reality resembling art, Ethan Krupp, who posed for the ad, was an employee of the progressive Organizing for Action. He offered on social media a self-portrait of himself that confirmed the photo's stereotyped image. He claimed to be a self-described "liberal f***." And explained: "A liberal f*** is not a Democrat, but rather someone who combines political data and theory, extreme leftist views, and sarcasm to win any argument while making the opponents feel terrible about themselves." Krupp added, "I won every argument but one." When Krupp boasted about "making the opponents feel terrible about themselves," he was likely referring to people of his own narrow circle, rather than trying such verbal intimidation on the local mechanic or union electrician. An emblem of a majority party Krupp certainly was not.

Nor was a 2012 interactive Obama reelection campaign web ad, "The Life of Julia." Its dependency narrative defined the life of an everywoman character as one of cradle-to-grave government reliance—a desirable thing. Julia is proudly and perennially a near ward of the state. She can get through school only thanks to Head Start and federally backed student loans. Only the Small Business Administration and the Lilly Ledbetter Fair Pay Act enable her to find work. Though unmarried, Julia has one child—but no health care worries, thanks to Obamacare. And in her retirement years, only Social Security and Medicare allow her security, comfort, and the time and wherewithal to volunteer for a communal urban garden, apparently a hobby rather than a critical food source.

The subtext of Obama's message was the assumption of a demographically shrinking, urbanized country where liberated unmarried women find parity only through government dependence. The president was certainly not appealing, as some of his Democratic predecessors did, to a confident young married woman who, along with her husband, was struggling to start a family business while raising three kids and saving to buy a three-bedroom, two-bath house in the suburbs. Again, few in the progressive movement saw that progressive politics were insidiously prompting a political pushback.

By January 2014, Obama had lost the entire Congress. He was reduced to warning that he would now act legislatively, making as well as enforcing laws: "We're not just going to be waiting for legislation in order to make sure that we're providing Americans the kind of help they need. I've got a pen and I've got a phone . . . And I can use that pen to sign executive orders and take executive actions and administrative actions that move the ball forward."

That promise implied that he could make his own sorts of law if the obstructionist Republican-controlled Congress would not come along. And he did just that—and disastrously set an ironic example of presidential overreach that a later President Trump would find especially useful. Eventually, Obama reconfigured vast swaths of federal lands as sacrosanct national parks, while putting equally large areas off-limits to oil and gas exploration. He empowered the EPA to so enlarge its interpretation of existing environmental regulations that it de facto was creating its own legislation.

Over his tenure, Obama had nearly nationalized health care, now with strict government supervision of health insurance plans and doctor and patient obligations. He raised the top rates of income taxes. He raised capital gains taxes. And he raised corporate tax rates. Yet Obama, in the fashion of the prior Bush administration, still saw annual deficits explode and the national debt double over his two terms—given unprecedented increases in entitlement and discretionary spending in the years before congressionally mandated spending freezes.

With greater regulation and higher taxes, industries and commerce hunkered down. Zero-interest rates and massive quantitative easing likely stagnated economic growth, but also allowed massive federal borrowing to be serviced through low payments on the debt. Middle-class passbook savings accounts earned virtually no interest, diminishing the idea of rewarding thrift, while rewarding the notion of cheap borrowing. Sharp downturns like the 2008 disaster usually prompt equally sharp subsequent recoveries. Yet the 2009 upswing proved the most anemic economic recovery in modern history. At the time, few—including most Republicans—realized that Obama's agenda was slowly kindling a rationale for a reappearance of populist nationalism, given job growth stagnation and redistributive government at home, and a perceived loss of influence abroad.

Obama's presidency was the first two-term tenure in modern history not to achieve 3 percent growth in annualized GDP. Part of the stagnation was surely psychological. If there were such a thing as "animal spirits" that stampede growth, Obama tranquilized them with sermons that seemed to castigate success: almost immediately he lectured companies in January 2009 that "there will be time for them to make profits, and there will be time for them to get bonuses—now is not that time."

In April 2010, Obama (who along with First Lady Michelle Obama on leaving the White House would sign joint book contracts for a reported $65 million—if true the largest book advance in history—and a Netflix hypercapitalist deal rumored to be almost as lucrative) sermonized: "We're not, we're not trying to push financial reform because we begrudge success that's fairly earned. I mean, I do think at a certain point you've made enough money."

During his reelection campaign in July 2012, Obama borrowed a theme from Elizabeth Warren in suggesting that ultimately the state—in "Life of Julia" fashion—was responsible for personal success: "There are a lot of wealthy, successful Americans who agree with me—because they want to give something back. They know they didn't—look, if you've been successful, you didn't get there on your own. You didn't get there on your own."

Unwillingly, Obama was prepping the 2016 race for any candidate who would brag in opposite fashion that wealth creation was good. For Trump, the more an individual could achieve riches, the better off was everyone around him. The individual certainly did build his own successful business. And the more that he did so, the better off everyone else would be as well.

There was a similar transformative effort abroad to radically recalibrate, or at least rhetorically reconfigure, US foreign policy. Apologies for purported past American sins, distancing from former allies such as the Gulf monarchies and Israel, new openings with Iran and Cuba, and efforts to reset Russian relations, cut back on defense, downsize the nuclear arsenal, and postpone missile defense all seemed to suggest a new overarching idea of how the world might become a safer place. These resets either were going to bring dramatic results or in their failure they would likewise invite radical pushbacks in 2016.

The mounting criticism of Obama's foreign policy was not only that it was utopian, self-righteous, and naïve. Rather, it also assumed that nations were not collections of people with predictable and all too human aspirations and behaviors, and subject to certain ancient rules of deterrence, balance of power, and mutual defense alliances. The result was a series of Russian aggressions in eastern Ukraine and Crimea as well as cyber intrusions, an ascendant China reforming the South China Sea region into something akin to the Japanese Greater East Asia Co-Prosperity Sphere of the 1930s, the rise of an ISIS "on the run" as a once "stable" Iraq crumbled, a spreading Iranian-Syrian-Hezbollah Middle East Axis, and newer versions of the old instability throughout North Africa and much of the Middle East.

As the Obama administration prepared to leave office, his transformation of the Democratic Party was completed in a number of symbolic ways well beyond its new minority status at the local, state, and federal levels. And these changes, like Obama's policies, would soon play into the hands of candidate and president Trump.

In sum, there was now no such thing as a centrist Democrat, much less a conservative working-class one. During the 2016 Democratic primary, the single old-style Truman Democrat in the race, former US senator James Webb, quit in disgust after just four months. He was all but humiliated for his calcified ideas (e.g., urging greater gas and oil production, redefining affirmative action as for blacks alone, and maintaining a strong deterrent foreign policy in the face of Chinese and Russian provocations).

Ironically, by 2018 a few smart Democrats in centrist states were winning local and state elections, as well as special-election house seats, by emulating Republican positions on abortion, guns, trade, and immigration. A cynic, however, would expect them to revert to the new doctrinaire progressive agendas once in office.

A second barometer of the new progressive takeover of the Democratic Party was the radical change in Hillary Clinton's 2016 campaign from her earlier run in 2008. The alteration was staggering. Clinton's 2016 primary rival Bernie Sanders was as left-wing as had been Obama himself eight years earlier. Yet this time around, Clinton foolishly did not tack rightward. She outdueled Sanders for the leftist base rather than moved to the center as she had in 2008.

No longer was Clinton promoting working-class issues or drinking boilermakers or bowling with blue-collar whites. She portrayed the socialist Sanders as unserious and Trump as scary. But mostly Clinton ran as the would-be first woman president ("I'm With Her"), who would energize the same identity politics as had Obama. Substitute female for African American, and surely a similar record number of minority voters would turn out to defeat yet another septuagenarian white, male, millionaire Republican—as if Trump were no more than a McCain or another Romney, to be smashed again by Hillary Clinton, a female updated Obama.

After the 2016 election a third troubling symptom of the Democratic Party's metamorphosis—and of why Hillary Clinton had lost—was seen in the strange January 2017 post-election race for chair of the Democratic National Committee. It was a minor but iconic affair. The progressive psychodrama offered a telling sign that the forces that had lost Hillary Clinton the 2016 election were not just still in play, but strangely were now in total control of the Democratic Party.

A wise observer of Trump's victory would have concluded that Hillary Clinton had foolishly ceded to Donald Trump the working-class blue-collar Democratic vote in a dozen or so of the most critical swing states. Instead, Democrats argued that the loss was because Hillary had not been progressive enough, a lapse that would be corrected immediately in 2017, as Democrats lurched even further leftward.

So the Democratic National Convention race soon became a two-person contest between radical progressive Tom Perez and even more radical Representative Keith Ellison (who would soon appear at a rally wearing a T-shirt with the Spanish logo *Yo no creo en fronteras* ("I don't believe in borders"). Yet a third candidate, the most radical, Sally Boynton Brown, perhaps best summed up the new Democratic identity politics gospel that would address the Trump victory:

> I'm a white woman . . . And my job is to shut other white people down when they want to interrupt. My job is to shut other white people down when they want to say, "Oh no I'm not prejudiced, I'm a Democrat, I'm accepting."

Again, Brown seemed oblivious that she might be a poster child for why Trump had just been elected.

A final indicator of the direction of the new Democratic Party was its growing failure in former swing states. That was nowhere more evident than in Ohio, the traditional bellwether arena for an Electoral College victory. Fifty-five percent of Ohio's population was white working class without college degrees, the erstwhile foundation of the Democratic Party. Yet by 2017, Ohio's congressional delegation was 12-4 Republican. Democrats held only about a third of the state's lower house seats, and a quarter of the state senate's.

The only major Democratic officeholder was Senator Sherrod Brown, who was known for his successful cultivation of Ohioans dispossessed by globalization. Again, Ohio was not a solidly red Texas or a safely blue California, but a more important battleground where presidential elections were won or lost. It had voted for Trump in 2016 by eight points and was becoming more Republican than at any time since 1932. Democrats seemed either clueless or uninterested as to why this had happened during its signature Obama administration. Instead, their default strategy was that an uncouth President Trump would wreck the Republican Party, and then voters would return to even a socialist Democratic Party as their only alternative.

Democrats, of course, would understandably argue that Hillary Clinton won the popular vote in 2016, proof of a healthy party, and did well enough in the 2018 midterm elections. Certainly, without the Electoral College Clinton would have been president. But aside from the truism that Trump, like all candidates, would have tailored his campaign according to constitutional realities not direct-election fantasies, the peculiar nature of California almost alone in some sense explains Clinton's popular vote plurality (Hillary Clinton won the 2016 national popular vote by 2,864,903 votes, mostly a result of an unprecedented 4,269,978-vote margin of victory in California alone).

Again, the mystery is not that Trump won. Instead, the paradox is that a candidate without any prior political experience or military service, the target of an overwhelmingly hostile press, with a partisan incumbent Democratic president, and with a nearly 2-1 disadvantage in campaign funding was still not defeated by Hillary Clinton—former First Lady, senator, secretary of state, and would-be first female president of the United States in the path-breaking tradition of Barack Obama. The 2016 campaign must be appreciated as the most asymmetrical presidential race in history, which ended in the most astonishing result imaginable.

What had happened to the Democrats? As we have seen in earlier chapters, for those in key midwestern swing states, identity politics had devolved from concerns for diversity to ranting against "white supremacy" and "white privilege." Democrats were apparently oblivious to the fact that 67 percent of the electorate was still white, and that most of that majority was neither wealthy nor especially privileged. The danger to Democrats was that, in their zero-sum logic, if all other tribes were supposed to vote by ethnic or racial solidarity, they did not yet have the numbers. Instead, they more likely were driving diverse Greek, Armenian, German, Irish, and Polish ethnics, and assimilated Latinos and Asians, into their own construct of a tribal white bloc that could not be easily countered by minorities, young urban professionals, single women, and Independents.

Equally troubling for Democrats was their idea that superficial appearance was easily definable and static, and trumped class. But were voters always predictable on the basis of their race and gender? Moreover, who can easily calibrate the exact pedigree or electoral mentality of someone one-half Mexican American, or a quarter Japanese, or three-quarters so-called Anglo?

When the Democratic Party began to ignore the common human condition of unique individuals, it could not fully allow for the effects of intermarriage, integration, and assimilation. Even without the fakeries of an Elizabeth Warren or Ward Churchill (the University of Colorado professor who also fabricated a Native American identity), twenty-first-century America was increasingly difficult to stereotype by neat racial categories.

When a person's class was factored into the tribal equation, even more paradoxes about identity politics arose. For example, were a privileged Eric Holder's children disadvantaged due to their African American ancestry, while the sons of poor, white coal miners in West Virginia were favored because of their "white privilege"? Did working waitresses with a husband and three kids really identify with multimillionaire Lena Dunham or university activist Sandra Fluke?

Given Obama's charisma and his success in two presidential elections, the country should have moved left with him. The idea of more entitlements and government services, coupled with high taxes on the rich, historically has won majority public support in democracies, from ancient Athens to the modern European socialist state. But the country did not quite follow the progressive redistributionist agenda, largely because of a stagnant economy; open borders; a sense that globalization had not benefitted half the country; record labor nonparticipation rates; an apologetic foreign policy; a series of scandals in the IRS, the Veterans Administration, and the Justice Department; and a general public weariness with 24/7 moral sermonizing on matters of gender and race.

African American Barack Obama, running as a traditional liberal, won 43 percent of the white vote in 2008. White female Hillary Clinton, newly incarnated as a leftist progressive, won only 37 percent in 2016. So the progressive problem was not that a supposedly racist white America had voted strictly along tribal lines. Rather the rub was that the working and blue-collar classes would only move so far left, before recoiling and heading back to the center. Again, year by year, month by month, Barack Obama was laying the foundation for the emergence of Donald Trump or something like him, through the polarization of the electorate and the absence of an ecumenical middle-class message.

To define the Obama era is to envision a sort of genie that brought all sorts of repressed unsustainable ideologies and politically unviable ideas out of the bottle. Given Obama's personal popularity, he made them for a while seem mainstream. Progressivism, however, inherently was a dynamic ideology that constantly rendered its prior recent manifestations as passé if not illiberal. In some sense, the Democratic Party was mimicking the cycles of European revolutions, from those in France to Russia, in which today's radicalism was almost immediatcly sccn as ycs- terday's counterrevolutionary sellout, to be followed by tomor- row's more authentic and strident leftism. In the 2016 campaign, there would not be a coherent message to counter Trumpism except a tired implied triad: We are the party of Barack Obama. Trump is satanic and must be destroyed. Hillary Clinton will be our first woman president, despite rather than because of what she says and does, or what she has said or done in the past.

Democrats had only sketchy ideas of how to define radical environmentalism as a boon to the middle classes of Ohio, or why their progressive anger at the rich did not also apply com- mensurately to Facebook billionaires, Jeff Bezos and George Soros, Malibu celebrities, elite anchor women, and wealthy es- tablishment Democrats. How could an open border be a boon to the job aspirations of inner-city youth, and minority and white working-class Americans?

If Donald Trump had wanted to construct anemic Demo- cratic agendas and opponents, he could not have done a better job than the Democrats themselves had after 2008. Thanks to the trajectory of the Democratic Party, Trump would be a ben- eficiary of not just his base's fealty of "I'm for Trump," but also make Independents ask, "What's the alternative?" And as we shall see in subsequent chapters, the remedy for a Democratic Party without new ideas and captured by the hard Left was cer- tainly not Hillary Clinton, whose negatives and inept campaign were tailor-made for a Trump candidacy.

Yet what ensured Trump's unlikely rise was not just Demo- cratic cluelessness in the general election. Trump had help from two other quarters as well. There was an equally confused Re- publican Party that handed him the nomination, and an admin- istrative state with overweening power and authority that was increasingly unpopular and considered dangerous.

Chapter Five

REPUBLICANS LOSE
WHILE WINNING

One day, all will be well—this is our hope.
All is well today—that is the illusion.
—Voltaire, *Poem on the Lisbon Disaster*

The national Republican establishment too often started with a weak agenda and then presented it even more weakly. The Republicans' crisis was that their orthodoxy did not appeal any longer to those in swing states of the Electoral College that increasingly chose the president. And to the extent that it might, the usual way their messengers delivered it confirmed that it would not.

During the 2016 primary campaign, most Republican candidates were privately depressed by the paradox that their party was winning at nearly every level while losing the presidency. Indeed, of the prior six presidential elections (and 2016 would be no different), Republicans had lost the popular vote in five of them. Yet, as noted, in just eight years Obama in some sense had all but wrecked the Democratic Party, at least for the next two years following his presidency. Remember that over his tenure the party lost seventy-nine House seats and twelve senators. With them vanished a ruling majority in both houses of Congress and any chance to transform the Supreme Court.

The Democratic Party's local and state implosions were even greater. In 2009, Obama's first year in office, Democrats controlled 59 percent of state legislatures. But by 2017, they had majorities in just 31 percent. Not since the 1920s had Democrats been weaker, losing thirteen governorships, to retain a mere sixteen of fifty. Nationwide, they had suffered net losses of about eleven hundred local offices.

As a general rule, political parties tend to lose down-ballot races when they hold the presidency. But rarely had there been such a disconnect between presidential popularity and party failure, although the verdict is out whether Trump eventually will trump the Obama model of getting reelected while losing the Congress.

What were the common explanations for these contradictions, and how would the latter play out in 2016 for Republicans, and Trump in particular? There were a number of them.

Core conservative messages and issues—less government, reduced taxes, strong defense, secure borders, fiscal prudence, the return of the melting pot—resonated despite the liberal power of popular culture. Republicans, members of the traditional minority party, in theory had the more persuasive message for the times and more dedicated grassroots operatives, despite less access to big-money donors. Democrats were moving further to the left, leaving ever more of the middle to Republicans. Yet Republicans seemed to field far poorer national spokespeople and dismal presidential candidates. And they seemed to be worried more about how they were perceived by the general culture than about winning national elections.

There were lots of unknowns as well in 2016. How well would record high minority bloc voting transfer from the nation's first black president to a fellow liberal, multimillionaire, white sixty-nine-year-old woman? Would assimilation, integration, and intermarriage somewhat nullify liberal bloc voting of minorities? Could Republicans appeal to voters on the basis of shared class worries about jobs and deindustrialization rather than race? What sort of Republican presidential nominee might beat a Democrat, and how would that occur, if he or she ran on an orthodox establishment agenda that had failed in the prior two elections?

Although there had been a number of Republican congressional victories—from slowing federal spending to denying Obama a liberal Supreme Court justice—the base of the Republican Party was growing frustrated over its leaders' perceived national impotence. Republicans had controlled the House since 2011. They had a firm majority in the Senate by early 2015. Yet Republicans had not been able to block Obama from doubling the national debt, raising taxes, all but nationalizing health care, slashing defense spending, and rewriting energy and immigration law through executive orders.

Conservative voters, for all their frustrations, were beginning to concede the new power of a "pen and phone" presidency of administration directives. With a compelling commander in chief like Obama, a president could frustrate even a hostile Congress, widen executive orders, create new laws under the guise of bureaucratic regulation, and redefine foreign policy. In other words, in a zero-sum game, the presidency could advance agendas far more successfully than a majority party in both houses of Congress.

But, more fundamentally, the proverbial Republican base grew increasingly angry that its party seemed willing to lose the presidency nobly rather than win in ugly fashion. The last time a Republican had run a sharp-elbows campaign was in 1988, when the coarse Lee Atwater managed the brutal but successful effort to elect the supposedly gentlemanly George H. W. Bush. By the time Atwater was through with a decorous

Michael Dukakis—running negative ads of him in military garb awkwardly driving a tank, clips of stinky debris floating in supposedly liberal and green Boston's harbor, and grainy videos of career criminal Willie Horton revolving in and out of prison to commit serial felonies—Bush had erased a ten-point deficit. He won by eight, in an Electoral College near landslide, and in a fashion more analogous to the tough Obama campaigns of 2008 and 2012 in which his Republican opponents were rendered as selfish and mean spirited.

Yet what followed after 1988 for the winning Republicans was reminiscent of the European reaction to the carnage of World War I. The victorious British and French had vowed to concede almost anything to the former losers to avoid another war and the perceived brutality necessary for victory, and therefore found themselves psychologically and materially unprepared for what followed. Meanwhile, the once defeated and humiliated Germans were determined to try almost anything to replay the war on their terms and to pay any price for winning it a second time around.

In 1992, Bill Clinton ushered in entirely new Democratic protocols, the antitheses of the loser Dukakis's soft approach: Atwater-like Democrats would run the sharpest attack ads. Democrats would set up a "war room" and rapid-response team. Democrats would court Wall Street and raise far greater cash. Democrats would field candidates who wished to win rather than be liked. Whereas Dukakis had been no doubt the more admirable gentleman, Clinton was clearly far more willing to do and say what he felt necessary to win. Both he and running mate Al Gore laid their southern drawls on thickly and to purple-state voters posed as conservative good ole boys.

In contrast, complacent Republicans were rejecting the prior slash-and-burn pathway of Lee Atwater, who had died at forty of a brain tumor in March 1991, and just as the 1992 Bush reelection campaign heated up. Atwater himself had later expressed profound apologies over his past "naked cruelty" shown Michael Dukakis: "I would strip the bark off the little bastard and make Willie Horton his running mate." By his own later admission, the Atwater winning style of 1988 was now seen as something to be avoided rather than repeated.

It is often forgotten that in the pre-Trump years, mostly disasters followed for Republicans at the national level. The future slate of presidential candidates of George H. W Bush in 1992, Bob Dole in 1996, John McCain in 2008, and Mitt Romney in 2012 were almost stereotypes of wealthy white men or rather predictable establishmentarians. If they thought that "character matters" and the sterling personal records of such career politicians and multimillionaires would trump the new style of Democratic brawling, they were sorely mistaken. Even successful twice-elected George W. Bush had lost the popular vote in 2000. He was barely reelected in 2004 with a 50.7 percent majority of the popular vote and a slim victory in the Electoral College, against a weak John Kerry candidacy.

By summer 1992, incumbent George H. W. Bush was being reduced by the Clinton campaign to both an inept and callous president who had prompted a supposedly historically cruel recession ("It's the economy, stupid," the Democrats insisted). Bush had broken his melodramatic Clint Eastwood tough-guy pledge not to raise taxes ("Read my lips: no new taxes") and had left incomplete an otherwise brilliant victory over Saddam Hussein in the 1991 first Persian Gulf war.

The facts that Bush was hardly a "wimp" but instead a war hero, and Clinton a supposed draft dodger, or that Bush was purportedly an ideal family man, Clinton a womanizer, or that Bush was drug free, Clinton a dabbler in the sixties drug culture, actually meant very little to traditional voters. When conservative Texan and Bush-hater Ross Perot entered the race as a third-party, anti-Bush candidate, Bush was essentially through, garnering only 37 percent of the popular vote to Clinton's winning 43 percent. Future Trump voters either stayed home, voted for Perot, or supported Clinton as a perceived southern Democratic centrist.

Some of the same routine played over the next two decades. Republicans nominated more wealthy and seasoned party men, the Democrats younger and supposedly cooler candidates—Clinton, Gore, Obama. Again, the one exception was George W. Bush's squeaker reelection in 2004. Bush survived an unpopular war and smears over his National Guard service to edge out a stodgy and often sanctimonious and off-putting John Kerry, on the basis of incumbency, his post 9/11 steadiness, a strong economy—and Karl Rove's transient efforts to revive some of Lee Atwater's "naked cruelty" sort of negative advertising.

The 2012 primaries would see some of the weakest and wackiest Republican candidates in memory. Aside from veteran career politicians such as Mitt Romney, Rick Santorum, and Newt Gingrich, there were plenty of oddball outsiders whose political eccentricities were not mitigated by commensurate charisma, such as Ron Paul, Herman Cain, and Michelle Bachman. For a while, a canny Newt Gingrich had run on an imaginative sort of populist appeal to the working class. But for Republican free marketers, Gingrich's often effective class attacks ("vulture capitalist") mostly were derided as bitter and envious of Mitt Romney's personal financial success that had led to an insurmountable lead in fundraising over his poorer rivals. The net effect of all these Republican losses was a growing grassroots anger at purported Republican softness. Fairly or not, conservative voters felt that their candidates were far more apt to back off from confrontations, Democrats to incite them.

In 2008, it was deemed dirty to play clips of the Reverend Jeremiah Wright screaming "God damn America," but not so to suggest that John McCain was nearly senile and supposedly could not remember how many homes he owned (eight)—or that he was a veritable racist in seeking to deny the first serious

African American presidential candidate the White House. In contrast, one can imagine what a candidate Trump would have done with the Wright-Obama connection had he been the 2008 Republican nominee.

In 2012, Barack Obama's checkered youth, dubious past friends and associates, and family were still off limits. Not so those of Mitt Romney. He was serially trashed as a high-school hazer of a half century earlier, and a callous sort who put his own dog on his car's roof, pushed the disabled over cliffs, cut off health insurance to the cancer stricken, installed an elevator in his home, and never much talked to his garbage man. Romney's wife, a cancer and multiple sclerosis survivor, was reduced to a stay-at-home, dilettante tony equestrian. Michelle Obama's past bitter editorializing was considered ancient history ("America is downright mean." "For the first time in my adult life, I am really proud of my country.").

The conservative grassroots perception grew that the fault was again not so much Democrats for dishing it out, but Republicans for taking it—in the manner that Democrats felt they had done the same in the 1970s and 1980s. When Trump in 2016 began cruelly to dismiss Republicans as "low energy," primary voters, even if reluctantly, tended to agree.

The irate conservative base believed that politics had become a red-blue near civil war that was now engulfing their entire lives with little private space left. Progressive boycotts of corporations deemed illiberal had, they felt, turned CEOs into C. S. Lewis's "men without chests" and routine shopping into a political minefield of boycotts and petition grievance.

Entertainment was no relief either from constant progressive proselytizing. The Oscars were mostly progressive virtue-signaling, whose subtext was the hopelessness of white sexist illiberal men. Much later, during the 2018 Oscars, host Jimmy Kimmel, himself a former co-host of a raunchy and randy male pride show, pointed to the Oscar statue and declared that its eunuch appearance summed up the proper values of the new Hollywood: "Oscar," Kimmel preened, "is the most beloved and respected man in Hollywood. He keeps his hands where you can see them. Never says a rude word. And most importantly, he has no penis."

With the National Football League facing bend-the-knee national anthem protests since August 2016, and declines in viewership, with social media now a veritable Roman arena where thumbs-up/thumbs-down mobs instantly destroyed careers, and with nearly breaking-news events supposedly rooted in some purported conservative pathology, from guns to religion, the Republican base wanted fighters of any sort: sometimes the cruder, the more thick-skinned, and the louder the better.

Conservatives, of course, were not just furious over complacence and timidity. A perceived lack of conservative principles mattered too. George H. W. Bush had broken his promise and raised taxes. George W. Bush had vastly expanded government spending, and started new underfunded mandates like new prescription drug benefits, and federal education programs like Common Core and No Child Left Behind. John McCain ran as a new version of former liberal Republican vice president and multimillionaire Nelson Rockefeller. Despite his 2008 veneer of focusing on illegal immigration and a reluctance to send troops abroad, McCain was essentially for open borders and preemptive nation building overseas. Mitt Romney as governor of Massachusetts had birthed something similar to Obamacare. Fairly or not, hoi polloi conservatives felt that their party kept losing the presidency because too many polite millionaires or deep-state politicians, or both, favored progressive-lite policies geared to the very rich and poor, with far less regard to those in between.

In 2016, bruised and humiliated core Republicans were ready to try something new. Or perhaps they looked for something both new and old: if not novel conservative issues, then at least new, more dynamic, and sometimes nontraditional candidates. Young senators such as Marco Rubio and Ted Cruz were supposedly engaging in a way Bob Dole and John McCain had not been. Governors like Jeb Bush, Chris Christie, Mike Huckabee, Bobby Jindal, John Kasich, Rick Perry, and Scott Walker all had solid records of reform governance. Outsider nonpoliticians like Ben Carson and Carly Fiorina were far more impressive than the Herman Cain of 2012. Senator Rand Paul was deemed moderate in a way his father, Ron Paul, often was not. In terms of "diversity" the Republican field had more women, Hispanics, and blacks than in the Democratic primary race, which was soon to be a two-person race of two elderly white people—Bernie Sanders and Hillary Clinton—and a sometimes rigged one at that.

Pundits praised the field as the best in recent Republican memory. Rumors of a Trump entry were written off as a stunt to spread the Trump commercial trademark and gin up his various merchandising efforts. To the extent that he would be a serious candidate, Trump would either crash and burn quickly (akin to something like fellow New Yorker Al Sharpton's 2004 primary bid), or linger to prove a third-party nuisance in Ron Paul or Ralph Nader fashion.

Yet almost immediately, Donald Trump even at sixty-nine years of age proved somehow more energetic and politically savvy than his sixteen Republican rivals, all younger and with more political experience. Again, given his television past, Trump was better at repartee. He proved as good or better a formal speaker. He went from low farce to high comedy with ease. And rather than hedge about his riches in Romney style, Trump exaggerated his net worth. Trump gambled that Republicans might prefer blowhard billionaires to diffident or guilt-ridden multimillionaires.

Of his campaign Trump had earlier on promised, "I'm going to pull up in my 757 and we're going to have the most expensive cars." If others frowned, Trump scoffed, "Do you want someone who gets to be president and that's literally the highest-paying job he's ever had?" Rarely before had any wealthy Republican candidate bragged about his financial success ("I represent traditional conservative values. I get up every morning and go to work. I work hard. I've been honest and I'm very successful. The billions I have? I earned every penny."). Trump reasoned that their reluctance to self-promote was "weakness," or betrayed guilt rather than pride. And to Trump's deterrent mind, such timidity only encouraged cheap criticism.

The result was an escalation of insults and counterslights. As an example of the devolving campaign tempo, at the beginning of the first primary debate Senator Rand Paul took easy aim at Donald Trump, suggesting that he was "used to buying politicians." The charge was likely true (or as Trump once had put it of politicians: "When I need something from them—two years later, three years later, they are there for me"). But Trump turned it upside down. He chided that Paul himself had once begged for a donation from Trump! And Trump had freely given it (whether he actually did was a matter of later contention). Trump assumed, as in the manner of a foul parasite to the burdened host, that the public hated hypocritical money-begging politicians far more than they did cynical entrepreneurs like himself, who saw quid pro quo favors as the price of doing business in a place like Manhattan.

When Rubio logically went after Trump's hypocrisy for hiring illegal aliens while damning illegal immigration, Trump brushed off the quite accurate charge, but with a weirder and wiser taunt of his own: "I've hired tens of thousands of people [in] my job. You've hired nobody. You've had nothing but problems with your credit cards." Trump seemed to be saying that if it was a sin to hire illegal aliens, it was a still greater sin to lack the wherewithal to do so!

More importantly, Trump talked like a brawler, not a Republican polite politician. He assumed the role of the flawed man of action, overshadowing his rival ankle-biting critics who scored points, but only in the context of Trump. Voters saw advantages in unleashing such a pit bull in the general election, even if they were unsure where he would stray or whom exactly he would bite.

Moreover, Trump implied that his problems arose from multimillion-dollar gambles, Rubio's from thousands of dollars in spendthrift purchases. But most importantly, much of America was tired of phoniness. Whatever Trump was—and he was many things—he was at least transparently authentic and sometimes self-deprecating. At times, such transparency bordered on deliberate self-parody, as when he bragged about his huge plane and limo. Later as president, the teetotaler Trump could turn on himself in matters of drinking: "I can honestly say I've never had a beer in my life. It's one of my only good traits. Can you imagine if I had, what a mess I'd be? I'd be the world's worst."

Rubio later would understandably blast Trump for his monotonous "Make America Great Again" boilerplate: "I see [Trump] repeat himself every night. He says five things: Everyone's dumb, he's gonna make America great again, we're gonna win, win, win, he's winning in the polls." All of Rubio's charges may have been true (and indeed New Jersey governor Chris Christie would wound Rubio with the same charges of scripted talking points), but they were also irrelevant, given that Trump was successfully sticking to one message of winning against all odds in service to American renewal. Trump's thinking was that Rubio's idea of more diverse bullet points could always be acquired, but his own innate audacity not so much.

When Ted Cruz (presciently) mocked Trump's "New York values" (likely a reference to Trump's personal business and sexual scandals), the brawler Trump suddenly demolished him in unexpected high fashion with references to the September 11 terrorist attacks: "The people in New York fought and fought and fought, and we saw more death, even the smell of death—no one understood it. And we rebuilt downtown Manhattan, and everyone in the world watched and loved New York and New Yorkers. And I'll tell you, that was a very insulting statement that Ted made."

Here Trump revealed a rare reflective side that would occasionally reappear when he was president, one that warred with his greater propensity for rough language. When Trump of all people could deal the stronger moral card, then his opponent would be wise to cash out. Some of Trump's later supporters would often harken back to these revelations of the "good" Trump, in hopes that he would cease the invective and go high. They might, however, have lacked appreciation that Trump's more frequent habits of going low could make his exceptions of aspirational prose seem more moving than the usual therapeutic boilerplate of scripted politicians.

The problem with the Republicans in the 2016 primaries was not just limited choices between accomplished but otherwise predictable businesspeople and career politicians. There was also the predominance of stale, blah, blah, blah messaging: always free and unfettered trade, always more unquestioned global commitments, always unquestioned nation-building interventionism, and, of course, always "comprehensive immigration reform" in the fashion of the Democrats' open borders/amnesty/guest worker agenda that Jeb Bush and Marco Rubio had more or less signed on to.

Republican voters were not necessarily buying messages that did not seem to take account of people in need. Instead, many had already squared the circle of both supporting a conservative agenda but making allowances for Trump's signature renegade issues of fair trade, harmful globalization, unnecessary foreign interventions, and illegal immigration—as well as his most non-conservative and randy personal life.

Conservatives increasingly were even confused as to whether they themselves really believed any longer in traditional Republican globalism. They were waking up to the fact that campaigning on orthodox conservatism did not necessarily have a connection with later conservative governance. George W. Bush had run up far more red ink than had Bill Clinton. His education policies could have been championed by John Kerry. Ronald Reagan, George H. W. Bush, and George W. Bush, eager to ensure cheap labor for corporate interests, had been laxer on border enforcement than had Bill Clinton.

Democrats always appointed hard-core liberals to the Supreme Court—Stephen G. Breyer, Ruth Bader Ginsburg, Sonia Sotomayor, and Elena Kagan. Republicans too often settled for liberals or centrists, such as Harry Blackmun, William Brennan, Anthony M. Kennedy, Sandra Day O'Connor, Lewis F. Powell Jr., David H. Souter, John Paul Stevens, Potter Stewart, and Earl Warren—or nominated nonentities such as George Harrold Carswell, Clement Haynsworth, or Harriet Miers. Republicans liked to be called "flexible" and "bipartisan" for their appointments, Democrats "faithful," "loyal," and "principled."

But mostly, conservatives like George H. W. Bush had wished to be liked and respected by liberals. Often George W. Bush had not replied to scurrilous attacks that had unfairly reduced him to a near war criminal, and that he allegedly had deliberately allowed blacks to be inordinately harmed by Hurricane Katrina. In contrast, when liberals like Barack Obama won, they taunted conservatives that they really had won the election ("Elections have consequences, and at the end of the day, I won," Obama reminded Republican lawmakers), and so had little desire to bring on board Republicans by cutting taxes or raising defense spending. "Bipartisan legislation" was signing on to liberal agendas, or so disgruntled conservatives seethed.

We have seen how Trump recalibrated just a few issues to appeal to red-state America and to take advantage of the latitude ceded to such positions, and to a candidate such as himself, by progressive, left-wing Democrats and orthodox Republicans. But why did not Republican rivals at least expropriate, massage, or otherwise subvert Trump's issues that by early 2016 showed real traction in large rallies and through strengthening polls?

In a nutshell, they were captive to a doctrinaire Republicanism, even as its dogmas had alienated many of its own base. There was no longer a viable social and cultural conservativism of the sort outlined by Edmund Burke and Alexis de Tocqueville or, for a time, embodied by Ronald Reagan, himself a self-made man from the Midwest.

The idea of protecting customs, traditions, and the continuity of a broad landowning and small business middle class had been essential to classical Republicanism from Roman agrarians who built the Republic and defeated Hannibal to England's working-class citizens who had resisted the siren songs of European revolutions from the late eighteenth to early twentieth centuries. In such a conservative tradition, the hallowed and vibrant middle class was more grounded than the often self-indulgent rich, and more careful and commonsensical than the poor. As we have seen in chapter 1, part of this red-state chauvinism was grounded in the idea that cities were the habitats of rich and poor, the country more the domain of those in between. Small towns and rural life were traditional incubators of moderation, where airy theory met earthy practice and muscles grounded the mind. Republicans forgot all that, in their fealty to the no-laws-in-the-arena doctrines of globalized capitalism.

These were not mere abstractions. In the 2016 primary, the Republican field preferred allegiance to time-honored and principled conservative theories from Adam Smith to Austrian American economist Joseph Schumpeter's "creative destruction" of constant constructing and demolishing businesses, farms, and companies in endless pursuit of greater productivity in the market. Such an organic market—call it cruel but not illogical—created economies of scale and efficiency.

True, supply and demand, and rules of the marketplace eventually enriched all members of society in a way command or structured economies could not. When borders were secured according to the demands of the market, wages, and capital flows, then traffic to and fro would eventually stabilize. In practical terms, once Mexico copied US capitalist and political paradigms and was enriched by billions in expatriate remittances, it too would reform and soon resemble Canada. And Canada and America did not have to export their citizens to neighboring countries.

In such pure Republican commercial orthodoxy, free trade encouraged competition. Competition ensured greater efficiency. Efficiency brought lower prices and better living standards for everyone. It was almost as if lower-middle-class Americans on part-time wages and federal and state subsidies were better off shopping at Walmart for cheap, mostly Chinese-made products than working for good wages, supporting themselves, and paying higher prices at the local True Value–affiliated family hardware store.

Republican elites believed that the more democracies that arose, the less likely were wars, given consensual societies' greater reluctance to provoke and preempt conflict. If oversight of the global liberal order meant that the United States would have to occasionally get taken in trade deals or to pay through the nose for freeloading allies and neutrals, then the long-term benefits were well worth the bothersome costs.

The richer and more free market a China or Russia became, the more they would become internationally reasonable or perhaps even soon democratic. And the better off the world, including America, would be. Increasing federal debt to pay for open borders, "free" trade, and an imperial military did not matter so much. America was endlessly opulent and powerful. Or so Bush Republicanism seemed to assume.

These ideas were institutionalized in conservative media like the *Wall Street Journal*, the *Weekly Standard*, and *Commentary* because, in terms of economics at least, they worked, at least in the long term and for many Americans. They were the stuff of the Washington think tanks, including the American Enterprise Institute and the Heritage Foundation that so often supplied working papers and appointees to incoming Republican administrations.

The Austrian school of economic theory, which produced singular thinkers like Ludwig von Mises and Friedrich Hayek, and influenced Milton Friedman, had largely won the neoliberal argument over socialism, communism, and Keynesian government-controlled economies. But such free-market theories soon became holistic and were stretched too far to explain politics, culture, and social life in a way they were never intended. Economists were no longer single-minded hedgehogs, but prided themselves in thinking that they were all-knowing foxes.

Their free-market dogmas offered answers to far wider social and cultural questions, from immigration and the role of government to education and defense. Summed up brutally, it meant that for the market to enrich society, champion the individual, and protect liberty, there would have to be short-term winners and losers—players who were constantly engaged in a cauldron of modification, rejection, and adaptation of their very lives.

Nothing was static; nothing sacred. The quaint idea of a sixth-generation family farm as something of intrinsic value to grounding regional society depended only on how wise each generation was in adapting to market realities. A single generation of starry-eyed romantics could easily destroy the romance of their legacy; cold pragmatists would perpetuate it. If preserving the linchpin steel mill of the community meant ten cents more in the price of steel per pound over competing South Korean imports, then such an iconic plant needed to rust away.

Social scientists as diverse as Daniel Bell (*The Cultural Contradictions of Capitalism*), Christopher Lasch (*The Revolt of the Elites and the Betrayal of Democracy*), and Robert Nisbet (*The Quest for Community* and *The Present Age*)—well before, but unknown to, Trump and most of his advisors—had cautioned that conservatives were headed for a collision between their two mutually exclusive signature ideologies. Free-market capitalism's rising standard of living and empowerment of the individual could undermine society's need to preserve traditional social and conservative cultural mores that alone moderated ever-growing reckless material and sensual appetites, which in turn undermined capitalism's work ethos.

The dilemma for Trump's Republican critics, both during the campaign and in his presidency, was not the same as Trump's, but in some ways worse. True, they did not need, like Trump, to dig up new issues and cobble together theories to make coherent Trump's often scattered themes of restoring red-state America from avoidable decline. Establishment Republican candidates in the era of Trump were left with repackaging and salvaging old dogma and tired orthodoxy to suspicious voters, in ways that did not seem increasingly callous or certain to lose national elections.

Trump abruptly had reversed equations. He would *first* appeal to voters and then stitch together the necessary canons to systematize and make coherent his scattershot appeals. That is, he would promise out-of-work lathe operators that he would bring back jobs that China "had stolen." Coal miners were put out of business by the EPA, not the heartless competition of cleaner-burning and increasingly cheap natural gas. American kids were killed by illegal alien drunk drivers or robbed and assaulted by illegal aliens, who should never have been allowed so freely to ignore federal immigration law and so clearly belonged back in their own country. The extent to which cheap laborers helped to lubricate the economy (and Trump's own construction projects) was a secondary consideration.

As we have also seen, the electoral advantages of Trump's messaging were obvious. Trump, the billionaire sybarite and Manhattan fixer, ostensibly put people first. The convenient orthodoxy followed. In July 2018, Trump bragged to a reopened steel plant in Granite City, Illinois, that his unpopular steel tariffs—leverage to gain his art-of-the-deal reciprocity with foreign producers—had given American steel workers parity and, with it, lost jobs: "After years of shutdowns and cutbacks, today the blast furnace here in Granite City is blazing bright, workers are back on the job and we are once again pouring new American steel into the spine of our country." Cogent but abstract counterarguments that tariffs in the long run might depress global trade and lose American jobs did not resonate with the out of work or those tired of subsidized foreign steel dumped onto the US market.

Trump's opponents appeared less empathetic. They seemed to put orthodoxy first, and then made the people follow it. Where Trump had a new theory for every perceived loser; his Republican rivals pigeonholed supposed losers into existing and narrow set remedies. The media predictably fixated on Trump's money, his crudity, his questionable ethics, his past bankruptcies, his loose mouth, his lack of political experience, and his amateurish staff, and never saw what was right before their eyes: Trump of all people talked of people as people, especially those often forgotten if not despised.

Or as a rabid Trump supporter and lifelong friend put it to me during the primary when I grilled him on Trump's ideas and past: "Do you ever wake up without a job? Why can't someone in China or Vietnam write a book or one of your columns just as good as you can for half the cost? Why doesn't everybody get tenure like yours? Why doesn't a college just bring in cheaper people from overseas to replace you guys at half the cost?"

Trump had no history of major loyal donors. He had no career after the White House—or one before. He rarely visited think tanks. He probably did not subscribe to conservative magazines and opinion journals. There was no "conservative movement" of intellectuals in his circle. He had so many dramas—business, taxes, sexual—in his past that he scarcely feared another one. Suing and being sued were his mother's milk. He certainly had no allegiance to or much knowledge of the status quo Republican Party. Most of the status quo Right avoided his campaign and later his presidency.

Fair trade, legal immigration only, Jacksonian defense policy of helping friends and hurting enemies, and American chauvinism were synthesized by Trump himself, and later by advisors such as Stephen Miller and Stephen Bannon, into a supposedly new national populism. The great strength of Trump was that he operated outside the Republican Party's intellectual and political apparat. His great weakness was that when in extremis he had no such institutional support invested in his candidacy or presidency, and thus few ancillaries to defend his agendas or explain his bad behavior as was true of past administrations.

In truth, the "Make America Great Again" campaign was just the political extension of the way Trump had done business. He operated by undeniable cunning. He understood human nature, respected perceived quiet strength, and had contempt for loud weakness. Trump admired the multibillionaire in the conference room who sat quietly and nodded to confirm a decision; he oddly respected less the multimillionaire who talked loudly (like himself) among the wealthier, and assumed a predominance his riches had not earned.

Trump understood that people did not wish to hear long-term solutions for short-term problems, especially from those who always seemed to have the clout to avoid any downside from their own abstract theories. By process of trial and error, and seeking soft spots, Trump had through sudden failure and bankruptcies, but even quicker recalibration and restoration, become rich and learned that sheer willpower, bluster, and audacity were surprisingly rare traits among the elite. And like the middle classes, the restless Trump had always distrusted banks, the Federal Reserve, and Wall Street. Such institutions were often impediments to his wild-eyed projects and dreams, or dealt with money in the abstract rather than in its concrete manifestations of office buildings, golf courses, and resorts.

On almost any issue, the ad hoc Trump could outmaneuver his rivals often by ignoring research, data, and conventional wisdom, and reducing an issue simply to relative self-interest and throwing it back on the critic. Free trade is great? If so, then why didn't China follow it? NATO is crucial? Then why didn't the frontline members most in need of it pay as much as America did? Illegal immigration doesn't really matter? Then why does Mexico police its own border with Guatemala? Globalization is essential? But why should China be building new factories while we were closing them?

On and on, month after month, during the campaign and right on through his presidency, Trump hammered these "but then why do they do it?" reductionist issues. What made them resonate was a central truth that all the Republican candidates and presidential critics could never completely answer: ultimately, America willingly allowed others to take advantage of the global trade, commercial, and military post-war rules it had fostered on the supposition that the United States would always be so wealthy and powerful that it could and must afford the underwriting to keep the global project viable.

Trump insisted otherwise: we were broke. Others freeloaded or cheated. And the world was a mess. Or rather, he told America, this system broke you and enriched those who perpetuate it:

> Our politicians have aggressively pursued a policy of globalization, moving our jobs, our wealth and our factories to Mexico and overseas. Globalization has made the financial elite,

who donate to politicians, very, very wealthy. I used to be one of them. I hate to say it, but I used to be one. But it has left millions of our workers with nothing but poverty and heartache. When subsidized foreign steel is dumped into our markets, threatening our factories, the politicians have proven, folks, have proven they do nothing.

Besides Democrats and Republicans, however, Trump had one more and perhaps even greater challenge to winning the presidency: the so-called administrative or deep state, also known as "the Washington swamp," "the bureaucracy," "the Beltway"—the entire permanent, ever-growing regulatory and administrative octopus that ultimately outlasted administrations, terms, and tenures and had developed a life of its own.

Trump was not the swamp's own. It hated him perhaps even more than did his party rivals and Democratic opponents. And it has insidious power to thwart outsiders in ways unimaginable to even Donald Trump.

But what exactly is the deep state? Why did it begin to despise Donald J. Trump? And how could he possibly circumvent it?

Chapter Six

THE ANCIEN RÉGIME

*Whether the mask is labeled fascism, democracy, or
dictatorship of the proletariat, our great adversary
remains the apparatus—the bureaucracy, the police,
the military.*

—Simone Weil, "Reflections on War"

On September 5, 2018, the *New York Times* published an
anonymous editorial by a supposed "senior official" in
the Trump administration. In astounding fashion, the unnamed
writer claimed that he/she was part of a legion of administration
appointees and government officials who were actively working
to undermine the Trump presidency by overriding his orders,
keeping information from an unknowing Trump, or acting inde-
pendently of his directives. Or as Anonymous unapologetically
put it:

> Trump is facing a test to his presidency unlike any faced by a
> modern American leader.
>
> It's not just that the special counsel looms large. Or that the
> country is bitterly divided over Mr. Trump's leadership. Or

even that his party might well lose the House to an opposition hell-bent on his downfall.

The dilemma—which he does not fully grasp—is that many of the senior officials in his own administration are working diligently from within to frustrate parts of his agenda and his worst inclinations.

I would know. I am one of them.

The *Times* author then continues by confessing to a sort of slow-motion coup to undermine the Trump presidency:

It may be cold comfort in this chaotic era, but Americans should know that there are adults in the room. We fully recognize what is happening. And we are trying to do what's right even when Donald Trump won't.

The result is a two-track presidency.

The writer then lists the supposed Trump sins and offers the following rationale for such extraordinary subversion on the part of self-elected conspirators:

This isn't the work of the so-called deep state. It's the work of the steady state.

Given the instability many witnessed, there were early whispers within the cabinet of invoking the 25th Amendment, which would start a complex process for removing the president. But no one wanted to precipitate a constitutional crisis. So we will do what we can to steer the administration in the right direction until—one way or another—it's over.

The bigger concern is not what Mr. Trump has done to the presidency but rather what we as a nation have allowed him to do to us. We have sunk low with him and allowed our discourse to be stripped of civility.

Most telling, however, given the supposed plethora of Trump sins, the author *never* cites a particular presidential act that by any coherent definition could be called illegal, dangerous, or unethical, much less unprecedented in presidential history. Indeed, Anonymous concedes that Trump has often been successful in his tenure: "Don't get me wrong. There are bright spots that the near-ceaseless negative coverage of the administration fails to capture: effective deregulation, historic tax reform, a more robust military and more."

Yet Anonymous then boasts that such landmark success came because of others and in spite of Trump: "But these successes have come despite—not because of—the president's leadership style, which is impetuous, adversarial, petty and ineffective."

Trump's purported sins then arise largely in matters of executive "style" and supposedly unpresidential character: "Meetings with him veer off topic and off the rails, he engages in repetitive rants, and his impulsiveness results in half-baked, ill-informed and occasionally reckless decisions that have to be walked back." Anonymous did not square the circle of how such an incompetent and dangerous leader had accomplished such admittedly good things, often well beyond the ability of prior and supposedly better qualified and more sober Republican presidents.

The author concludes his opinion editorial by promising the country that like-minded unelected officials and bureaucrats have formed a "resistance" that will do its best to nullify the directives of the elected president and instead implement policies that they believe will take the country in the "right direction"—and are the product of their apparently superior professionalism and a proper presidential tone that they associate with their own:

There is a quiet resistance within the administration of people choosing to put country first. But the real difference will be made by everyday citizens rising above politics, reaching across the aisle and resolving to shed the labels in favor of a single one: Americans.

What neither the opinion writer nor the *New York Times* disclosed about their joint efforts of producing an anonymous op-ed on September 5 were some obvious considerations of sourcing, timing, and objectives.

First, the editorial appeared on the eve of a much publicized tell-all about the Trump White House by *Washington Post* investigative journalist Bob Woodward, whose latest book, *Fear*— his nineteenth such exposé mostly based on undisclosed and unnamed sources and without citations—was scheduled to come out just six days later. Advance excerpts largely dovetailed with Anonymous's argument of a president whose inexperience and temperament "scare" those in government and force them to find ways to circumvent or obstruct his wishes.

The opinion piece also coincidentally was published just four days after the late Senator John McCain's funeral. McCain is lionized in the anonymous op-ed as the proper antithesis to Trump ("We may no longer have Senator McCain. But we will always have his example—a lodestar for restoring honor to public life and our national dialogue").

At the funeral, eulogist after eulogist used the solemn occasion not just to praise John McCain, but also to blast Donald Trump. Oddly, McCain's final deification by his erstwhile critics and enemies was mostly a result of his own bitter and ongoing feud with Donald Trump that in his eleventh hour sanctified him to past presidents George W. Bush and Barack Obama. Both their earlier presidential campaigns had once smeared McCain as a libertine and reckless (the Bush effort in 2000, especially during the South Carolina primary), and vilified him in 2008 as a near-demented racist (the Obama 2008 campaign). Due to his feud with Trump, in death McCain was transmogrified into angelic status by the very architects who in life were sometimes responsible for his demonization.

Finally, the McCain funeral and anonymous op-ed marked the return of former president Barack Obama to the campaign trail, as he began to give a series of angry and often bitter speeches on the eve of the 2018 midterms—ironically both blasting Trump as dangerous and incompetent while taking credit for the apparently quite competent Trump handling of the economy. The common thread in all these coincidental events was not just collective hatred of Trump on the part of the establishment, but also the extraordinary means by which a proverbial deep state sought to subvert a supposedly extraordinarily dangerous outsider.

Usually ex-presidents do not blast their successors at funerals. A prior president customarily does not hit the campaign trail to level charges against a sitting president. State funerals are not regularly transmogrified into pep rallies. And anonymous members of an administration usually do not have the connections to publish lead *New York Times* editorials that channel Bob Woodward's sensational but unsourced allegations.

A cynic might have believed there had been some sort of collusive effort ahead of the 2018 midterm election to create a simultaneous and force-multiplying demonization of Trump— almost as if there was a common effort coordinated by the major media, journalists, establishment politicians, and supposedly dozens of officials within government. But that idea would not completely be a conspiratorial conclusion, because Anonymous boasted of the presence of such an organized "resistance" inside the government.

A final, even more disturbing note: the deep state is neither transparent nor confident in its criticisms, at least enough to name names in its near-subversionary efforts. Both past presidents and Megan McCain, daughter of John McCain, in their funeral eulogies trashed Trump—to the glee of editorials in the major papers.

But none of them completed their politicization of the service by mentioning Donald Trump by name. Nor did Anonymous ever disclose his name or come forward publicly to present particular examples of documented wrongdoing. Nor did Bob Woodward cite most of his sources, name his informants, or produce footnoted data to assure the readers of the veracity of his sensational charges. Instead, the premise was that the establishment has such power, prestige, and authority that it has no need to reveal its methodologies and sources—once it claimed the higher moral ground and felt that it had not just the right, but indeed the duty, to overturn the verdict of the 2016 election.

All great empires of the past created such deep states.

The permanent bureaucracies and elite hangers-on adapted as imperial conditions dictated. Imperial Spain's El Escorial outside Madrid, the courts of Renaissance Venice, and Byzantium's Constantinople, or the thousands who lived at eighteenth-century Versailles, were all thronged with court functionaries. They were the embryos of nonstop dramas of intrigue and coups, and often immune to periodic changes even in autocratic heads of state.

The Byzantine emperor Justinian savagely curbed the influence of his bureaucratic opponents only through the infamous slaughter of the Nika riots of AD 532. The key for the deep-state careerist was always survival, even more than public service. The ubiquitous fifth-century Athenian Alcibiades was variously an Athenian democratic imperialist, a suspected oligarchic sympathizer, a wanted outlaw of the Athenian state, a turncoat working for Sparta, a returning Athenian democrat, and an aristocratic exile under the protection of Persia—the common denominator being a manipulative skilled survivor of the politics of the Greek city-state.

Similar was the much later example of the "versatile" French minister Charles Maurice de Talleyrand-Périgord. Talleyrand for more than forty years was a fixture of the permanent Paris court and thus in succession an advocate and betrayer of the Ancien Régime, the French Revolution, Napoleon, and the restored monarchy. His loyalty was to the career of Monsieur Talleyrand rather than to France, much less to monarchy, the revolution, republican government, or dictatorship.

Since the US post-war era, the yearly growth of American state and federal government has been exponential. By 2017, there were nearly 3 million civilian federal workers, and another 1.3 million Americans in the uniformed military. Over 22 million local, state, and federal workers had made government the largest employment sector. The three largest American unions were respectively the National Education Association (mostly teachers and public education staff), Service Employees International Union, and the American Federation of State, County & Municipal Employees. All routinely endorsed progressive candidates.

Unions as a rule in the twenty-first century have grown only among government workers. Over the last four decades, the vast majority of public employees without masters or doctoral degrees have usually achieved compensation packages higher than their private-sector counterparts. Union membership until 2018 was mandatory for many public employees. Until stopped by a Supreme Court decision, dues had pro forma been automatically deducted by their unions, regardless of actual membership status.

Bureaucracies had become politicized on the premise that big government both required high taxes that Democrats more than Republicans ensured, and could be weaponized to further political agendas and avoid cutbacks in state employment and its compensation. Most federal unions gave far greater donations to Democratic than Republican candidates. According to a report in the *Hill*, in 2016 about 95 percent of all donations from federal workers to the two presidential campaigns went to Hillary Clinton—apparently on the premise that her agenda of greater regulation, higher taxes, and more entitlements would, in particular, translate into more federal jobs and higher salaries, and in general support a shared philosophy that the administrative state plays the central role in American life and culture.

The insidious power of the unelected administrative state is easy to understand. After all, it governs the most powerful aspects of modern American life: taxes, surveillance, criminal justice proceedings, national security, and regulation. The nightmares of any independent trucker or small-business person are being audited by the IRS, having communications surveilled, or being investigated by a government regulator or prosecutor.

The reach of the deep state ultimately is based on two premises. One, improper government worker behavior is difficult to audit or at least to be held to account, given that it is protected both by union contracts and civil service law. And, two, a government appointee or bureaucrat has the unlimited resources of the state behind him, while the targeted private citizen in a federal indictment, tax audit, or regulation violation not only does not, but is assumed also not to have the means even to provide an adequate legal defense.

Lois Lerner, director of the Exempt Organizations division of the IRS, more or less got away with targeting mostly conservative groups before the 2012 election. She had ensured that dozens of nonprofits would not receive prompt tax-exempt status and ostensibly oppose Obama's agendas. Eric Holder's Justice Department surveilled various Associated Press reporters and especially Fox News's James Rosen—on the suspicion that they were receiving leaked information from Obama administration sources.

The so-called deep state is often weaponized to reflect current orthodoxies. In the last thirty years its operating premises have embraced multiculturalism, feminism, and identity politics diversity—more or less the sacred tenets that Trump has targeted. Between 2009 and 2016 the Obama administration, to take one example, had recalibrated the war on terror, and had hoped to change its reality through the use of state-sanctioned euphemisms. Obama sought to use the apparat to institution-alize the notion that radical Islam had no intrinsic connection with terrorism, and that adherents of Islam had no greater pro-pensity to incite violence against Westerners than did follow-ers of other religions—political correctness that Donald Trump campaigned against throughout 2016.

Nonetheless, the deep state used its considerable influence to change language and realities. Note the consistent themes emanating from bureaucracies as diverse as the CIA and NASA. John Brennan, a Washingtonian insider and the former CIA chief and at one time the president's chief counterterrorism ad-visor, once asserted: "Nor do we describe our enemy as 'jihad-ists' or 'Islamists' because jihad is a holy struggle, a legitimate tenet of Islam, meaning to purify oneself or one's community." Jihadists themselves such as those of ISIS in Syria would have objected to Brennan's therapeutic and ignorant portrait of them.

Former director of National Intelligence James Clapper in-sisted that "the term Muslim Brotherhood is an umbrella term for a variety of movements. In the case of Egypt, a very hetero-geneous group, largely secular." Of course, the Muslim Broth-erhood would also have protested the changing of its name to something like the "secular brotherhood" to reflect a "largely secular" role.

"When I became the NASA administrator," NASA direc-tor Charles Bolden told *Al Jazeera* in 2010, President Obama "charged me with three things." Bolden added, "Perhaps fore-most, he wanted me to find a way to reach out to the Muslim world and engage much more with dominantly Muslim nations to help them feel good about their historic contribution to sci-ence, math, and engineering." Nowhere in any founding NASA charter had there been an agenda item to promote Islamic psy-chological well-being.

Army chief of staff General George Casey, in the aftermath of the Fort Hood shootings, sought to embrace the correct deep-state orthodoxy: "Our diversity, not only in our Army, but in our country, is a strength. And as horrific as this tragedy was, if our diversity becomes a casualty, I think that's worse." The real horror was that Major Nidal Hasan's radical Islamic demons had been known and ignored by many in the US Army.

Director of Homeland Security Janet Napolitano thought she could mitigate radical Islamic–inspired terrorist attacks by changing the very meaning of words: "In my speech, although I did not use the word 'terrorism,' I referred to 'man-caused' disasters. That is perhaps only a nuance, but it demonstrates that we want to move away from the politics of fear toward a policy of being prepared for all risks that can occur."

Apparently, oil spills were not to be different from blowing up a US military barracks overseas. The Office of Management and Budget sent a memo to the Pentagon: "This administration prefers to avoid using the term 'Long War' or 'Global War on Terror.' Please use 'Overseas Contingency Operation.'" Anti-terrorism was now akin to generic efforts such as operations to help flood or drought victims abroad.

No one in Washington called Donald J. Trump a "god" (as journalist Evan Thomas in 2009 had suggested of Obama) when he arrived in January 2017. No one felt nerve impulses in his leg when Trump talked, as journalist Chris Matthews once remarked had happened to him after hearing an Obama speech. And no newsman or pundit cared how crisply creased were Trump's pants, at least in the manner that *New York Times* columnist David Brooks had once praised Obama's sartorial preciseness. Instead, Trump was greeted by the Washington media and intellectual establishment as if he were the first beast in the book of Revelation, who arose "out of the sea, having seven heads and ten horns, and upon his horns ten crowns, and upon his heads the name of blasphemy."

Besides the Washington press and pundit corps, Donald Trump faced this third and more formidable opponent: the culture of permanent and senior employees of the federal and state governments, and the political appointees in Washington who revolve in and out from business, think tanks, lobbying firms, universities, and the media. Or as the legal scholar of the administrative state Philip Hamburger put it: "Although the United States remains a republic, administrative power creates within it a very different sort of government. The result is a state within the state—an administrative state within the Constitution's United States." The power of the deep state was twofold: it had the unlimited resources of government at its call in any fight against individuals. And it knew how government worked and could be manipulated far better than the citizens whom it supposedly for a brief time served.

In theory, the deep state we have described should have been a nonpartisan meritocratic cadre of government officials who were custodians of a civil service that had often served Americans well and transcended changes in presidential administrations. The ranks of top government regulators, justices, executive officers, and bureaucrats would take advice, and often be drawn, from hallowed East Coast, supposedly apolitical institutions—the World Bank, the Council on Foreign Relations, the Federal Reserve, the Ivy League faculties, Wall Street, and the blue-chip Washington and New York law firms.

In fact, the deep state grew increasingly political, progressive, and internationalist. Its members and cultural outlook were shaped by the good life on the two coasts and abroad. And every four or eight years, it usually greeted not so much incoming Republican or Democratic presidents as much as fusion party representatives with reputable résumés, past memberships in similar organizations, and with outlooks identical to its own.

Then the disrupter Trump crashed in.

Trump was not so much critical as ignorant of deep-state rules and its supposed sterling record of stable governance. Trump proved willing to fire lifelong public servants. He ignored sober and judicious advice from Washington "wise men." He appointed "crazy" outsiders skeptical of establishment institutions. He purged high government of its progressive activists. And he embraced deep-state heresies and blasphemies such as considering tariffs, questioning NATO, doubting the efficacy of NAFTA, whining about federal judges, and jawboning interest rates. And he also left vacant key offices on the theory that one less deep-state voice was one less critic, and one less obstacle to undoing the Obama record.

It was easy to dismiss Trump as unorganized or uninformed for leaving thousands of federal positions of such a state unstaffed, even by the middle of his second year in office. Indeed, almost 250 White House appointments requiring congressional confirmation were still unfilled by summer 2018. Most of the four thousand political appointed jobs in his administration were also still vacant. Only 26 percent of Trump's executive branch appointees had been confirmed after six months.

Trump had also brought a number of controversial characters into his 2015–16 campaign that horrified the administrative state. Trump had seemed to mirror-image his own flaws by seeking subordinates who shared them, even if his questionable circle served for only brief periods and often at the periphery— from the soon to be indicted and disloyal Michael Cohen to the soon to be fired Corey Lewandowski, and the soon to be indicted Paul Manafort to the soon to be indicted George Papadopoulos. Once elected, Trump staffed his White House with newcomers who, as we will see in a subsequent chapter, came and went with increasing frequency: the fired Stephen Bannon, the resigned Hope Hicks, the forcibly resigned Robert Porter, and the fired Anthony Scaramucci.

Given his dearth of experience and the absence of the establishment's willingness to work for Trump, he often relied on his own daughter Ivanka and her husband, Jared Kushner, as loyalists. Trump cared little or did not know that there was a reason in the past why presidents had not brought into the White House too many presidential family members—whether Donald Nixon, Billy Carter, Roger Clinton, Neil Bush, or Malik Obama.

There were some understandable reasons for so many vacancies, both explicit and implied, as well as for the number of political novices. Trump ran as an outcast. He promised to "drain," not to perpetuate, the swamp. In other words, by his own definition, there were already too many federal employees, and far too many career bureaucrats of the apparat. Deserving workers in the ranks could easily step up, be internally promoted, and preclude the need for hiring more overtly political appointees.

Trump replied to his critics in October 2017 with the dismissive, "I'm generally not going to make a lot of the appointments that would normally be—because you don't need them. I mean, you look at some of these agencies, how massive they are, and it's totally unnecessary. They have hundreds of thousands of people." Yet an exasperated presidential advisor Stephen Bannon would later claim that a frustrated and isolated Trump had later reconsidered leaving vacant so many positions and instead concluded: "I've got really to staff up something. I need to embrace the establishment."

Because Trump ran against Democrats, the Republican establishment, and the deep state, in victory he had few Washington insiders left to pick from, other than those at the marquee cabinet secretaryships. Again, there was certainly no Trump-supporting apparatus of conservative pundits and Washington old hands to systematize his agendas, issue position papers—and recommend battle-hardened "Make America Great Again" adherents to serve in the White House. In some

cases where Trump found qualified outsiders, deep-state bureaucrats often held up their appointments or sought to classify
them as lower-paid employees.

In the meantime, establishment institutions provided the
seasoned opposition to almost everything Trump did. They
were likely the "senior officials" to whom the anonymous *New
York Times* op-ed writer referred, when he talked about an ongoing "resistance" inside the government to thwart the Trump
agenda. In the conservative old days, a Republican president
could call upon New York and Washington pundits and insiders—in the present generation names like David Brooks,
David Frum, Jonah Goldberg, Bill Kristol, Bret Stephens, or
George Will—for kitchen-cabinet advice. But now they were
among Trump's fiercest critics. Only in the matter of judicial
appointments could Trump find seasoned and experienced
conservatives eager to be appointed or advanced, and respected
organizations like the Federalist Society eager to help him ensure conservative justices.

As an initial result, Obama holdovers lingered everywhere
in the executive branch and cabinet offices. They had no immediate desire to leave, when obstruction, if caught, only won ac-
colades. Almost immediately, Trump's private phone calls with
foreign leaders such as with Mexican president Enrique Peña
Nieto and Australian prime minister Malcolm Turnbull were
leaked to the press only to appear as transcripts in the *Washington Post*.

Bruce Ohr, an Obama appointee and the fourth-ranking official in the Trump Justice Department, had continued to meet
with FBI informant Christopher Steele, *after the election*, concerning lingering lurid rumors about Trump. Ohr, whose wife
had worked for Steele (a fact not disclosed by Ohr to his supe-
riors), still privately funneled Fusion GPS opposition research
to the FBI, which earlier had supposedly severed relations with
Steele for violating FBI agreements concerning his use as an

informant. Rarely has a president had a top-ranking official in a cabinet agency actively working with the FBI jointly to undermine his tenure.

Almost every episode of the newly inaugurated Trump eventually leaked out, whether his private conversations with congressional leaders or conferences with his own staff. Nonstop, Trump was said to have yelled, threatened, sworn, and lied to those around him. Rumors from insiders spread that he was unbalanced and mentally impaired. It would be as if every profanity and threat Lyndon Johnson ever had thundered in the White House were broadcast in real time around the world or salacious accounts of John F. Kennedy's sexual antics in the White House pool leaked and appeared daily in the news, or a group of LBJ insiders had concluded any president who would conduct business while on the toilet or who would expose himself to staff members was unhinged and should be thwarted by a "resistance" in any manner possible.

The Washington media fixtures sensed that Trump threatened to pollute the entire sea in which they swam. And so they aired so-called fake news stories that Trump had removed the bust of Martin Luther King Jr. from the West Wing, or that his rallies were lightly attended, or that he had buffoonishly overfed fish during a visit to a koi pond with the Japanese prime minister. Sometimes opinion journalists offered apocalyptic scenarios of Trump's fate. David Brooks reassured his depressed readers that Trump would likely either resign or be removed from office before his first year was over.

When Melania Trump took time off after kidney surgery and was not seen publicly, Never Trumper David Frum wondered whether Trump had struck his wife and sought to cover up the ensuing crime ("Suppose President Trump punched the First Lady in the White House (federal property = federal jurisdiction), then ordered the Secret Service to conceal the assault?"). Frum was on record as seeing Trump as some sort of righteous collective punishment for the moral failings of the American people: "We got Donald Trump in the first place as a punishment for not being good enough citizens."

In contrast to his unproven allegations, Frum had written that Trump's opponents such as himself were engaged in a sort of self-righteous moral crusade: "As President Trump is cruel, vengeful, egoistic, ignorant, lazy, avaricious, and treacherous, so we must be kind, forgiving, responsible, informed, hardworking, generous, and patriotic. As Trump's enablers are careless, cynical, shortsighted, morally obtuse, and rancorous, so Trump's opponents must be thoughtful, idealistic, wise, morally sensitive, and conciliatory. 'They go low, we go high,' a wise woman said."

But was going "high" or being "kind" and "informed" falsely implying that the president of the United States had engaged in spousal battery?

This multifaceted opposition to Trump from the administrative shadow government and its media enablers in Washington was both ideological and careerist. Again, the deep state increasingly had grown more statist than libertarian, and in general more progressive rather than conservative. It was not always so.

Not long ago, liberals had echoed outgoing President Dwight Eisenhower's warning about the "military-industrial" complex. They had been apprehensive of the supposed right-wing overreach of the CIA and FBI and the threats to civil liberties posed by the National Security Agency and the Internal Revenue Service. Once upon a time, civilian libertarians worried over Woodrow Wilson's propaganda machine, the eerily labeled "Committee on Public Information" so redolent of French Revolution euphemisms. They had pushed back at FDR's congressional allies who tried to pass a "Libel Bill" to silence critical journalists and to "pack" the Supreme Court with additional justices to ensure favorable New Deal rulings. They were aghast when learning of John F. Kennedy's successful efforts to wiretap prying reporters.

Again, now not so much. In the last decade, on questions of diversity, gender, gay rights, political correctness, and social activism, the unchecked and unaccountable powers of the deep state were envisioned as more an ally than a threat. Few cared much when Barack Obama's Justice Department investigated the communications of Associated Press reporters. Weaponizing the Obama IRS at least was seen as going after the right people. Court packing was once again discussed as a legitimate alternative to Trump's increasingly conservative Supreme Court. After all, the powers of government could often enact needed cultural, political, and social change by fiat rather than see it stall amid messy legislative compromise, shutdowns, and filibusters.

On matters far transcending the euphemisms used in the war on terror, antidemocratic means were seen as a useful way of implementing what were felt to be radically democratic (though ironically often unpopular) agendas. The US military by fiat could allow women in combat units and the transgendered in the military. And the Department of Justice might sue banks for alleged discrimination or mortgage abuse, then force the targeted banks to settle the cases by donating to politically correct, third-party nonvictims, almost always progressive social justice organizations.

In the 1970s, the military officer corps and the top ranks of the CIA, DOJ, and FBI were, in the eyes of the Left, synonymous with *Seven Days in May*—and *Manchurian Candidate*–like conspiracies. Yet in 2016, these same institutions had been re-calibrated by progressives as protectors of social justice against interlopers and bomb throwers like Donald Trump. Whether it was scary or needed to have a secretive, unelected cabal inside the White House subverting presidential agendas depended on who was president.

During the Robert Mueller investigations, progressives usually defended the FISA court-ordered intercepts of private citizens' communications, despite the machinations taken to deceive FISA court justices. Indeed, liberal critics suggested that to question how the multitude of conflicts of interest at the Obama DOJ and FBI had warped their presentations of the Steele dossier to the courts was in itself an obstruction of justice or downright unpatriotic.

News of FBI informants planted into the 2016 Trump campaign raised no eyebrows. Nor did the unmasking and leaking of the names of US citizens by members of the Obama National Security Council. Ex-CIA director John Brennan and ex-director of National Intelligence James Clapper soon become progressive pundits on cable news. While retaining their security clearances, they blasted Trump variously as a Russian mole, a foreign asset, treasonous, and a veritable traitor.

Both became liberal icons, despite their lucrative merry-go-rounds between Washington businesses and government service, and they sometimes lied under oath to Congress about all that and more.

While the deep state was far too vast to be stereotypically monolithic in the Obama and Trump years, it was a general rule that it had admired Obama, who grew it, and now loathed Trump, who promised to shrink it. Moreover, Trump did not, as most incoming and outgoing politicians, praise in Pavlovian fashion the institutions of Washington. As we have seen, nothing to Trump was sacred. During and after the campaign, he blasted the CIA, the FBI, the IRS, and Department of Justice as either incompetent or prejudicial.

When Trump cited the Veterans Administration, it was to side with its victims, not its administrators or venerable history. In Trump's mind, the problem with federal agencies was not just that they overreached and were weaponized, but that their folds of bureaucracy led to incompetency. Take almost any recent terrorist incidents—the Fort Hood shootings, the Boston Marathon bombing, the San Bernardino attacks, or the Orlando nightclub killings—and the perpetrators were in some fashion already known to either the FBI or local law enforcement or both, who nonetheless did not take preemptive action.

Trump was the first Republican candidate by design to campaign against the deep state as some sort of tumor that grew and devoured the flesh of the country. At campaign rallies, he deliberately bellowed out "radical Islamic terrorism!" to mock the bureaucracy's use of euphemisms, and promised to bring back the free usage of the word "Christmas" as a Christian holiday, rather than a secular seasonal celebration during the end of the year holidays.

On March 17, John Brennan, in objection to the firing of deputy director of the FBI Andrew McCabe (who shortly would be found by the nonpartisan inspector general to have lied on four occasions to federal investigators, and was soon reportedly in legal jeopardy from a grand jury investigation), tweeted about the current president of the United States: "When the full extent of your venality, moral turpitude, and political corruption becomes known, you will take your rightful place as a disgraced demagogue in the dustbin of history . . . America will triumph over you."

In mid-April, Brennan followed up with another attack on Trump: "Your kakistocracy [rule of the "worst people"] is collapsing after its lamentable journey. As the greatest Nation history has known, we have the opportunity to emerge from this nightmare stronger & more committed to ensuring a better life for all Americans, including those you have so tragically deceived."

If such hysterics from the former head of the world's premier spy agency and current MSNBC/NBC pundit seemed a near threat to a sitting president, then Samantha Power, former UN ambassador and a past ethics professor on the Harvard faculty, sort of confirmed that it really was: "Not a good idea to piss off John Brennan."

Power herself was found to have requested transcripts of FISA court-ordered surveillance of Trump associates in the 2016 campaign. Indeed, she had gone further and made over 260 requests to have the redacted names of American citizens in these files "unmasked," many of which were mysteriously leaked to the press. Aside from the enigma of why a UN ambassador needed to know the whereabouts and the names of Republican officials in the midst of a campaign—*and after the election*—Power simply denied under oath to a House Intelligence Committee, without explanation, that the requests made under her name were really made by Samantha Power herself! Who had made them, or why, or if she had allowed others to make them, was never disclosed.

Brennan had been initially appointed as President Obama's top counterterrorism advisor, and then had taken over the CIA—during the abrupt and mysterious post-2012 election resignation of General David Petraeus. Over the next eight years of the Obama administration, Brennan was caught in a remarkable series of lies and perjuries, all without much lasting consequence. In 2009, Brennan falsely claimed that intelligence agencies had *not* missed clear indications that Umar Farouk Abdulmutallab, the so-called underwear bomber, would try to take down a US airliner. Just days later, when his denials were ridiculed, Brennan flipped and blasted intelligence agencies for their laxity. In 2011, Brennan falsely alleged under oath to Congress that Obama's drone program in the last year had not caused a single civilian death in Pakistan. In truth, scores had been killed. The same year, Brennan offered various versions of the American killing of Osama bin Laden. His misleading narratives required constant revisions.

In March 2014, Brennan denied accusations that he had illegally ordered CIA analysts to access the computers of US Senate staffers to find out what exactly they knew about possible CIA roles in enhanced interrogations. When he was once again caught outright lying by a CIA inspector general, Brennan was forced to apologize to the members of the Senate Intelligence Committee. In May 2017, Brennan testified under oath to Congress that he had no knowledge during the 2016 campaign of the origins, nature, and paymasters of the Fusion GPS Christopher Steele dossier. Nor, Brennan claimed, was he aware that both the FBI and the Department of Justice had used the infamous file to obtain FISA court-ordered surveillance before and after the election. All those statements were questionable assertions.

Several sources had reported that Brennan was not only aware of the Steele document, but had wanted the FBI to use the Steele document to pursue rumors about Trump. He reportedly briefed Senator Harry Reid (D-NV) on the dossier. Armed with those rumors, Reid then became insistent that they be leaked before the 2016 election. Remember that by long-standing laws and presidential directives, Brennan was prohibited from using the CIA to monitor the activities of US citizens.

I emphasize Brennan only because he was iconic of the deep-state careerists who had mobilized against Trump, especially in their expectation that he would never face charges such as lying to Congress or its investigators. Former National Security advisor Susan Rice, a fierce Trump critic, likely lied about the Benghazi tragedy, the Sergeant Bowe Bergdahl desertion in Afghanistan, and hostage swaps that followed the so-called Iran deal, the presence of weapons of mass destruction in Syria, and her role in the unmasking of names of surveilled Americans. She too never suffered career damage from her serial prevarication.

Fired and would-be martyred FBI deputy director Andrew McCabe openly admitted to misstatements ("I was confused and distracted"). He had falsely assured investigators ("Some of my answers were not fully accurate") that he had not been a source for background leaks about purported Trump-Russian collusion, all of them negative to Trump. The inspector general released a report condemning McCabe for his serial false statements. McCabe was leaking FBI business to deflect from charges that he had ignored conflict of interest charges arising from his own investigation of Hillary Clinton—after his wife, a candidate for the Virginia legislature, had been a recipient of hundreds of thousands of dollars in campaign donations from Clinton-affiliated political action committees.

Former FBI director James Comey likely misled a FISA court by not providing the entire truth about the Steele dossier—and then later probably lied under oath to Congress that the dossier was not the prime evidence for collusion submitted to the court.

Comey's sworn statements to Congress that he had not written a summation about the Clinton email scandal until he had interviewed Hillary Clinton and that he had never leaked FBI information to the media were likely also false. Comey had assured the president that he was not under investigation while leaking to others that Trump, in fact, was. His sworn testimonies could not be reconciled with either those of former attorney general Loretta Lynch or former FBI deputy director Andrew McCabe.

During his spring 2018 book tour, Comey was giving nonstop interviews, critiquing everything from Trump's spotty tan to the only moderate size of his hands. In his memoir, *A Higher Loyalty*, Comey dubbed Trump a "liar" and asserted that "Donald Trump's presidency threatens much of what is good in this nation." Meanwhile, Comey had admitted that he calibrated his investigation of Hillary Clinton to perceptions that she would likely win the election, and by summer 2018 was under investigation by the inspector general for improper leaking of likely confidential documents.

Former director of National Intelligence James Clapper lied under oath to the Senate Intelligence Committee when on March 12, 2013, he assured its members that the National Security Agency did not collect data on American citizens. Months later, Clapper claimed that he gave "the least untruthful" answer.

By late 2017 Clapper too was blasting Trump, claiming that the president of the United States was a veritable traitor and a Russian stooge without offering any proof: "I think this past weekend is illustrative of what a great case officer Vladimir Putin is. He knows how to handle an asset, and that's what he's doing with the president."

Later, Clapper likely lied again when he testified under oath to the House Intelligence Committee, claiming that he had not leaked the contents of the Steele dossier to the media, although later he confessed that he had done just that to CNN's Jake Tapper. Clapper later became a CNN analyst, criticizing those who had alleged that he had been serially untruthful.

Brennan, Clapper, Comey, McCabe, and Rice were never held to account for their distortions. The first three, long after being fired or retired, had still held security clearances. In television appearances, they often leveraged their knowledge of inside information to substantiate the validity of their attacks on Trump. Apparently, it was understood that once a professional bureaucrat or revolving-door appointee reached a senior level in the government, he was immune from the sort of perjury charges or ostracism that most all Americans would face.

A characteristic of the deep-state careerist is the psychological condition known as "projection." To square their own circle of untruth, our so-called best and brightest accuse others of precisely what they do as a matter of habit. I select this small sample of deep-state careerists because they have held various positions of power in Washington, all became fierce critics of Donald Trump, all lied either publicly or under oath, or both, and all expected that their positions or their politics would provide them the very exemption they expected did not exist for the targets of their invective. And all were absolutely right in those presumptions.

Another one of the administrative state's signature traits was conceit. Those who consult, who revolve in and out of government, who profit from their insider contacts, and who exercise enormous but unelected and unaccountable power develop a sense of entitled privilege and belong to a mutual admiration society. A characteristic disdain grows for the public who pays them.

Ironically, the former unpopularity of a rogue deep state made its antipathy to Trump a political asset with progressives. A few examples of administrative state hubris explain why Trump thought attacking it was good politics.

Do we still remember Jonathan Gruber? He was the self-absorbed MIT professor who later became the architect of Obamacare. Gruber was caught on tape bragging how he had supposedly hoodwinked dumb Americans in order to ram down their throats the Affordable Care Act—while he was paid nearly $300,000 to talk the bill through Congress as a contract analyst for the Department of Health and Human Services.

President Obama had early on falsely assured the American people that they could keep their doctors and their health plans. They would see their premium costs decreased. After all such presidential assurances proved untrue, Gruber boasted that voters were simply too stupid to figure out how they had been had by the passage of the Affordable Care Act: "And basically, call it the stupidity of the American voter or whatever, but basically that was really, really critical for the thing to pass."

Ben Rhodes—assistant to the president and deputy national security advisor for strategic communications and speechwriting, and one of the authors of President Obama's "A New Beginning" June 4, 2009, speech in Cairo, and the Benghazi false talking points that misled the press about the actual events of the attack on the American consulate—was especially cynical in boasting how he had manipulated what he thought were a mediocre media to ram through the Iran deal concerning Teheran's ongoing nuclear weapons program. Rhodes related to the *New York Times Magazine* that he seeded administration strategies about passing the Iran deal among the field of novice and compliant wannabe Washington–New York foreign-policy "experts"—on the expectation that such progressive journalists were rank amateurs who would naïvely take his bait.

Rhodes elaborated: "The average reporter we talk to is twenty-seven years old, and their only reporting experience consists of being around political campaigns. That's a sea change. They literally know nothing." Rhodes went on to explain that he easily could manipulate pseudo-experts to complete his circular con of feeding and spreading the news: "We created an echo chamber. . . . They were saying things that validated what we had given them to say."

Because the post-modernist Rhodes was apparently contemptuous of the value of traditional firsthand experience and contemporary journalistic education, he felt he could construct almost any bureaucratic reality he wished. And he too was largely right. "In the absence of rational discourse, we are going to discourse the sh*t out of this . . ." Rhodes elaborated: "We had test drives to know who was going to be able to carry our message effectively, and how to use outside groups like Ploughshares, the Iran Project, and whomever else. So, we knew the tactics that worked . . . We drove them crazy."

In the end, nemesis caught up to Rhodes's hubris. His Iran agreement, which by intent circumvented the Senate's constitutional duty to ratify such treaties, and which was based on not being fully candid with the public and the media, was finally overturned by Donald Trump through the same means of administrative fiat that Obama had used to conclude it.

In a larger sense, when Trump despaired that the media despised him, he was only half correct. *Both* the media and the deep state—and the weld between both—loathed him. Of course, that reality was in part because they were often one and the same thing.

The supposedly street-smart and savvy rogue Manhattan developer Donald Trump, nonetheless, initially was without political, military, and Washington experience. Trump had no real appreciation of the tentacles of the deep-state octopus. They were many. Consider a few of the most prominent examples.

Rhodes himself was the brother of CBS News president David Rhodes. He was married to Ann Norris, a chief foreign policy advisor to former US senator Barbara Boxer (D-CA) and a principal deputy assistant secretary in the State Department under Secretary John Kerry. What Rhodes had failed to note in his brag about the "echo chamber" was that some of the reporters whom he found obsequious and compliant worked for his own brother and covered his wife.

The former president of ABC News Ben Sherwood was the brother of Elizabeth Sherwood-Randall. She had served in various offices as one of the top national energy and security advisors to President Obama. Note the incestuousness: two-thirds of the major nightly network newscasts were overseen by siblings of close advisors of the president of the United States. Had Donald Trump's closest advisors had siblings who were the respective presidents of ABC and CBS news networks, his coverage might not have been 90 percent negative.

Obama's second White House press secretary, Jay Carney, was married to Claire Shipman. She was a veteran reporter for ABC. The deputy Washington bureau chief of CNN, Virginia Moseley, was married to Tom Nides. He had served as the deputy secretary of state for management and resources under Hillary Clinton. Former ABC News executive producer Ian Cameron was married to Susan Rice, who—pre-Benghazi—was a regular on the Sunday talk shows.

NPR's White House correspondent, Ari Shapiro, is married to a lawyer, Michael Gottlieb, formerly of the Obama White House counsel's office. *The Washington Post*'s Justice Department reporter, Sari Horwitz, is married to William B. Schultz. He was the Obama general counsel of the Department of Health and Human Services. Vice President Joe Biden's former communications director, Shailagh Murray (also a former *Post* congressional reporter), is married to Neil King Jr., formerly one of the *Wall Street Journal*'s top political reporters. King worked for Fusion GPS, which had hired the anti-Trump Christopher Steele to compile a dossier to thwart Trump's election.

Power couples and siblings are a Washington staple. Infamous Clinton aide Huma Abedin had married the more infamous deviate, and later felon, former congressman Anthony Weiner. CNN's Christiane Amanpour was the spouse of former State Department spokesman Jamie Rubin. Both former reporter and Harvard professor Samantha Power and her husband, Cass Sunstein, served in the Obama White House. Andrea Mitchell reported on administration news that sometimes her husband, economist Alan Greenspan, had made. The daughter of Univision anchor Jorge Ramos, who loathed Trump, had worked for Hillary.

These are mere random examples of the incestuous relationships of the deep state. In 2010, a more systematic stealth email list, "Journolist," was finally revealed. It proved a veritable electronic chat room for Washington's progressive reporters so that they could communicate privately and off the record about ways to help the 2008 Obama campaign and marginalize conservatives.

The WikiLeaks trove of the emails of the chairman of the 2016 Hillary Clinton campaign, John Podesta, revealed, *inter alia*, that blue-chip journalists such as *Politico*'s Glenn Thrush and the *Washington Post*'s Dana Milbank had colluded with the Clinton campaign to align some of their news accounts and commentaries with orthodox Democratic talking points. Campaign reporter Thrush had infamously self-described himself in one of his communications to Podesta: "Because I have become a hack I will send u the whole section that pertains to u . . . Please don't share or tell anyone I did this. Tell me if I f****d up anything."

The CNBC chief Washington correspondent and *New York Times* contributor John Harwood was often found out to be both reporting on and serving as an informal advisor to the Clinton campaign. Donna Brazile, a onetime head of the Democratic National Committee and also a former CNN analyst, lied about tipping off the Clinton campaign before an impending CNN-sponsored town hall debate during the 2016 Democratic primary. And then she initially flat-out further fibbed about her collusions ("We have never, ever given a town hall question to anyone beforehand").

In another WikiLeaks email revelation, *Politico* reporter Ken Vogel gave Democratic National Committee press secretary Mark Paustenbach a chance to read over and "fact-check" his story prior to publication. Mark Leibovich, a senior reporter for the *New York Times Magazine,* was likewise swept up in an email dump, asking the Clinton campaign to read over and approve his quotes before publication.

Especially influential in the deep state were the revolving-door multimillionaires who came into both Republican and Democratic government from, and went back to, the big banks and Wall Street—the Tim Geithners, Jack Lews, Hank Paulsons, and Robert Rubins. There were also the lesser satellites of the quasi-public lending agencies Freddie Mac and Fannie Mae (to melt down in the 2008 financial crisis), such as Franklin Raines (earning $90 million in "bonuses") and a Jamie Gorelick ($26 million), who, like Raines, had lots of government service but very little knowledge of the financial industry. Former Clinton and Obama aide, former congressman, and now Chicago mayor Rahm Emanuel had somehow, between his White House and House of Representatives tenures, garnered $16 million for his financial "expertise."

The *locus classicus*, of course, of swamp profiteering was the Clinton power marriage itself. It invested nearly forty years of public service in what proved to be an unmatched pay-for-play payoff, when the former First Couple parlayed Hillary's political trajectories into a personal fortune of well over $100 million. Hillary Clinton in between her secretary of state tenure and her presidential candidacy often was paid $10,000 to $60,000 *a minute* for private Wall Street riffs. After her defeat, the market value of her honoraria mysteriously plunged to $25,000 per speech.

Again, the administrative state was not entirely liberal. The above examples could easily be matched by permanent Republican fixtures who were deeply embedded into the Washington landscape and considered Trump as much a threat as did his progressive opponents. Many of the Never and pro-Trump conservative pundits themselves had served in Republican governments, had spouses and family members who were Washington journalists and media players, and went in and out of campaigns as consultants and advisors every four or eight years.

The swamp usually took care of itself. When Hillary Clinton found herself in an ethical bind, given her record on the Libyan intervention and an embarrassing communication trail about four American deaths in Benghazi, the Obama administration jailed a video maker, Nakoula Basseley Nakoula, on trumped-up probation violations. He was falsely blamed for the debacle on the dubious claim that his obscure film clip had caused a spontaneous riot in Benghazi—despite on-the-scene evidence of a preplanned, al-Qaeda-affiliated terrorism operation.

In response, the administration also green-lighted an in-house investigation to be led by the sober, judicious, and appropriately unimpeachable DC figure Thomas Pickering. He proved to be emblematic of the establishment state. Pickering was a respected career diplomat, bipartisan Council on Foreign Relations fixture, co-chairman of blue-ribbon investigative committees—a multilingual veteran of hazardous diplomatic posts, confidant to presidents of both parties, and octogenarian "wise man." In other words, Pickering had the proper credentials to be appointed to conduct an internal investigation of

Clinton and the Benghazi debacle as chairman of the Benghazi Accountability Review Board.

Four of the five members of this board, including Pickering, were apparently recommended by Hillary Clinton's own State Department team. No one would dare suggest that Pickering, appointed as an undersecretary of state and an ambassador by Bill Clinton, and a well-known Clinton friend, might have various conflicts of interest. He was, after all, investigating the allegations that Hillary Clinton refused to beef up security at the consulate in Benghazi, or falsely claimed in public that the loss of four Americans was the result of an inflammatory video, just hours after she confided in email communications that it was a preplanned al-Qaeda attack.

Instead, Pickering decided that Clinton would *never* appear before his committee. Clinton aide Cheryl Mills, in deep-state fashion, found a way to preview the board's findings before publication and ended up making critical decisions affecting the scope of the investigation. In the end, the State Department chastised and put on leave lowly subordinates, even though they seemed only to have worked within the security parameters established by the sacrosanct secretary of state.

Nor would anyone suggest that the temperate and esteemed Pickering, as a vice president of Boeing from 2001 to 2006, and then a "consultant" to Boeing from 2006 to 2015, had any special financial interest in promoting the Clinton, and then the John Kerry, policy of outreach to Iran. Indeed, Pickering testified before Congress and wrote elegant op-eds about why the Iran nonenrichment accord was a good deal. But he never quite informed the country that a liberated and cash-flush Iran was also considering a $25 billion purchase of aircraft (with potential dual use as military transports) from Boeing—which just happened to be Pickering's quite generous corporate client.

Was it all that strange that when such Washington fixtures like Pickering signed outraged collective op-eds about the "ignorant" and "unqualified" Donald Trump (who had promised on the campaign to cancel the Iran deal), no one seemed to listen anymore?

Did a deep-state Hank Paulson—former assistant to former Nixon aide John Ehrlichman, former CEO of Goldman Sachs (a firm that had given over $800,000 to Hillary's campaigns as well as $675,000 in speaking fees), former treasury secretary, and of some $700 million in net worth—ever sense that his assurances that Hillary was both presidential and not corrupt were not especially believable?

Trump was warned by friends, enemies, and neutrals that his fight against the deep state was suicidal. Senate minority leader Chuck Schumer, just a few days before Trump's inauguration, cheerfully forecast (in a precursor to Samantha Power's later admonition) what might happen to Trump once he attacked the intelligence services: "Let me tell you: You take on the intelligence community—they have six ways from Sunday at getting back at you."

Former administrative state careerists were not shy about warning Trump of what was ahead. The counterterrorism analyst Phil Mudd, who had worked in the CIA and the FBI under Robert Mueller, warned CNN host Jake Tapper in August 2017 that "the government is going to kill" President Donald Trump.

Kill? And what was the reason the melodramatic Mudd adduced for his astounding prediction? "Because he doesn't support them." Mudd then elaborated: "Let me give you one bottom line as a former government official. The government is going to kill this guy. The government is going to kill this guy because he doesn't support them." Mudd further clarified his assassination metaphor: "What I'm saying is government—people talk about the deep state—when you disrespect government officials who've done thirty years, they're going to say, 'Really?'" It was difficult to ascertain to what degree Mudd was serious or exaggerating the depth of deep-state loathing of Trump.

A writer for the *London Review of Books*, Adam Schatz, seemed even more direct. He reported a supposed conversation that he had with an American political scientist knowledgeable of the Washington permanent caste. He purportedly had assured Schatz that if Trump were elected, he would likely not survive his full term: "He will have to be removed from power by the deep state, or be assassinated."

Another progressive, the former Cleveland mayor, presidential candidate, and congressman Dennis Kucinich (D-OH), confessed in 2017: "The intention is to take down our President. This is very dangerous to America. It's a threat to our Republic. It constitutes a clear and present danger to our way of life. So, we have to be asking, 'What is the motive of these people?' . . . This is a problem in our country. We've got to protect our nation here. People have to be aware of what's going on, we need to protect America. This isn't about Democrat or Republican. This is about getting what's going on in the moment and understanding that our country itself is under attack from within."

Even more dramatic were comments made during the Trump presidency by the ever ubiquitous and always more loquacious John Brennan about the vengeance of the deep state. Brennan insisted that the permanent bureaucracy had an "obligation . . . to refuse to carry out" any orders from President Trump that it deemed anti-democratic. In normal times, that boast would be interrupted as an insurrectionary call to all but remove a president or at least nullify his office. In Brennan's mind, a career bureaucrat could arbitrarily decide a Trump presidential executive order was unconstitutional and then refuse to obey, or even block it. All of these threats were the more serious deep-state side to the popular bombast of actors and celebrities who routinely weighed in with more candid conspiracy talk, such as Alec Baldwin ("We need to overthrow the government of the United States under Donald Trump") or Rosie O'Donnell ("I want to send the military to the White House to get him").

The Robert Mueller investigation of Donald Trump for allegedly colluding with the Russians will be treated in a subsequent chapter. But the composition of Mueller's special counsel
investigatory team was almost a caricature of the nature and
composition of the deep state. It need not have been, given the
polarization over the special counsel appointment and the importance of avoiding even the hint of any conflicts of interest—
another testament to the power of New York–Washington
received wisdom and protocol.

The announcements of initial appointments made the Washington and New York media become giddy, as if they were
assured that those of their own tribe would be unleashed on
Trump. *Wired*, for instance, published this headline on June
14, 2017: "Robert Mueller Chooses His Investigatory Dream
Team." *Vox*, on August 22, was elated: "Meet the all-star legal
team who may take down Trump." The *Daily Beast*, two days
later, saw the team in military terms: "Inside Robert Mueller's
Army."

The "army's" soldiers possessed all the right résumés, with
many of the requisite degrees from the right universities, the
right revolving-door histories of government and private-sector
employment, and the right ideology—not so much progressive as wedded to the idea that the administrative state was the
true sober and judicious expression of the values of the United
States. Otherwise, in almost every imaginable context, the special counsel's team was compromised at its very beginning
through its own incestuousness and anti-Trump bias—almost
in the Soviet-style certainty of Lavrentiy Beria's "Show me the
man and I'll find you the crime."

How exactly had former FBI director Robert Mueller been
selected as special counsel to investigate Trump? Recently fired
FBI director James Comey had testified that he was so exasperated with the president that he had leaked his own confidential memos of presidential meetings via a friend in order that

it "might prompt the appointment of a special counsel." And
the appointed special counsel was soon none other than Robert Mueller, with whom Comey had worked professionally in a
variety of contexts for nearly twenty years and who had an interview with Trump as a possible replacement for the fired Comey!

Two of Mueller's lead FBI investigators, Lisa Page and Peter
Strzok, had a long-concealed amorous relationship characterized in their thousands of text messages by an overriding hatred of Donald Trump and a desire to ensure that he was not
elected president or barring that, that he did not prove a successful president. In various text exchanges, they referenced an
"insurance policy" to prevent a Trump presidency, as well as
deliberate efforts to leak classified information to the press, also
in the context of harming the 2016 Trump campaign.

Strzok interviewed Michael Flynn (January 24, 2017) to learn
about possible Trump-Russian collusion, and earlier Clinton
aides Huma Abedin and Cheryl Mills in connection with the
Clinton email scandal. All three had apparently given misleading information; only the first Trump advisor so far has been
charged for lying to the FBI.

Both Page and Strzok communicated with Deputy Director
Andrew McCabe concerning the "insurance" idea that might
suggest efforts to stop Donald Trump's election, or thwart his
presidency. When the inspector general released evidence of
their prejudices and romantic involvement, the two were reassigned. But Robert Mueller apparently did not immediately announce why they were taken off his investigation. In deep-state
style, their staggered departures were reported in the press as
normal reassignments and not connected—as if to inform the
public *why* they were leaving would somehow not be in the
Mueller investigation's interest.

In May 2018, Page finally resigned during the controversy
over her venomous anti-Trump text message exchanges with
Agent Strzok, and in anticipation of a supposedly devastating

forthcoming inspector general's report. In it, Strzok is quoted in a previously undisclosed August 2016 text reassuring Page that he would prevent Trump from becoming president: "No. No he's not. We'll stop it." Remember, this quote came from an FBI investigator who would shortly be appointed by Mueller to investigate possible Trump-Russian collusion.

In similar fashion, only through the inspector general's report of June 2018 did the public learn that another of Mueller's FBI lead attorneys—who earlier had been assigned to the Clinton email investigation—after the election had bragged in a text to an FBI attorney of his opposition to Trump: "Viva le [*sic*] resistance." Again, Mueller did not disclose whether he knew of any such prejudice when he hired the unnamed FBI attorney, much less why he had retained him until early 2018, or why the public once again was not apprised of the circumstances of this lawyer's belated departure.

Deputy Attorney General Rod Rosenstein appointed the special counsel Robert Mueller. Yet Rosenstein while in the Obama Department of Justice had once been a supervisor of the highly controversial Uranium One investigation headed by none other than then FBI director Robert Mueller—an investigation that may be currently connected with efforts to find Russian collusion with American elected or appointed officials.

Rosenstein also, during his tenure in the Trump Justice Department, in June 2017 signed at least one of the surveillance requests to a FISA court. Those applications came under a cloud of suspicion for allegedly not disclosing the unverified nature of the Steele dossier, the Clinton campaign's payments to Steele, the departure of Steele from FBI association, or the circular nature of news accounts concerning the dossier.

Four members of the original Mueller team arrived as former associates at his law firm of WilmerHale. Some of them were now investigating former Trump campaign chairman Paul Manafort, Trump's daughter Ivanka, and Jared Kushner, the president's son-in-law, who were supposedly also represented by WilmerHale attorneys. Of the initial fifteen appointed Mueller team lawyers, at least seven were known to have contributed money to the Democratic Party or Hillary Clinton or both.

Another Mueller appointee was Andrew Weissmann. He was also a former partner at WilmerHale. Weissmann had emailed applause to Obama DOJ holdover Sally Yates when, as an acting attorney general, she had tried to block her then new boss President Trump's immigration moratorium. Like other Mueller team members, Weissmann was a donor to Democratic causes and an admitted Hillary Clinton partisan. Sally Yates reportedly had co-signed one of the FISA court requests, again without disclosures of the full nature of the Steele dossier, to surveil Trump campaign associates.

Aaron Zebley, another Mueller team member, had served as Mueller's chief of staff while Mueller was FBI director, and yet another former partner at WilmerHale. In the past, Zebley had represented Justin Cooper, who had testified to the House Committee on Oversight and Government Reform that he had set up Hillary Clinton's private server and then destroyed with a hammer some of Clinton's mobile devices when there was already investigatory interest in their contents. Indeed, Clinton's email server in question—the domain clintonemail.com—used by Hillary Clinton was, in fact, registered to Cooper himself, not to Bill or Hillary Clinton, while she was secretary of state.

If Mueller wished to have ensured that his team had clear conflicts of interest, he could have done no better than to have selected an attorney who had represented one of the chief participants in the Clinton email scandal. Neither Mueller nor the media ever voiced much worry about the appearance of conflicts of interest.

Then there is special counsel investigation member Jeannie Rhee. Rhee, another WilmerHale alumna, another sizable contributor to the Clinton campaign effort, is yet another attorney who had represented someone deeply involved in a recent Clinton scandal. She had recently defended not only the Clinton Foundation, but also Obama deputy national security advisor Ben Rhodes during hearings conducted by the US House Select Committee on Events Surrounding the 2012 Terrorist Attack in Benghazi, Libya, in relationship to his alleged role in providing narratives about the attack that were later proven to be inaccurate.

Was the United States so short of legal talent that special counsel Mueller could not find lawyers from a law firm other than his own, or who had not contributed to the Clinton campaign, or who had not represented clients in ongoing Clinton-related scandals, or who did not live in Washington or New York?

Donald Trump, throughout his brief political career, had feuded with Jeff Bezos, Amazon owner and the richest man in history, largely because Bezos's *Washington Post* daily damned Trump and was deeply embedded in Washington politics in a fashion that Trump could only have dreamed of. Moreover, in the 2016 campaign, Silicon Valley money had poured into the Clinton campaign in stunningly asymmetrical fashion. According to data gathered on the eve of the election by Crowdpac (which claims in nonpartisan fashion to monitor sources of campaign donations), technology companies' employees donated overwhelmingly to Hillary Clinton by a 95 percent margin over Donald Trump.

Crowdpac estimated that 99 percent of all political donations from "Silicon Valley" (i.e., Palo Alto, Menlo Park, Mountain View, and their environs) were given to the Clinton campaign. Alienating Silicon Valley could be disastrous politically, given its huge capital resources, its control over the internet and social media, and its insidious cultural influence.

Google, Twitter, and Facebook had often been accused of employing political bias in the operation of their products according to their own progressive tastes. Civil libertarians have faulted the social-media and internet giants for violating rights of privacy and for monitoring the shopping, travel, eating, and entertainment habits of their unwary customers to the extent that such corporations knew where and when Americans traveled or communicated with one another. Trump's nemeses—Apple, Alphabet (Google), Amazon, Microsoft, and Facebook—were the world's five largest companies in terms of stock value. Together they enjoyed market capitalizations of over $3 trillion. That sum was about the net worth of the entire country of Switzerland.

Until the rise of high-tech companies in the 1980s, there were, for better or worse, certain understood rules that governed the behavior of such large corporations. Anti-trust laws prohibited corporations from stifling competition. Price cutting and fixing, dumping, and vertically integrating to ensure monopolies were once mostly illegal. The government broke up large "trusts." The public looked askance at the power of megacorporations and their ability to sway public opinion through the monopolistic purchases of media and advertising, and their ability to liquidate smaller rival companies. Product liability laws, if often punitively and unfairly, nevertheless held corporations accountable even for the deliberate misuse of their products.

Yet by the election of 2016, Silicon Valley and related high-tech companies were exempt from such traditional regulations and without much fear of retaliation from the political party they loathed. After all, Facebook and Google ran veritable monopolies. Facebook alone controls an estimated 40 percent of the world's social-media market. It has more than 2 *billion* monthly users.

Google has gobbled up about 90 percent of the world's search-engine market. Apple earns $230 billion in annual revenue and is nearing a market value of $900 billion. Microsoft controls about 85 percent of the word-processing personal and business markets. Amazon alone was responsible for about 45 percent of all online sales in 2017. It has huge contracts with the Pentagon.

Google News is one of the nation's larger aggregators of daily media reports. When competitors to Big Tech arise, they are offered billions of dollars, then cashed out and absorbed. Facebook has bought over fifty rival companies. It acquired former competitor WhatsApp, the world's leader in messaging platforms, for a staggering $19 billion. Alphabet/Google has bought over two hundred companies, among them YouTube.

By itself, Facebook, which the government does not regard as a public utility, can adjudicate tasteful—or "proper" political—expression. Google alone determines each day what sort of imaging—much of it ideologically driven—billions of internet users will see on their screens. Yet its management is unapologetically partisan. In September 2018, a pirated video appeared of a Google "all hands meeting" following the Trump victory. Sergey Brin, co-founder of Google, remarked to the audience: "I certainly find this election deeply offensive, and I know many of you do too." Brin attributed Trump's victory to voter "boredom" and then editorialized that in general "data shows that boredom led to fascism and also the communist revolutions." Google vice president for global affairs Kent Walker attributed the Trump victory to self-destructive tribalism: "We're trying to figure out, how do we respond to that, what are the next steps for us before the world comes into this environment of tribalism that's self-destructive [in] the long-term." Walker also cited "fear, xenophobia, hatred, and a desire for answers that may or may not be there" for the rise of Trump.

Disagree with Facebook, Twitter, YouTube, or Google, and you will learn that it's hard to find commensurate alternative services. If a particular historical video does not meet Silicon Valley's correct narratives, YouTube will stifle it through "restrictive mode filtering," as it has with many offered by nonprofit conservative Praeger University.

None of these tech giants are held to the same oversight that monitors transportation, drug, oil, or power companies. Why was that, and what then had Trump got himself into by feuding with Silicon Valley?

The Big Tech corporations certainly provided cool twenty-first-century products. People were mostly happy with the way they word processed, searched, emailed, posted, and bought online—at least until they butted up against the power of these monopolies and found their social-media accounts arbitrarily frozen, their private habits and data sold to other companies and operatives, their internet use constantly interrupted by ads and messaging, or their providers using their patronage to advance agendas about the larger culture.

Unprecedented capital and revenue mattered—both the fear of governments losing it and the hope of acquiring it. Jeff Bezos was worth in summer 2018 over $140 billion. Bill Gates of Microsoft is second at $90 billion, and Facebook's Mark Zuckerberg ($71 billion) is fifth. Civilization has never seen such Croesus-like concentration of personal wealth. And it remains dumbfounded by it. By comparison, Trump's entire fortune was comparable to what Bezos or Zuckerberg made or lost some days on the stock market.

In inflation-adjusted dollars, these new billionaires dwarfed the nineteenth-century so-called robber-baron fortunes of the Rockefellers, Carnegies, Fords, and Mellons that once prompted a cultural revolution of muckraking and trust-busting. Such huge amounts of capital, coupled with monopolies over the way much of the world communicates, gives just a handful of people never before seen political power. And after July 2016 much of it was aimed against conservatives in general, and in particular, Donald J. Trump and his agendas.

Nationalism ironically explains why Big Tech remained mostly unregulated. Why would Americans wish to hamstring some of the world's largest companies when they ensured that American culture and practice saturated the cyber world? Trump himself as a nationalist accepted that Big Tech earned the nation money and prestige. He naturally bragged that his new tax reform bill would allow Silicon Valley to bring back hundreds of billions of dollars without the tax consequences of the past. Yet it was unlikely that those who were thereby even further enriched would remember Trump's magnanimity on Election Day.

High-tech companies had also long managed to navigate the straits between the two political parties. Democrats, the traditional trust-busters and hyperregulators, appreciated the progressive politics and West Coast hip culture of corporations such as Facebook and Amazon. Why would they have ever wanted to regulate entities that were a reliable cash cow for the Democratic Party and that pushed progressive agendas insidiously through daily internet use?

On the other hand, pre-Trump Republicans and conservatives were rigidly wedded to doctrinaire free-market economics and were ideologically averse to intruding into the marketplace— even when they were often at odds with high-tech monopolies and sometimes targeted by them. Silicon Valley cynically manipulated both parties: Democrats would drop their muckraking tendencies given Big Tech lucre and progressive cool; blinkered Republicans were so ideologically straitjacketed that they were simply incapable of biting the hand that starved them.

Trump did not quite fathom that he was up against not just the media and the Beltway swamp, but also against a brave new world of mobile communications, computers, the internet, and social media without guidance from the past about whether these international and global megacompanies qualified as public utilities, monopolies, or trusts. As progressive quasi-independent and autonomous states, they made their own laws. Silicon Valley and its affiliates hardly feared what they felt was the passing irritant of a Trump presidency, despite their zealous efforts to have prevented it and now to derail it. Meanwhile, that they hated Trump was enough for the media and the Democratic Party to overlook business practices that made those of Exxon or General Motors seem parochial and naïve. Establishment Republicans for the most part kept out of the fray and either felt that Trump had bitten off more than he could chew or that their own free-market orthodoxy precluded a trust-busting crackdown on Silicon Valley.

Often Silicon Valley proved the receptacle for the revolving-door careerists of progressive Washington. When Obama EPA director Lisa Jackson stepped down after being caught using a pseudonymous email account, she was quickly hired as Apple's environmental director. When Jay Carney, Obama's press secretary, left the administration, after a short stint at CNN he became Amazon's senior vice president of worldwide corporate affairs. Obama's campaign advisor David Plouffe was hired by Uber. Gene Sperling, an Obama administration economic advisor, joined the board of directors of Ripple Labs, an American high-tech financial services corporation. And on and on.

In the first two years of his presidency, Trump has not resigned. He has not been impeached. He has not been indicted. He has not died or been declared *non compos mentis*. Trump did not govern as a liberal, as some of his Never Trump critics predicted. He had not been driven to seclusion by lurid exposés of his past womanizing a decade earlier as a Manhattan television celebrity. Predictions of all that and more were no more accurate than earlier prognostications that Trump would never be nominated and certainly never elected.

An administrative state, swamp, deep state, call it what you wish, was wrong about Trump's nomination, his election, and his governance. It was right only in its warnings that he could be crude and profane, with a lurid past and an ethical necropolis of skeletons in his closet—a fact long ago factored and baked into his supporters' votes.

At each stage, the erroneous predictions of the deep state prompted ever greater animus at a target that it could not quite understand, much less derail, and so far has not been able to destroy. By autumn 2018, the repetitive nightly predictions of cable news pundits that the latest presidential controversy was a "bombshell," or marked a "turning-point," or offered proof that "the walls were closing in," or ensured that "impeachment was looming on the horizon" had amounted to little more than monotonous and scripted groupthink.

Never before in the history of the presidency had a commander in chief earned the antipathy of the vast majority of the media, much of the career establishments of both political parties, the majority of the holders of the nation's accumulated personal wealth, and the permanent federal bureaucracy.

Why such aversion, such fear and loathing?

In the next three chapters, we will learn why and how Trump, and those around him, defined America's decline, envisioned its renewal, and thus haphazardly tried to "Make America Great Again."

These ideas and agendas, and the people who embraced them, were antithetical to the status quo of both parties and the administrative state itself.

PART THREE

TRUMP METAPHYSICS

The lion cannot protect himself from traps, and the fox cannot defend himself from wolves. One must therefore be a fox to recognize traps, and a lion to frighten wolves.
—Niccolò Machiavelli, *The Prince*

Chapter Seven

TRUMP ON DECLINE

The Western world has lost its civic courage. . . .
Such a decline in courage is particularly noticeable
among the ruling and intellectual elite, causing an
impression of a loss of courage by the entire society.
—Aleksandr Solzhenitsyn,
Harvard commencement address, 1978

None of the more than twenty candidates running for president in 2016 claimed that America was in good shape—except perhaps Hillary Clinton, who advertised herself as the first female president and the progressive guarantor of Barack Obama's successful eight years. Yet Donald Trump's notion of decline was different from both the pessimism of his Republican rivals and Bernie Sanders's vision of a wretched society in need of a radical socialist cure.

Instead, Trump's upbeat "Make America Great Again" was a simplistic tripartite message about decline: America was once great. Now it is not. But under Trump it will be great again. Trump promised such renewal on the first day of his campaign—as he has continued to do almost every day since.

But has Trump ever fully defined what he meant by "decline"? Were Americans really materially or spiritually poorer than in the 1990s, the 1970s, or the 1950s? And were *all* Americans so suffering, or just half the country?

Why did the richest generation in the history of civilization, or again at least half of it, find Trump's gloomy diagnosis of decline and his therapy of renewal so persuasive, even optimistic?

Trump, of course, was saying nothing new in a presidential campaign.

Almost *every* presidential candidate has run on the idea of an America gone wrong under the incumbent. Usually the fault was due to someone of the opposite political party—more recently from the Left's "A Time for Greatness" (John F. Kennedy, 1960), "To Begin Anew" (Eugene McCarthy, 1968), and "Come Home, America" (George McGovern, 1972) to the Right's "Let's Make America Great Again" (Ronald Reagan, 1980) or Mitt Romney's "Restore Our Future" (2012).

Ronald Reagan started off his 1980 campaign with a pre-Trumpian rallying call: "For those who've abandoned hope, we'll restore hope and we'll welcome them into a great national crusade *to make America great again* [italics added]."

Such promises of restoration are also very Western. Long before Trump or Reagan, railing about decline was inherent in the mentality of Western civilization. Given the culture's allegiance to freedom of expression, self-critique, rationalism, and scientific progress, life should always prove materially richer, or at least be so perceived by each generation. And woe to all when it does not.

The ancient Greeks saw a state's rise, fall—and rise again—as an organic cycle, analogous to human aging, dying, and birthing. The late-eighth-century BC poet Hesiod railed at the dawn of the age of the city-state that his own Askra, a rural hamlet in Greece, was already mired in moral decline.

That was also the theme of Homer's contemporaneous epics. The age of epic heroes of the *Iliad* and *Odyssey* was coming to a close. The heroic era had already fallen far into near mediocrity from the lost Heroic Age of supermen and demigods. Old Nestor sounded like Trump, lamenting the passing of an earlier better age and how successful men like himself had once been responsible for it.

No two adages in Roman literature resonate Trumpism better than the first-century BC poet Horace's lament of his generation, "Worse than our grandparents' generation, our parents' then produced us, even worse, and soon to bear still worse children," or his contemporary, the historian Livy's pessimistic conclusion that Romans of his war-torn and depraved age could "bear neither our diseases nor their remedies."

Rome, in fact, would endure for another half millennium after the worrisome Livy—and a millennium and a half in the East at Byzantium. Arthur Herman's *The Idea of Decline in Western History* focused especially on the Enlightenment's cultural glumness. In the subsequent nineteenth and early twentieth centuries, ideas of near-imminent collapse of civilization were thematic in the writings of such historical pessimists as Friedrich Nietzsche and Oswald Spengler.

Given Americans' restlessness, their reliance on ever better technology and machines, and their sense of manifest destiny, everything always just had to become better. And when it sometimes did not seem so in American history, furor ensued.

Yet Trump's blame gaming was quite unlike the sermons of Barack Obama. He had in his accustomed careful manner faulted Americans for a variety of their own pathologies, from past biases ("The United States is still working through some of our own darker periods in our history") to laziness ("But we've been a little bit lazy, I think, over the last couple of decades." "If you're in the United States, sometimes you can feel lazy and think we're so big we don't have to really know anything about other people.").

In contrast, Trump loudly condemned others, but *not* even softly his fellow citizens. He focused on economic "cheaters" abroad like the Chinese and the Mexicans. Then there were the supposedly free-loading and pampered Europeans. Worse were our own clueless leaders who made "dumb deals" and thereby let more cunning foreigners take America to the cleaners ("We've made other countries rich while the wealth, strength, and confidence of our country has disappeared over the horizon").

Trump was on to something, at least politically, in scapegoating foreigners rather than Americans for their country's perceived shortcomings. Voters were tired of accepting blame for their own malaise, never more so than during the Obama administration.

Yet the alternative of praising foreigners as somehow superior had a long history in the United States. In the 1930s, declinists had moaned that fascism supposedly had provided a unique model of government/free market partnerships based on scientific principles that had far better than the United States weathered the Great Depression. Mussolini was often popular in Depression-era New York saloons. Post-war communism supposedly had passed America by, given its resonance with the awakening post-colonial third world. *Sputnik* and the domino theory seemed to prove that.

After the implosion of Nazism and Soviet communism, next came 1970s Japan, Inc. The more disciplined and thrifty Japan would, in its own way, bury a decadent United States. As the Japanese economy ossified, the post-modern European Economic Community and later the twenty-first-century European Union were praised as the next paradigm superior to the free-market democracy of the United States. The wiser soft-power EU was doing away with pernicious American ideas like nationalism, unfettered capitalism, and hyperindividualism.

As the EU soon in its turn stagnated, a rising China—indeed, with the largest population in the world—was the next-in-line usurper of US dominance. It supposedly enjoyed more rapid if not effective governance. Op-ed writers such as the *New York Times*'s Thomas Friedman praised its high-speed rail and new airports, heralding the efficiency of its autocratic decision making. And China exuded an upbeat confidence of ascendency (even as it was facing political challenges and demographic and environmental disasters).

All these delusional paranoias of relative decline shared the common symptom that Americans had never fully appreciated the singular genius behind their founding and the Constitution, the immense national wealth and advantageous geography of North America, or the amazing resilience of uniquely American institutions such as the melting pot, the ethos of rugged individualism, upward mobility, and American obsessions with self-improvement, home improvement, and career improvement.

Forgotten also in these common American postmortems was the characteristic American ability to modify, adapt, reinvent, and rebirth in a way not possible in more rigid societies. Again, what saved Trump from becoming just another cultural doomster was his particular sectarian take on the old saw.

Decline, as Trump framed it in his January 20, 2017, inauguration address, was now a different sort. It was a symptom of what foreign nations, hand in glove with "a small group of American" connivers, had done to other Americans to damage the whole:

> . . . a small group in our nation's Capital has reaped the rewards of government while the people have borne the cost. Washington flourished—but the people did not share in its wealth. Politicians prospered—but the jobs left, and the factories closed. The establishment protected itself, but not the citizens of our country. Their victories have not been your

victories; their triumphs have not been your triumphs; and while they celebrated in our nation's Capital, there was little to celebrate for struggling families all across our land.

In the pre-Trump era, Democrats defined decline through traditional progressive and redistributionist lenses. Of course, they focused on inequality and the current *relative* plight of the poor compared to the rich, rather than the *absolute* condition of the impoverished compared to the indigent of the past.

Supposedly too many Americans were without government help. And far too few controlled the nation's wealth. Therefore, in the progressive mindset, a radical increase in taxes, government, and entitlements was needed to ensure "fairness" and bring America home again. That a poor person with an iPhone had more computing power and access to culture in his palm than a billionaire did in 1990 was irrelevant. Apparently, it did not matter that a cheap Kia had more appurtenances and luxuries than did a top-of-the-line Mercedes twenty years ago.

Another progressive take on decline was the purported decadent tastes and appetites of the lower middle and working classes. The gullible deplorables were supposedly hooked on consumerism, the rat race, reality television, fast food, and easy credit and debt.

Books like Cullen Murphy's *Are We Rome?* had focused on America's material excesses and cultural insularity that suggested that we were eroding like the late Roman Empire. In this regard, it was not an accident that Trump appealed to the lower and middle classes on the argument of unfairness, appropriating left-wing class politics, but situating them within the promise of capitalist cures.

For example, the way to help the struggling in wealthy cities such as Los Angeles, Portland, San Francisco, or Seattle who could not afford housing was *not* to let the wealthy continue (for a variety of self-interested environmental, financial, and political reasons) to zone them out or to write off their own considerable property taxes and jumbo mortgages, but rather to build vast new housing tracts that would bring down the price of a home, and start eliminating tax deductions for the exclusionary blue-state affluent. How odd that the wealthy wanted fewer houses built, the poor more. And the former were called liberally correct, and the latter conservatively wrong on environmental, cultural, or self-interested grounds.

Progressives also believed that out-of-control defense spending of the military-industrial complex marked a slide into mindless warring and needless investments in weaponry. According to Paul Kennedy's canonical *The Rise and Fall of the Great Powers*, for example, defense spending supposedly had all but doomed the United States in the way it had purportedly exhausted prior empires like those of the Hapsburgs and Britain.

Finally, the most recent progressive declinist theme was environmental collapse as inevitable fallout from laissez-faire capitalism. In the various works of the anthropologist Jared Diamond (*Guns, Germs, and Steel*; *Collapse*), Western civilization was intrinsically invested in resource depletion and unsustainable exploitation. Global warming, overpopulation, and scarcity were the ultimate apparitions of the Western lifestyle and its inevitable instability and transience.

Trump, of course, would discount all such pessimism as ridiculous, especially the near glee with which the elite Left sometimes welcomed the fated end of supposedly toxic middle-American consumerism. Trump, unlike progressives, believed that what was needed was not less, but *more* consumerism, on the chance that the middle class could have access to some of the same stuff as the wealthy.

Yet Trump was not quite an orthodox conservative declinist. True, like most conservatives he believed that America was naturally rich and its economic system unmatched. Recessions and downturns must be due to incompetent social and cultural engineers who had unnaturally shackled America's free-market, free-trade traditions, and allowed it to stagnate at home. Think of the stagflation and oil embargoes of the Jimmy Carter era or the perceived calcified annualized GDP stagnation and "lead from behind" recessional foreign policy of Barack Obama.

Yet Trump was also quite unlike conservatives who railed against moral decline—usually defined as a growing agnostic and atheistic spiritual emptiness, the sexual revolution, the dissolution of the nuclear family, crime, hedonistic license, anti-Americanism, cultural relativism, and utopian pacifism. Trump, of course, supported conservative issues that evangelicals embraced. But his own checkered past, Manhattan excesses, three marriages, and chronic womanizing made him an unlikely reactionary moralist.

In contrast, Trump certainly felt that making everyone wealthier would make them stronger and happier and thus the country as a whole more united, safer, and more stable—without regard to whether they were gays, divorced, adulterers, single parents, or traditional households. Material progress led to universal American happiness and healed wounds. It did not contribute to decadence.

Trump's idea of decline, then, was not quite either the economic pessimism of the Left or the cultural rot of the Right. As a capitalist-nationalist-populist, he instead complained of a rigged decline for some as the tab for the prosperity of others—in some ways not unlike the charges of unfairness from his doppelganger Bernie Sanders, which made their parallel ascendances in 2016 not all that mystifying.

For Trump, the problem with the United States was not capitalist-inspired inequality, but the lack of nationalist patriotism of capitalists (even, as he admitted, such as himself). The elite and rich no longer cared about other Americans as much as they did others abroad—supposedly Chinese eager for American trade advantages, purportedly poor Mexicans in need of a new start in the United States, wealthy Europeans who claimed that they could not afford their own NATO protection, and assumed deprived Middle Easterners who expected the United States to rebuild their nations.

Trump's theory of decline was caused by a sort of willing betrayal of the elite clerks. And decline was worse than prior bouts of erosion, because it was alleged to be a *deliberate* choice. It was not intrinsic and fated, one that pitted coastal winners against interior losers. Trump laid out the writ against the status quo in his inaugural address:

> For many decades, we've enriched foreign industry at the expense of American industry. . . . We've made other countries rich while the wealth, strength, and confidence of our country has disappeared over the horizon. One by one, the factories shuttered and left our shores, with not even a thought about the millions upon millions of American workers left behind The wealth of our middle class has been ripped from their homes and then redistributed across the entire world.

Such blanket accusations often enraged the establishment. At the height of the campaign in June 2016, incumbent president Barack Obama dismissed Trump's earlier declinist charges. Indeed, he had become so irate that he promised his audience that he would not even use Trump's name and thus "do his advertising for him":

> Even though we've recovered, people feel like the ground under their feet isn't quite as solid. If they're feeling insecure, and they're offered a simple reason to be more secure, people are going to be tempted by it . . . He just says, "I'm gonna negotiate a better deal." Well how? How exactly are you going to negotiate that? What magic wand do you have? And usually the answer is, he doesn't have an answer.

Trump no doubt liked the reference to a "magic wand." He certainly believed that he had just that in his use of deregulation, tax cuts, energy production, investment credits, trade fairness, and reductions in illegal immigration. And he assumed that he could negotiate "a better deal" by using the power and influence of the United States to insist on reciprocal trade.

Here Obama seemed once again almost to blame the victims of globalization, which he apparently felt was an organic and therefore unstoppable, fated process that would require some sort of magic to arrest. Demanding fair trade, or only legal immigration, or more contributions from NATO members, or producing more gas and oil was doable only in the unhinged fantasy of waving a "magic wand." Translated to red-state America, that was interpreted as something like "get over it."

Yet despite Obama's charges, just a few weeks earlier during the ongoing 2016 campaign, in a Caddell & Associates poll, 56 percent of Americans agreed that "in the 15 years since 9/11, the power and prestige of the United States as an international leader and power ha[d] declined." Less than 10 percent believed America's stature had increased. Only about a fourth of those polled thought it had remained about the same. Obama strangely seemed to have little clue as to why and how he had left the Democratic Party, at least at the congressional and state levels, weaker than at any time since 1920.

Implicit in Obama's rebuttal was that, for all the perceptions of the embittered, things were always getting better. Indeed, there was no denial in some areas that sunny appraisals were well founded. Empiricists like the political scientist Josef Joffe (*The Myth of America's Decline*) and the psychologist Steven Pinker (*The Better Angels of Our Nature*; *Enlightenment Now: The Case for Reason, Science, Humanism, and Progress*) amassed a great deal of data to show that in a material sense most Americans were now better fed, better educated, healthier, richer, and safer than ever before. Certainly, the current generation lives during a blessed era in which the individual has more choice, faces less physical danger, and has more rights than in previous eras of history. Such an upbeat picture may have been accurate in both relative and absolute senses. For example, that Apple, Facebook, Google, and Amazon are all American companies is no accident. And if cancer or heart disease, as in the manner of polio or AIDS, is to be cured or controlled, the answers will likely come from American researchers.

Americans have never led such affluent material lives—at least as measured by access to cell phones, big-screen TVs, cheap jet travel, and fast food. Obesity rather than malnutrition is the greater bane. Occasional urban mobs swarm electronics stores, not food markets. Americans spend more money on Botox, face-lifts, and tummy tucks than on the age-old scourges of smallpox and malaria.

If arriving space aliens looked at the small houses, one-car families, and primitive consumer goods of the 1950s, they would have thought the post-war United States, despite a balanced budget in 1956, was impoverished in comparison with an indebted contemporary America where consumers jostle for each new version of the iPhone and Air Jordan sneakers.

By any historical marker, the United States has it all: undreamed of new finds of natural gas and oil, the world's preeminent capacity for food production, continual technological wizardry, demographic growth, a superb military, the world's top-ranked research universities, and constitutional stability. How then did Trump the declinist explain to America that it was in deep trouble without his leadership?

Trump argued that what was wrong was not America's morality, but its spirit. The thrice-married Trump's personal life, suspect business ethos, and conspicuous appetites and tastes may have been right out of the Roman novelist Petronius's *Satyricon*. But Trump retained the American can-do confidence of building a huge border wall, or bringing back ossified industries, or sparking a manufacturing renaissance, of flooding the world with American oil and gas, or rebuilding airports, bridges, and roads as quickly and competently as he had the skating rink in New York's Central Park.

So Trump's point was not that America was not rich, but rather that it deserved to be even richer than it was—or at least that those Americans who were not now rich could be. To the degree homes were less safe than in the 1950s, streets were dirtier, homelessness more rampant, the culprit, in Trump's reductionist view, was not enough jobs and economic growth. Work in Trump's view was the font from which all cures flowed.

In his first speech to Congress in late February 2017, Trump made a sweeping promise: "To launch our national rebuilding, I will be asking the Congress to approve legislation that produces a $1 trillion investment in the infrastructure of the United States—financed through both public and private capital— creating millions of new jobs. This effort will be guided by two core principles: buy American, and hire American."

In sum, Trump's reductive decline was a writ against the present establishment that simply was psychologically unable to define victory, much less achieve it over America's rivals anymore. Trump saw his mission as replacing a "don't dare" timidity with a "can do" confidence.

For Trump, elite prognostications about the need for various reductions, rationings, or cutbacks were largely reflections of elite utopian planning that either did not understand or was repelled by American genius and confidence. After only weeks in office, Trump was claiming to a joint session of Congress that he had already changed the American mentality of inaction:

The time for small thinking is over. The time for trivial fights is behind us. We just need the courage to share the dreams that fill our hearts. The bravery to express the hopes that stir our souls. And the confidence to turn those hopes and dreams to

action. From now on, America will be empowered by our aspirations, not burdened by our fears—inspired by the future, not
bound by the failures of the past—and guided by our vision,
not blinded by our doubts.

Millions of voters had agreed with Trump that Americans
might have been the richest and freest generation in history,
but they were increasingly the most neurotic and mercurial as
well—and in need of a jolting recharge. Americans overthink
and triple-guess things to the point of paralysis. The majority
of Americans no longer worked with their hands, grew food,
or built things, and many were paid quite handsomely to avoid
such drudgery. But the result for society at large in terms of
lawmaking, education, and social planning was that abstraction
ruled over practicality. Nature remained theoretical and deified
rather than concrete and thus sometimes feared. Or so Trump
seemed to sense in his trust in the curative powers of industrial
production, manufacturing, and construction. In April 2017,
Trump had boasted to construction kingpins: "We're a nation
of builders, and it was about time we had a builder in the White
House."

Trump's theory of declinism originated from a variety of
sources. First was Trump's take on the 2016 election. In Electoral College terms, he thought that he had monitored the pulse
of the country far better than did his Republican primary opponents, and crafted messages that would resonate in swing states
of the deindustrialized Midwest. In the eyes of his orthodox
Republican rivals, Trump's chief heresy was his view that, despite an always expanding capitalism, in the here and now he
still believed in a peasant static notion of limited good: the pie
did not always get bigger, but rather some gorged more of its
slices at the expense of others. In electoral terms, the globalized
success of one nation often came at the expense of another not
so fortunate. In other words, he would get tough on our rivals

and enemies abroad, but not on other Americans, the victims of globalized forces beyond their control.

Trump drew some of his declinist and doctrinaire ideas from 2016 campaign advisors like the eccentric Stephen Bannon and Stephen Miller, two of the media's most caricatured and disliked politicos in America. Both were not initial Trump supporters. Yet by summer 2016, they had helped to codify and square the Trump circles. How could an undeniably wealthy America be doing terribly? How could a sybarite Trump credibly deplore spiritual decay? And how could conservative Republicans question the free-market doctrine of a beneficent unfettered capitalism?

For Miller and Bannon, who was fired by Trump (in August 2017 for allegedly chronically leaking to the press), the answer that resolved Trump's paradoxes was that the unrestrained personal indulgence and cultural leftism of the 1960s never quite died. True, protesters of the sixties had long ago outgrown their superficial indulgence. Most ex-hippies had never really absorbed much of the dogma anyway. The majority became traditionalists ("sold out") when they began working and supporting families. But some of the most influential college radicals had never evolved from their adolescent left-wing activism and doubled down on the political and personal indulgence of their youth.

The millionaire and thrice-divorced Bannon believed that these aging radicals had weaponized their sixties pop theories of radical economics and permissive culture as they grabbed the reins of twenty-first-century establishment power during both Republican and Democratic administrations. Just as those of the protest generation did their own thing as twentysomethings, now that same ethos of excess and selfishness had transmogrified from jeans, long hair, and T-shirts into buccaneer capitalism: the counterparts in business to what the essayist Roger Kimball had once called the "tenured radicals" from the sixties who now ran the universities.

The Trump team complaint continued that former leftist counterculture types had superimposed their values of the me generation onto—and thereby commandeered—Hollywood, Wall Street, Silicon Valley, and the deep state. These had become anti-Trump bastions where elitists made up rules that benefitted themselves at the expense of working-class Americans.

Trump's populist idea of cultural decline as a product of rigged economic, social, and trade policies caused a furor. It seemed to elevate Trump's attacks on China, an open border, deindustrialization, and the evil of globalism into some sort of unified theory of exploitation, almost in the traditional conspiratorial leftist sense. The old "hate America" crowd, according to Bannon, had gone from outsiders to insiders, and therefore caused a lot more damage in the boardrooms than they ever did in the streets.

In a 2017 *New Yorker* essay, Ryan Lizza offered a particularly hostile sketch of Bannon, after his departure from the White House, whom he saw as a two-bit Trump Svengali turning Trump's "mob of malcontents" into some sort of pseudo-political movement:

> Bannon saw it as his role to infuse Trump's victory with more meaning than the random result of the rise of a mob of malcontents. During the campaign last year, Trump would frequently ask Bannon and Miller, now Trump's top policy adviser in the White House, for quotes from the Founding Fathers or nineteenth-century Presidents that link them to Trump's policies. Aside from Jackson, they frequently leaned on Alexander Hamilton and Abraham Lincoln.

In an equally critical view in the *Guardian*, the political scientist Thomas Frank summed up Bannon's earlier declinist documentary, *Generation Zero*, as a crude stereotype:

Generation Zero asserts that history unfolds in a cyclical pattern, endlessly repeating itself. Historical crises (such as the Depression and Second World War) are said to give rise to triumphant and ambitious generations (think Levittown circa 1952), who make the mistake of spoiling their children, who then tear society apart through their decadence and narcissism, triggering the cycle over again. Or as the movie's trailer puts it: "In history, there are four turnings. The crisis. The high. The awakening. The unravelling. History repeats itself. The untold story about the financial meltdown."

Such observers had sought to demonize Bannon as a crank and a bigot, and his influence on Trump as dark and dangerous. Lizza claimed Bannon was, in fact, a white chauvinist and xenophobe. Frank thought him an embarrassing lightweight dabbling in ideas mostly beyond his half-educated reactionary mind.

The Trump team's sometime employment of the supplementary slogan "America First" was supposedly a window into its soul, given that the slogan only provided further ammunition to critics. The isolationist, anti-war, noninterventionist, and often anti-Semitic 1940 movement of Charles Lindbergh (which included at one time the likes of John F. Kennedy and Frank Lloyd Wright) had alleged that Jews and British imperialists had sought to force America into another war on the continent. Trump supposedly resurrected it.

Of course, Bannon likely would have seen such establishment progressive critics and purveyors of "fake news" as indicative of the very symptoms of the indulgent culture of the deep state that he had sought to indict. Lizza, for example, would shortly be forced to resign from the *New Yorker* and dismissed as a lecturer from Georgetown University for alleged sexual misconduct. Another journalist, Thomas Frank (not the political scientist mentioned above), was fired from CNN after he and two colleagues could not support their allegations in a story (later retracted by CNN) of a supposed ongoing investigation into some sort of pre-inaugural meeting, organized by Trump campaign advisor Anthony Scaramucci, between Trump officials and a purported director of a Russian-related investment fund.

What was revolutionary, however, about the Bannon thesis of decline was its purported right-wing solidarity with the working class, the traditional bread-and-butter constituency of the Democratic Party. In an interview with *Gentleman's Quarterly* after his firing, Bannon claimed: "The elites do not mind if we're on a decline. What is going to save this country is the working-class people and the lower middle-class people in this country who refuse to accept that America is in decline."

Translated, that meant that Trump's *conservative* declinists claimed the elites had brought the country down at the expense of the working class of its interior, a dogma that in political terms raised the specter of winning away blue-collar Democrats. Yet, far from being jaded, Trump's advisors were upbeat, even confident about restoring the fortunes of the red-state middle class, and, with it, America's as well. The muscles of America, Pennsylvania and Michigan, would rise again—and with them the United States itself!

So would Youngstown and Milwaukee. Perhaps the declinists saw that the culprit of inescapable national regression is rarely external causes like war, disease, or environmental catastrophe. Instead, states insidiously wither away from complacency and ennui brought on by globalized coastal affluence and leisure, which often lead to amnesia about the original sacrifices and protocols that were required for prosperity.

Yet throughout history, to the rare extent that declining nations have reversed course, their salvation was found not so much by reinventing themselves as by returning to the values that once made them singular—increasingly difficult in an age of affluence and bounty. Renewal focuses on investing more than consuming, limiting the size of state bureaucracies and en-titlements, restoring confidence in the currency, and avoiding costly optional wars. It also requires preserving the rule of law, enshrining meritocracy, and reinculcating national pride in an-cestral customs and traditions while ensuring citizens equality under the law.

In an age of instability—with China ascendant, rampant global terrorism abroad, and increasing racial and ethnic ten-sion and stagnant economic growth at home—could America return to its economic, cultural, and military preeminence while offering security, prosperity, and a continuation of American values to its citizens? "Make America Great Again" hinged on remembering what made America "great" in the first place, but also what has threatened to not make America great at various times in our recent history.

Also, implicit in Trump's message was that each generation chooses whether to unite around an ideal that transcends class, race, and regional divides, or to give in to the more natural state of tribal solidarities and prejudices. There is always a choice whether to abide by the Constitution or to "improve" and thus warp it. Americans are always pondering whether to liberate the American economy or to governmentalize it, and whether to honor or be ashamed of their all too human icons of the past. Can an often second-guessing, apologetic, and overly litigious America still feel confident that it can be good enough with-out having to be perfect? Every nation's next generation must decide whether to leave behind a country better than the one it inherited. And sometimes the resulting choices can either re-energize or finally put to rest their collective inheritance. Or so the Trump thinkers argued in their unifying theory of decline.

The media and the progressive movement, as well as Never Trump Republicans, intensely disliked Trump's populism and especially its declinist avatars like Stephen Bannon and Stephen Miller. Yet did it at least take seriously any of its writs—if for no other reason than to expropriate some of the more resonant themes as their own? Hardly.

The reaction again was predictable furor, or more often that in just a year Trump himself had sent the United States into decline! In an April 2016 essay, *New York Times* columnist David Brooks admitted that he was flabbergasted by the specter of his Republican Party nominating Donald Trump. He soon confessed that he had both missed his appeal and would try to understand it.

> The job for the rest of us is to figure out the right response. That means first it's necessary to go out into the pain. I was surprised by Trump's success because I've slipped into a bad pattern, spending large chunks of my life in the bourgeois strata—in professional circles with people with similar status and demographics to my own.

Yet subsequently Brooks would hardly venture outside his "bourgeois strata." When he did, he would confirm his earlier assumptions. Eighteen months after his confessional, in January 2018 Brooks would write of Trump's red-state base that questioned the wisdom of illegal immigration:

> It's more accurate to say restrictionists are stuck in a mono-cultural system that undermines their own values: industry, faithfulness and self-discipline. Of course, they react with defensive animosity to the immigrants who out-hustle and out-build them. You'd react negatively, too, if confronted with people who are better versions of what you wish you were yourself.

But objecting to illegal immigration and the widespread flaunting of US immigration law hardly equated to a psychological meltdown when "confronted with people who are better versions of what you wish you were yourself."

MSNBC news host Joy Reid (soon to face personal scandal with revelations of her past homophobic blog posts), however, had the most revealing pushback against Trump's idea of decline. Almost inadvertently, she seemed to agree with his symptomology and diagnosis, while arriving at a radically different prescribed treatment and prognosis. In short, Trump's notion of an imperiled traditional America was actually a good thing if it had at last ended the diseased norms of the past:

> In every way, Donald Trump is a president built for the past; a benighted, late 19th Century figure who spun his supporters a tale that he could restore a bygone era when coal fires burned, factories hummed, steel mills belched out soot and opportunity and a (white) man with a sturdy back, a high school diploma and a song in his heart could buy a little house, marry a little wife and have 3 cherry-cheeked kids he didn't ever have to cook or clean for, plus if he can afford it, a hot mistress on the side.

Reid went on to suggest that Trump's base was at long last dying. The present and future correctional trajectory of the country as a loose confederation of competing identity groups was long overdue. Obama's visions would supposedly survive Trump's brief detour.

Somehow Reid, whose immigrant father and mother came to the United States respectively from the Democratic Republic of Congo and British Guiana, had never quite reflected upon why they had done so. What was so attractive about an America before the age of Obama that had drawn them to its shores? Why did Reid assume that she had garnered such career and financial opportunities as a black woman and as the child of immigrants, even in a country so apparently flawed at its inception and irredeemable until its very recent history? Who, after all, had written America's singular constitution or created a uniquely stable and just political system, and what tradition in particular had established such a self-critical and constantly reinventive and adaptive culture?

Were there preferable less racist, less sexist, less homophobic, and more prosperous, more tolerant, and greener cultures and paradigms in anti- and non-Western cultures in Latin America and Africa? Where did Reid think the unique ideas of constitutional republicanism, individual rights, market capitalism, self-critique, and the idea of equality under the law derive? And why did she herself enjoy such freedom of speech in the past, even if to slur cruelly, first homosexuals, and then those who objected to her bigotry?

In conclusion, most Beltway insiders and New York grandees wrote off Trump's declinism as sophomoric. It was supposedly crafted and guided by a motley group of half-educated, would-be Nietzcheans. These autodidacts supposedly had painted a thin veneer of respectable thought onto what otherwise was a xenophobic, nativist, and racist red-state whine.

In that regard, they were as blind to the scope and resonance of Trump's signature ideology as they were to the inherent weakness and vulnerability of Hillary Clinton's candidacy. Trumpism, after all, did not exist in a vacuum. On Election Day it was also simply an alternative to something else. And that something else was increasingly seen to half the country as toxic by late 2016.

Democrats still needed something to beat Trump in 2016. As they would soon discover, that something was rapidly turning out to be a sort of nothing.

Chapter Eight

NEVER HILLARY

She was not happy—she never had been. Whence
came this insufficiency in life—this instantaneous
turning to decay of everything on which she leaned?
—Gustave Flaubert, *Madame Bovary*

How strange that Democrats during the primary were worried that Hillary Clinton was the only candidate who
could win the presidency, while Republicans were equally convinced that Donald Trump was the only one of their own who
could lose the general election. More likely, *any* major Democratic figure other than Clinton might have won, and *all* other
Republicans other than Trump might have likely lost.

Yet if the Republicans were to nominate Donald Trump, then
the sins of Hillary Clinton uniquely would cancel out his own.
And if Trump were to run as the fresh outsider sent in to drain
the swamp, then Clinton was the most likely among Democrats
to represent the tired landlord of the miasma.

If Trump seemed too old and unfit, then Clinton all the
more so. And if rumors of Russians tainted Trump's campaign,
then they were predated by Russian operatives angling with

the Clintons throughout Hillary's government service. In some sense, Hillary Clinton created the Trump presidency.

So aside from Trump's contentions that the United States was in decline and that only if Americans elected him could this regression be arrested, there was the matter of Hillary Clinton, his 2016 campaign opponent—and by July the only impediment between Trump and the presidency.

Trump certainly campaigned on issues. We have seen that he embraced existential themes and concrete wedge issues. And he had a divided and volatile electorate to leverage further. But Trump also had the controversial opponent Hillary Clinton, or rather the explicit argument that whatever Trump was, he certainly was not Hillary Clinton. The two were certainly a pair of contradictions in almost every aspect.

Physically, Trump's bulk fueled a monstrous energy; Hillary's girth sapped her strength. The reckless Trump did not drink; the careful Hillary freely did so. Hillary's "good-taste" carefully tailored suits and tastefully coiffed hair did not seem natural. Trump's "bad-taste" mile-long tie, orange tan, and combed-over yellow mane appeared paradoxically authentic.

Clinton was a creature of government, he often at war with it. Her misdeeds were far worse than her reputation; his reputation far worse than his misdeeds. He could be authentically gross, she inauthentically prim. And his low cunning was usually prescient, her sober assessments usually erroneous. Trump could certainly be cruel to individuals, but he was kind to the public. Clinton was kind to her particular friends, but cruel to people.

Trump not being Hillary proved to be a reassurance to half the country, in a way it might not have if another Democrat (a Joe Biden perhaps) had won the nomination. Indeed, Trump was clairvoyant about how the power of Hillary's negatives would empower his own candidacy (and later his presidency), and how the classical fallacy of *tu quoque* ("you do it too!") would help to nullify his own shortcomings and scandals.

Remember, there were always two Hillary Clintons who faced Donald Trump, both before and even after the election.

The first was her official persona. Clinton's résumé by summer 2015, at least in political terms, was far more impressive than Trump's: Yale Law graduate, accomplished female attorney, First Lady of Arkansas, First Lady of the United States, US senator from New York, former presidential candidate, and four years as secretary of state. By Washington's traditional standards of comparison, she was clearly more qualified than Donald Trump for the highest office in 2016. But, then again, she was also clearly more qualified in 2008 than had been Barack Obama.

Clinton was bright, savvy, a veteran campaigner, politically malleable, combative, and as knowledgeable of how Washington worked as any. For most of her life, Clinton's résumé had won raves. She was usually praised as an ideal candidate in the abstract, in the subjunctive, and in the future—but not so much when in the concrete, the indicative, and the present.

Her wayward spouse, Bill Clinton, was many things. But one thing he was *not* was politically obtuse. In fact, his innate political guile rivaled or surpassed Trump's own. Yet given his marital shortcomings and public scandals, Hillary bragged in the abstract about her husband's rare electoral savvy as much as in the concrete she ignored it—fatally so in 2016.

In private interviews with sympathetic hosts or at small gatherings of Wall Street investors and bicoastal progressives, Hillary Clinton often wowed her audiences by resonating favorite left-wing themes—studded with wink-and-nod reassurances that she was still neither a Bernie Sanders socialist nor an Elizabeth Warren bomb thrower.

Her money-raising shtick was to run to the left of where Bill Clinton had governed. Yet privately she kept assuring moneyed

interests that his 1990s tenure would be her own model once
she was elected. Indeed, in May 2016 she had overtly promised
that she would put Bill "in charge of revitalizing the economy,
because, you know, he knows how to do it"—an odd admission
of spousal dependency from the likely first female president and
an avowed feminist.

But mostly Hillary in 2016 sought to emulate Barack Obama's
landmark pathway to the presidency by becoming by near ac-
clamation the first female commander in chief. Her identity politics signature slogan "I'm With Her" reminded voters of their
chance for the third time in eight years to again make history.
Her twin campaign themes for supposedly radically new times
were (1) her gender, and (2) not being the uncouth and typical
rich white male Donald J. Trump.

But whereas Trump also found not being Hillary Clinton
useful to his campaign's other benchmark agendas, she had few
other alternative themes than being female and not Trump.

Did Clinton have issues that polled over 50 percent with the
American public? Was she for fixing or expanding controversial Obamacare? Should taxes under a president Clinton go up
or down? More or less fracking? How was she going to restart
a sluggish economy? Was she for or against NAFTA and the
Trans-Pacific Partnership trade deal? What exactly, if anything,
would she do about illegal immigration and a veritable open
border—given her past calls for strict border enforcement? And
given Clinton's tenure at the State Department, were the Libyan intervention and the Russian reset something to run on or
refute? Were "strategic patience" and "lead from behind" viable
foreign policy strategies to be continued in her presidency? Did
she intend to defang Kim Jong-un or renounce the Iran deal, or
continue the Barack Obama/John Kerry protocols? Was she for
a smaller or larger Pentagon budget, more or less NATO contributions? For most of the campaign such questions were never
raised, much less answered.

Then there was the flip side of Hillary, a quite different public persona altogether. In a December 2015 CNN poll, at her zenith of overwhelming positive publicity, and possessing a huge war chest, Hillary still only led an already pilloried Trump in an envisioned matchup by 49 percent to 39 percent. In that same CNN poll, Hillary Clinton's favorability ratings were underwater: 47 percent unfavorable versus 39 percent favorable. She was not yet as polarizing as Trump and would not be until late 2018 when her favorability ranking dipped to 36 percent, but she was also not nearly as likeable as other Democrats such as Joe Biden.

Americans had first been introduced to this other side of Hillary in the 1992 campaign when her husband, Arkansas governor Bill Clinton, beat incumbent George H. W. Bush, mostly by running as a centrist, capitalizing on Ross Perot's third-party candidacy that was bleeding Bush's working-class conservative support dry, and ignoring Hillary's social agendas in favor of "it's the economy, stupid" bread-and-butter issues. In her initial political incarnation in the early 1990s, Hillary had represented the left wing of the Democratic Party. She had sought to reassure progressives in private that behind her southerner husband's centrist pivots was a hardcore liberal such as herself.

On the primary stump in 1992, Hillary had tangled with rival California governor Jerry Brown, who questioned her past ethics at the Little Rock, Arkansas, Rose Law Firm. In her contorted defense, Hillary somehow had managed gratuitously to offend 30 or 40 percent of the electorate with a condescending putdown of stay-at-home moms: "I suppose I could have stayed home and baked cookies and had teas, but what I decided to do was to fulfill my profession, which I entered before my husband was in public life."

Clinton seemed dense to the riposte that staying home and raising America's future generations was far preferable to venturing out to engage in questionable ethics. Hillary's ability to alienate and offend in gratuitous, *ex tempore* generalizations would be her trademark for the next three decades—*and reappear with catastrophic results in 2016*. Indeed, off-the-cuff venting about the parochial habits of average Americans was Hillary Clinton's *hamartia*, her "fatal flaw" that fueled her hubris and earned nemesis at the appropriate future moment.

As First Lady, Hillary was engulfed in periodic controversies that still have not all abated a quarter century later. They were legion, both those committed before the 1992 election and afterward: cattlegate, Whitewater, filegate, travelgate, the missing Rose Law Firm documents, and on and on. These were real abuses and shortcuts, and they did not cease when Clinton left the White House.

After her run for the Senate in the 2000 Democratic primaries, almost immediately charges arose that husband and president Bill Clinton had earlier pardoned Puerto Rican and Hasidic Jewish lawbreakers who would likely support her candidacy. Her former finance director David Rosen was once indicted on criminal charges alleging a variety of unethical fundraising schemes.

There were *three* chronic themes in all of Clinton's lifelong imbroglios. One, she not only lied about them, but prevaricated to such a degree that her various narratives could never be reconciled. Claiming that she beat four-trillion-to-one odds in parlaying a $1,000 investment into a $100,000 payoff in less than a year on the cattle futures market was absurd. More absurd was suggesting that she had learned to become such a sophisticated speculator by making trades herself and reading financial newspapers. Most absurd was not paying taxes on her profits.

Two, Hillary never seemed to learn from her scandals. They instead were chalked up to a "vast right-wing conspiracy" or some sort of dark reactionary forces that had conspired against her. Yet, for example, in the Monica Lewinsky debacle, neither the *American Spectator* magazine nor special counsel Ken Starr had forced her husband to have carnal relations with a young intern in a room off the Oval Office, or to have allegedly groped another job seeker in a White House corridor, or to have lied under oath about such misadventures.

If the nation was given absurd explanations about cattle futures in 1993, it was given even more ridiculous alibis a near quarter century later about an improper private email server while she was serving as secretary of state. When asked by reporters whether Clinton had wiped clean any of her home-brew-server emails currently under FBI subpoena, she laughed as if the question was absurd: "What? Like with a cloth or something? I don't know how it works digitally at all." But, in fact, her aides were to employ an open-source cleaning software known as BleachBit that would make it almost impossible for federal investigators to recover over thirty thousand deleted emails under subpoena.

When Bernie Sanders ran a serious campaign against Hillary Clinton in 2016, it was inevitable that there were going to be attempts to use the Democratic establishment to warp the primary process to ensure a Clinton victory. And according to former Democratic National Committee chairwoman Donna Brazile, the party and the Clinton campaign colluded to create conditions favorable for her nomination.

Three, Hillary assumed that her exalted position and deep-state credentials gave her exemptions from accountability, to the point that she grew irate at even the thought of an accusation. If Donald Trump had to be stopped, then what was so wrong about hiring Fusion GPS to enlist Christopher Steele to draw on Russian dirt mongers for fake intelligence and to get the FBI and DOJ involved, and thus find ways to leak rumors before the election?

Why could not her husband meet Attorney General Lynch in a secret tarmac meeting while she was under investigation by Lynch's subordinate, FBI director James Comey—given everyone involved likely hated Donald Trump? If Bernie Sanders would surely lose the 2016 election and thereby ensure a Trump presidency, then what was wrong with warping the Democratic National Committee oversight of the primaries or receiving a CNN town hall question in advance?

Hillary, a persuasive talker in preset televised interviews, was nonetheless unimpressive in press conferences, and a poor public speaker, both in how she spoke and what she said. Once she left the womb of sympathetic interviewers and audiences, Hillary often sounded shrill rather than resonating on the campaign trail. In front of a black audience, she adopted an inner-city patois. Before white working-class voters she fell back on her "y'all" Arkansas mode. But often Clinton just seemed tone deaf. When asked whether the mob's macabre execution of Gaddafi had anything to do with her own visit to post-Gaddafi Libya, she rolled her eyes and said, "No," and then followed that sarcasm with her signature off-putting laugh. "I'm sure it did."

Clinton offered contradictory narratives about the causes of the killings of four Americans in the September 11, 2012, pre-election attack on the consulate in Benghazi, by attributing—in public and personally to the families of the deceased—the attack to a spontaneous riot over a provocative but otherwise mostly irrelevant internet documentary. That story fobbed the cause off on a supposedly right-wing provocateur, rather than on the failure of Obama administration intelligence and security officials—and would linger as a 2016 campaign issue.

Yet prior to that version, Clinton had already been briefed that the assault was a preplanned al-Qaeda-related hit, made possible by poor security preparations, in part arguably due to her own laxity of oversight. In fact, right after the attack she had likely assured the Egyptian prime minister Hisham Qandil and her own daughter, Chelsea, that the deaths were due to a terrorist assault.

During the Benghazi congressional hearings, Clinton grew frustrated that she could never quite square the circle that she or her subordinates had not acted on pleas for beefed-up security long before, and even right during, the firefight. Whether by intent or not, she almost sounded irritated by the deaths of the four Americans: "With all due respect, the fact is we had four dead Americans. Was it because of a protest or was it because of guys out for a walk one night who decided that they'd go kill some Americans? What difference at this point does it make?" The latter unfortunate callous sentence, especially when blared out of context, would also become a Trump 2016 sound bite.

In 2008, Clinton had been accused by the Obama campaign of fueling rumors that he might be a Muslim, while clumsily appealing to "white" working-class voters. In the 2016 election she simply wrote off her former would-be constituents as "deplorables."

Clinton dismissed coal miners as doomed, and seemed fixated on blaming red-state electorates that had never appreciated her candidacy. Nonetheless, through most of the summer of 2016 she led Trump in various polls by between eight and ten points—and was weekly pronounced as the sure next president. But such a substantial lead was never stable, given that Hillary Clinton—every bit as much as the volatile Donald Trump—always had the ability to say or do something that might bring her opponent within striking distance, usually in a way connected with her most recent scandals.

Hillary, as the non-Trump, usually made four charges against Trump: (1) he was a shady businessman; (2) he had lied about his past personal and professional scandals; (3) he seemed to be a beneficiary of Russian collusion; and (4) he was a chronic womanizer and sexual harasser.

The problem with all such charges was not that they were all necessarily false. Rather, the likelihood was that even if true they would easily boomerang back on Hillary herself—and thereby have the perverse effect of almost exonerating the less reputable Trump. Trump campaigned as if he were a known sinner, Hillary as an underappreciated saint. Sinners sin; saints do not.

During the 2015–16 campaign, it became clear that Russian-related interests had purchased a Canadian energy corporation, Uranium One, as a clumsy means to gain some access to strategic North American uranium deposits. During and after these negotiations, Russians with ties to the Kremlin mysteriously had given multimillion-dollar gifts to the Clinton Foundation, and an exorbitant honorarium of $500,000 to Bill Clinton to speak just once in Moscow. For the next three years, the scandal was fought in the media. The Clintonites claimed that either Hillary, as secretary of state, had only minimal authority to approve the deal, or that the sale did not threaten America's rather limited strategic reserves of uranium, or that gifts and honoraria were unrelated to those with stakes in the transaction.

Critics pointed out that when the sale was pending and finished, money flowed in various ways to the Clinton Foundation and Bill Clinton. But well before—and well after—the election? No one was interested in paying the Clintons or their affiliates much at all.

The real political problem for Hillary Clinton, however, was that such deals made it hard to find sufficient resonance with the charge that Trump's various suspect and often failed brand deals—Trump University, Trump beverages, Trump steaks, *Trump* magazine, Trump airlines—were all either poorly run or unethical enterprises. Indeed, Uranium One was emblematic of how Clinton herself had seen her own net worth soar from near zero in 2001 to $50 million in 2010, while the Clinton Foundation had raised over $2 billion by 2016—and those facts mitigated the charges that Trump, Inc., was singularly crooked.

Hillary and Bill Clinton since 2000 together had made a quarter billion dollars in gross income, without directly being involved in any businesses other than consulting and speaking or renting out their public name in the fashion that private citizen Trump more ostentatiously sold his. The subtext for potential investors was always that one day Hillary would follow Bill into the White House, where scandals died and patronage was reborn.

Donald Trump may have played fast and loose when asked about his net worth, his income tax returns, his charitable contributions, and the size and nature of the suspect Trump Foundation. But when Clinton understandably tried to press him on those vulnerabilities, he hit back with the much better publicized Clinton stonewalling about using a private and illegal email server while secretary of state, destroying over thirty thousand emails, some of which were requested by investigators, smashing mobile devices, transmitting classified information on an unsecured server, and lying about such wrongdoing.

Again, the subtext was that voters knew Trump was a known sinner, while Hillary—as an ex–First Lady, senator, and secretary of state—was supposed to be something more above reproach. Once more, it would have been far more difficult for Trump to have run against a putative "Crooked Joe Biden" or "Crooked Bernie Sanders."

The more Hillary tried to explain the inexplicable, from bleaching hard drives to communicating only about yoga and weddings on her destroyed emails, the less she seemed believable—and thus the less credible she found herself in impugning Trump's business ethics. Trump constantly hammered her on the issue of fairness—why had national hero General David Petraeus had his career ruined for showing a private citizen (and biographer and paramour) his classified notes, while Hillary Clinton was exempt from the greater sin of sending classified documents over an unclassified server? Trump argued that whereas no known damage to US security came from Paula Broadwell's illicit use of Petraeus's notebooks, the Russians and others likely read Hillary's emails, including those touching on US security. Note as well that in 2016 Rod Rosenstein, deputy attorney general in the Obama administration, prosecuted marine general James Cartwright on charges of either by intent or clumsily leaking information about cyberattacks on Iranian nuclear facilities—a charge Cartwright denied, but later pled guilty to making false statements to federal investigators.

On the collusion issue, Hillary was also especially vulnerable and hardly in a position to suggest that Trump worked with the Russians. She, not Trump, had pushed the mistranslated "reset" button in Geneva, Switzerland, in 2009, memorializing the new Obama administration outreach to Vladimir Putin as a rejection of George W. Bush's supposedly prior and unnecessary polarizing punishment of Russian aggression against Georgia on behalf of South Ossetia.

In fact, as secretary of state, Hillary Clinton had carried out reset as near appeasement of an aggressive Vladimir Putin. The Obama administration had looked the other way as Putin annexed Crimea and eastern Ukraine. It had dropped missile defense plans with Eastern Europe. Barack Obama, in the third 2012 general election debate, had mocked Mitt Romney for suggesting that Russia was a current existential enemy ("When you were asked, what's the biggest geopolitical threat facing America, you said 'Russia.' Not Al-Qaeda; you said 'Russia.' And, the 1980s are now calling to ask for their foreign policy back, because, the Cold War's been over for twenty years.").

Obama also had been caught on a hot mic seemingly promising a quid pro quo collusionary deal with outgoing Russian president Dmitri Medvedev, apparently to back off from missile defense in Eastern Europe in exchange for quiet Russian behavior during the Obama reelection effort (Obama: "On all these issues, but particularly missile defense, this, this can be solved, but it's important for him [Vladimir Putin] to give me space . . . This is my last election. After my election, I have more flexibility.").

No one quite knew why and how the Obama administration had been so passive in the face of Russian hacking and cyberattacks. Certainly the 2014 tepid response to the invasions of Crimea

and eastern Ukraine came after Obama's reelection promise that
"after my election, I have more flexibility." It was a hard sell for an
architect of Russian reset and a purchaser of Russian campaign
dirt to accuse Donald Trump of being soft on Russia.

Yet it was on matters of sexual impropriety where the compromised Clinton candidacy nullified much of her potential
leverage over Donald Trump's randy past. Trump had likely
had several affairs and may well have paid to keep them quiet
with purchased "nondisclosure agreements" concluded after
his decision to run for office. Trump had talked dirty. And he
was inadvertently caught on tape doing so in a cruel, often sexist
manner. He had been married three times and been in public
spats with females as diverse as Rosie O'Donnell and Megyn
Kelly. The *Access Hollywood* tape, released just hours before the
second presidential debate of 2016, revealed that Trump in private had crudely and callously joked about what he thought were
supposedly lusty perks—among them grabbing and groping—
that his celebrity status earned from allegedly sexually eager females. Tapes of long-ago appearances on Howard Stern's radio
shows did not suggest Trump would mature into presidential
timber. Later as president he got into a nasty spat with porn star
Stormy Daniels, which at one point saw Trump dismiss Daniels
as "horse face" in reply to her often ribald and media-driven
accusations against him.

Yet Hillary's attacks on Trump as a disgusting aggressive phi-
landerer ("This is horrific. We cannot allow this man to become
president!") earned her Trump ripostes that her husband Bill
was not just a womanizer, but often a violent one. Some of Bill's
transgressions, unlike Trump's, were not merely in his private
space, but inside the White House itself. And their cover-ups
were not just confined to him, but reliant on help from his government staff and, indeed, Hillary herself, who sometimes demonized Bill's lovers and encouraged the media to use the "nuts
and sluts" strategy of deprecating them. Hillary apparently

never appreciated that when she went after Trump's sins of the flesh, it would quickly prove a losing proposition.

In the age of Harvey Weinstein—a close Clinton supporter and associate—a president Trump by October 2017 should have been persona non grata. But the #MeToo movement of out-raged women coming forth in 2017 to castigate their sexual tor-mentors sometimes unexpectedly turned out to be an in-house progressive affair. Liberal male feminists often won the extra wage of hypocrisy once exposed as the most notorious gropers and grabbers. Feminists were especially outraged that supposed liberal sexual transgressors, on their side no less, like Al Fran-ken, Garrison Keillor, Mark Halperin, Matt Lauer, Ryan Lizza, Charlie Rose, and Tavis Smiley, had apparently relied on their progressive *fides* to deflect any thought that they were in fact sexual harassers, if not in some cases predators.

Trump, in contrast, was what he always was: a rich Manhat-tan player, not a traditional family man and husband. He con-fessed freely to "locker room talk" and almost seemed to admit that vulgar men like himself were always tempted to take liber-ties with aspiring quid pro quo models, job seekers, and beauty queens. More importantly, in political terms, Trump supporters had already calibrated Trump's indiscretions in their support for his populist agenda.

A few hours after the incriminating *Access Hollywood* tape went viral, at the second presidential debate the Trump team had not only brought into the front row of spectators Bill Clin-ton's past victims of alleged sexual violence and assault—Paula Jones, Kathleen Willey, and Juanita Broaddrick—but, far more importantly, also Kathy Shelton (the latter a victim of rape at age twelve by a former client of Hillary Clinton's). Clinton had cru-elly once bragged on tape about how she had gotten Shelton's obviously guilty attacker off with a light sentence. The preteen victim was supposedly "emotionally unstable." And Hillary added, "Children in early adolescence tend to exaggerate or romanticize." Or as a middle-aged Shelton put it at Trump's staged pre-debate press conference: "At twelve years old, Hillary put me through something that you'd never put a twelve-year-old through."

This was pure and shameless Trump showmanship—and a gambit beyond the imagination and ethos of any other Republican presidential candidate. Yet somehow a supposedly politically lethal revelation about Trump's crudity had now prompted a replay of the Clintons' own sexism and far greater callousness.

After the election, the sheer number of tabloid harassers identified in the age of Harvey Weinstein quite counterintuitively tended to contextualize Trump's former liaisons, even those with the porn star Stormy Daniels and Karen McDougal, a former Playmate of the Year. When liberal icons such as Tom Brokaw were demonized in the media, and Bill and Hillary Clinton were back in the news in the context of sexual harassment and sexual violence, who had time to worry about an old tape or a long-ago alleged consensual sordid moment with Stormy Daniels?

Some frustrated Democratic kingpins retroactively blamed Bill Clinton's recklessness of decades past (and by extension Hillary Clinton's empowerment of him) for so lowering the bar on matters of presidential sexual antics that progressives now had little ammunition against candidate and later president Donald Trump. Or as New York senator Kirsten Gillibrand, a former political client and follower of Bill Clinton and a would-be future presidential candidate, finally confessed a year after the election: "Things have changed today, and I think under those circumstances there should be a very different reaction. And I think in light of this conversation [her statement that President Bill Clinton should have resigned after the Lewinsky affair], we should have a very different conversation about President Trump, and a very different conversation about allegations against him."

Later in June 2018, Bill Clinton, on a book tour, would oddly confirm Gillibrand's charges, by defending disgraced groper former senator Al Franken and sanctimoniously revisiting his own Monica Lewinsky escapades. As feminists heightened their attacks against President Trump, Clinton, in clumsy fashion, inadvertently seemed to confess that he had once operated under standards in the past that would have earned him quite different consequences in the present. Indeed, he almost appeared to suggest that making women feel uncomfortable in the workplace was something that he himself had once not necessarily considered inappropriate: "I think the norms have really changed in terms of, what you can do to somebody against their will . . . You don't have to physically assault somebody to make them, you know, uncomfortable at work or at home or in their other—just walking around." At almost any moment, before or after the election, Bill Clinton referenced his past behavior in a manner that was almost always an embarrassment to Hillary Clinton.

In sum, Hillary Clinton's nomination served as a sort of scandal vaccination for Trump against a variety of accusations. Given the checkered Clinton past, her candidacy in one fell swoop had neutralized many of Trump's liabilities. Not being Hillary Clinton had at least become by November 2016 better even than not being Donald Trump. And by 2018, in the second year of the Trump presidency, Trump being President Trump in retrospect has seemed to voters at least preferable to Hillary being President Clinton.

By late 2017 and early 2018, defeated candidate Hillary Clinton was polling quite unfavorably. Oddly, she was still the subject of polls because in a series of endless book and speaking tours, she seemed to be replaying her loss each week—and thereby reminding half the country why they had been right to have gambled on Trump. In most polls by 2018, only 36–39 percent of the electorate viewed the ex-nominee positively. Indeed, her negatives had insidiously become higher than were Donald

Trump's own dismal ratings. Clinton's speaking fees had plummeted by 90 percent, from a high of $250,000 after she had left the office of secretary of state to $25,000 after losing the election. That drop-off had again suggested either that she had no further public offices to leverage for donors, or that her losing campaign had reminded the public how nondescript a personality she had become, or both.

Still, for the first two years following her November 2016 defeat, Hillary Clinton gave numerous interviews, public speeches, and book signings for her new memoir, *What Happened*. The common theme of her book and appearances was an ever-expanding array of excuses as to why she had lost the election—all of them omitting any mention that half the country over the past eight years had become alienated from progressives, or at least in November 2016 saw Clinton as more of the same problem rather than an innovative solution.

Indeed, the list of Clinton's culprits for her defeat kept growing in the months after her loss. She variously blamed (1) the Russians, (2) James Comey, (3) the cash-poor Democratic National Committee, (4) red-state racists and sexists, (5) the Electoral College, (6) the WikiLeaks email revelations, (7) right-wing media, (8) the mainstream media in general, (9) Republican efforts at voter suppression, (10) right-wing donors, (11) Stephen Bannon and Breitbart News, (12) Facebook, (13) Bernie Sanders, (14) Barack Obama, (15) Netflix, (16) fake news accounts, (17) the Republican National Committee, (18) her own campaign staff, (19) Jill Stein, a third-party left-wing 2016 presidential candidate, (20) Anthony Weiner, (21) socialist Democrats, and an array of more scapegoats.

Rarely did Clinton admit that she had proven a weak candidate: a poor speaker on the stump, reckless in her ad hoc quips, physically frail and secretive about her health, and a candidate without a message who relied on overwhelming cash advantages to foolishly seek to roll up a mandate by campaigning in solidly red states while neglecting purple states that would alone decide the election. Added to all that, she had neglected the most seasoned advisor in her circle: husband Bill Clinton. He had warned her young and inexperienced circle of tech and data "experts" that they needed to camp out in the Midwest swing states and craft messages for the middle class.

It was easy *post factum* to see why Hillary had tarnished her brand from a speech she gave in early March 2018 in Mumbai, India, explaining yet again why she had lost the 2016 election:

> If you look at the map of the United States, there is all that red in the middle, places where Trump won. What that map doesn't show you is that I won the places that own two-thirds of America's Gross Domestic product. I won the places that are optimistic, diverse, dynamic, moving forward. And his whole campaign, Make America Great Again, was looking backwards. You don't like black people getting rights, you don't like women getting jobs, you don't want to see that Indian American succeeding more than you are, whatever that problem is, I am going to solve it.

Here Clinton was reminding the public back home that her insulting "deplorables" and "irredeemables" rant of 2016 had been no accident. In her own narcissistic logic, a vote against Hillary, for any reason whatsoever, was a vote for racism or sexism or for purported economic losers in the red states. And the idea that a voter in Ohio or Wisconsin had voted for Donald Trump out of jealousy of a wealthier immigrant from India was simply preposterous.

Because 52 percent of married white women had voted for Trump, Clinton went on to blame supposedly complacent wives as mere appendages of their husbands. That was an ironic

charge from a spouse whose chronically philandering husband
had counted not just on Hillary's forbearance, but on her joint
efforts to demonize Bill's female liaisons:

> All of a sudden white women who were going to vote for me
> and frankly standing up to the men in their lives and the men
> in their workplaces, were being told "She's going to jail, you
> don't want to vote for her. That'd be terrible, you can't vote
> for that."

Note the eventual logic of Hillary's lose-lose dichotomy:
somehow, she had managed to infer that white women were less
autonomous than other nonwhite married women. At the same
time, she was charging that their white husbands cared more
about legal impropriety as a disqualifying presidential trait than
did other nonwhite men. In sum, Clinton had somehow suc-
ceeded in stereotyping the entire national demographic: both
men and women, white and nonwhite.

Seventeen months after her defeat, Hillary was still giving
new indications why she had lost the election. She often spoke
recklessly abroad as the 2018 midterm elections loomed at home.
Dozens of Democratic congressional and senatorial candidates
had long ago moved on and were at that moment running in districts and states carried by Donald Trump in the 2016 election.
It did them little good that Hillary Clinton, their former standard-bearer, was now on foreign soil trashing the very people
and regions necessary for their own upcoming elections. Democratic senator Claire McCaskill, in a tough reelection fight in red
Missouri (carried by Trump in 2016 by over eighteen points),
summed up their frustrations when she dryly noted of Hillary:
"For those of us that are in states that Trump won we would really appreciate if she would be more careful and show respect to
every American voter and not just the ones who voted for her."

Aside from pandering to a foreign audience at the expense of her own country, Hillary Clinton's lectures abroad also illustrated a few central narratives of her life after the 2016 election.

One, Clinton seemed obsessed with providing excuses why she had blown a supposedly huge lead.

Two, Hillary, like many conservative Never Trumpers, seemed to blame voters in red states for sharing the same pathologies as Donald Trump. In this way, her frenetic post-election and ad hominem barnstorming was an unexpected gift to a beleaguered President Donald Trump. It periodically reminded voters that for all Trump's early stumbling and setbacks, they had understandably voted for an alternative, any alternative, to Hillary Clinton. She certainly did not accept a stunning defeat in the professional and gracious manner of a Jimmy Carter in 1980, Mike Dukakis in 1988, George H. W. Bush in 1992, John McCain in 2008, or Mitt Romney in 2012.

Three, by never addressing candidly or transparently her own Uranium One, email, Clinton Foundation, and Fusion GPS scandals, Clinton's ongoing and unresolved liabilities deflected public attention from Trump's own ethical dilemmas. It was an irony of the Trump ascendency that Hillary Clinton, who had done so much to elect him as a candidate, now as a poor loser did even more for him as president by continuously regaming the lost 2016 election.

Finally, Hillary, as a Clinton, fed into the growing bipartisan consensus that the American presidency was not supposed to be a hereditary or dynastic office. Just as the implosion of the Jeb Bush candidacy had been an expression that two Bush presidencies were enough, so too Hillary's failure, both in 2008 and 2016, marked a similar popular pushback against a third-term Clinton presidency. In Hillary Clinton's case, in lieu of an agenda the candidate herself had remained the chief issue—a flawed messenger without a compensating message, and thus an unforeseen endowment to both candidate and president Trump.

In the next chapter, we shall see how some reluctant Trump voters were able to separate Trump the messenger from the Trump message, while other fervent supporters saw them as properly inseparable and complementary. Up to a point, most had overlooked Trump's character flaws to ensure new agendas and a long-needed pushback against a biased media, and would do so again during his presidency. But would that always be true? The media and the Never Trump camp kept waiting for that magical moment, the "bombshell" when the messenger finally destroyed rather than enhanced his message.

Chapter Nine

THE NEW/OLD CRUDE
MESSENGER

"I approve of almost everything he has done,"
my son remarked, "and I disapprove of almost
everything he has said."
— Joseph Epstein,
WSJ Opinion, February 27, 2018

In an earlier chapter, the "Modern Day Presidential," we
saw how Trump had used his tough tweets and unconven-
tional speech and behavior to his advantage. But was there also
a downside in the way he talked and acted that might nullify
his otherwise undeniable achievements, ensuring that he rarely
won a majority approval rating from the public?

Everyone agreed that Donald Trump could become crude.
A third of his supporters after the election expressed a personal dislike for Trump. But few could agree on whether his
crudity was unprecedented in presidential history, whether it
was a symptom of a crass society, or of an electronically wired
world in which presidential burps became internet headlines,
or whether it was long overdue retaliation. The debates framed

questions about whether Trump the messenger was separate from Trump's message, and whether Trump was new crude or just a newer version of the old crude.

For the Left, Trump's supposedly odious character—his comportment, vocabulary, feuds and fights—was a force multiplier of his purportedly odious message, a veritable repeal of much of the Obama agenda between 2009 and 2017. Yet for most of the Never Trump Right, the reprobate Trump messenger cancelled out what otherwise might have been his tolerably conservative message. And as we have seen previously, for nearly half the country who voted for Trump, his message was usually indistinguishable from Trump himself—or rather impossible without him.

The common denominator of all three of these positions is that Trump was not a neutral actor or subordinate to his message. In truth, he was one of the most controversial political figures in American post-war history—and he was inseparable from Trumpism.

The progressive writ against Trump the man was that he marked a new low in American political and presidential history, and similarly personified a singularly odious message. The supposedly socially aware could not stomach the fact that millions of Americans bought into a roguish messenger in the same manner that they mindlessly were deluded by ad men into going into hock for advertised consumer goods. But for this proposition of Trump's singular personal dreadfulness to be valid, a few corollaries also had to be true.

One, critics insisted that the sensationalism and tabloid stories that surrounded Trump were *not* mostly a result of our peculiar post-modern age. Much less were they artifacts of our present electronically connected era. Supposedly, the monster Trump had no one but himself to blame for his bad press: slanted coverage alone had not made a monster into a monstrous ogre.

Two, the progressive writ was also that even controversial past presidents had never reached Trump's ethical and spiritual lows. Trump was purportedly *sui generis*. Even had we known everything about a president Kennedy or the inner life of Woodrow Wilson, they still could not have possibly reached the nadir of Trump.

Three, his negatives were such that his personality could only cancel out his message. To the degree that the proverbial mob was fooled into liking Trump's agenda, it would have been fooled even more had he not been such an ignoramus and a knave. Eventually, Trump's personal negatives would come back to haunt him and derail Trumpism.

Were any of these progressive assumptions at all true?

Examine the present pantheon of progressive icons. Strip away their reliance on liberal media protection and transfer them instead into the present age of tabloid promiscuity and cyber omnipresence. Would we now have a very different view of their presidencies?

Prior to the late twentieth century, the press colluded with the office of the presidency to hide inconvenient realties from the public. The progressive Woodrow Wilson administration likely would never have completed its two elected terms had it operated on media protocols common just a half century later.

For nearly a year during the failing health and death of First Lady Ellen Axson Wilson, the president fell into a state of debilitating depression, carefully hidden from the press. Much later, during the last seventeen months of Wilson's presidency, despite valiant efforts, he was more or less unable to fulfill his duties due to a series of strokes that left him partially paralyzed and visually impaired. Those realities were carefully hidden from the public by the efforts of his second wife, Edith Bolling Wilson, and physician Dr. Cary Grayson. In the present case, we know that Trump is neither comatose nor is Melania running the country.

The country never learned the full extent of Franklin Delano
Roosevelt's paralysis. Much less did it know of FDR's past and
ongoing affairs—the mechanics of which were sometimes carried out in the White House, and with the skillful aid of his own
daughter Anna. By fall 1944, Roosevelt, seeking a fourth term,
was suffering from a series of life-threatening conditions. Wor-
rying that the public would not vote yet again for a terminally
ill president, sympathetic journalists and military physicians
covered up Roosevelt's illnesses—on the operating theory that
FDR would survive long enough to get elected to a fourth term
and ensure a continued Democratic administration.

Clearly in our age of the internet and social media, and an
inquisitorial media, Ivanka Trump could not have been helping
her father conduct a stealth affair in the White House, while
conspiring to hide his likely terminal illness from the public.

John F. Kennedy, by contemporary standards, was a serial
sexual harasser, if not a likely assaulter. While physically in the
White House he carried on sexual trysts with subordinates and
others without security clearances, mostly with the full knowledge of the complacent White House press corps. One former
JFK intern, Mimi Alford, later wrote a memoir describing losing her virginity at nineteen years of age to the president in the
White House presidential bed. On his direction and prompt,
and in his audience, she was leveraged into performing oral in-
tercourse in the White House swimming pool on his aide David
Powers, who routinely set up the president's extramarital trysts.
For all his alleged goatishness, Trump is currently not orches-
trating group sexual encounters in the White House basement.

Beneath JFK's cheery comportment and tanned physique
was a seriously physically ill president, dependent on a number of potent prescription painkillers and steroids, all carefully
hidden from public knowledge. We certainly know more about
the causes of Trump's strange skin color than we ever did about
Kennedy's.

Lyndon Johnson was not just a serial adulterer and often corrupt, but displayed a level of crudity that would now be seen as clinical, from conducting business while defecating on the toilet to exposing his genitals to staff—apparently as some sort of Freudian proof of his own, and by extension, his nation's, manhood. In a debate answer to a sneer from Senator Marco Rubio, Trump seems to have referenced obliquely his private parts ("I guarantee you there's no problem"), but never to our knowledge has he displayed them to staffers.

There is no reason to review the escapades of an impeached Bill Clinton. Despite the efforts of a sympathetic media, many of his transgressions were in part aired to the public. They ran the full gamut of a classical sexist and misogynist, from likely sexually assaulting chance acquaintances, to levering his advantages in age and power to win sexual favors from young subordinates, to attempting to defame and ruin the reputations of women deemed liable to disclose past liaisons. What differentiates so far, *inter alia*, Trump's womanizing from that of prior presidents, like Clinton's, is that his escapades were prior to, not during, his presidential service.

In all these examples of presidential excess, past and present, the progressive Left apparently determined that the flawed chief executive messenger should not endanger the flawless progressive message. Consequently, facts were either hidden or contextualized on the theory that sometimes noble ends excused the sordid means that accompanied them.

We can imagine what the Drudge Report and Fox News would have made of Woodrow Wilson's mysterious and lengthy public disappearance. A contemporary internet symposium of leading physicians would have made mincemeat of FDR's official medical reports. Moreover, had a John F. Kennedy operated in the age of Google, Facebook, Twitter, cable news, and cell phone cameras, his reputation would likely be roughly that of his younger libertine brother Teddy's.

Note that the lurid, but mostly now discredited exposé of the Trump White House, Michael Wolff's *Fire and Fury,* for most of early 2018 became a 24/7 staple of the mainstream media. Wolff's logical media successor was former White House staffer Omarosa Onee Manigault Newman, who claimed, often falsely, that her lurid tell-all memoir was based on secretly taped conversations of Donald Trump. Manigault Newman's sequel in turn was followed by another insider exposé from perennial White House muckraker Bob Woodward. In his summer shocker, *Fear,* Woodward quoted mostly unnamed sources and collected rumors from anonymous sources in the Trump cabinet and White House. His theme was that the administration was on the cusp of disaster, in "fear" that the incompetent and dangerous Trump might at any moment do something truly catastrophic. Woodward's warnings came at a time when the stock market had reached record highs, GDP growth was stronger than at any time in the last decade, unemployment was at a near record low, and abroad there was success in reworking NAFTA, in prodding NATO members to keep their budgetary commitments, and in recalibrating long overdue asymmetrical relationships with Turkey, Iran, and the Palestinians.

Quite different had been the reaction to Edward Klein's equally gossipy 2012 presidential tell-all, *The Amateur,* which was all but ignored by the press. Yet Klein nearly rivaled Wolff's and Omarosa's salaciousness, with charges that Obama operatives had bribed his former pastor Reverend Jeremiah Wright to ensure his silence, and that in general Obama was mostly as clueless and uninformed as he was narcissistic and self-absorbed.

If the charge of a Wolff, Manigault Newman, or Woodward against an often uncouth Trump is that his crudity and recklessness are frequent and insidious to a point never before seen by the standards of contemporary presidents, the argument is still not persuasive, given that we have rarely before experienced such biased and omnipresent media coverage, and we have never before had such purported access to the intimacies of a first family, certainly not during the Roosevelt, Kennedy, or Clinton administrations. By September 2017, the conservative media critics of the Media Research Center found that press evaluations of President Trump on the evening telecasts over the prior three months at ABC's *World News Tonight, CBS Evening News,* and *NBC Nightly News* were *91 percent negative.*

Those findings roughly coincided with an earlier study published by the liberal Harvard Kennedy School's Shorenstein Center on Media, Politics and Public Policy that found that coverage of the Trump presidency in its first hundred days was 80 percent negative, as evidenced in the *New York Times, Wall Street Journal,* and the *Washington Post,* in addition to CNN, CBS, Fox News, and CNBC parent NBC, as well as European news outlets the *Financial Times,* BBC, and ARD in Germany. The same researchers found that coverage of Trump was about twice as negative as had been true of reporting on Barack Obama. Those findings in turn corroborate earlier Pew Research Center results that reported that news accounts of the first sixty days of Trump's presidency were three times more negative than was true of the Obama administration's first two months.

Some journalists had even decided that the Trump aberration called for a reset of the journalistic ethos itself. Given Trump's purported odiousness, all reporters of conscience could no longer be disinterested about the threat he posed. Early in the 2016 campaign, the *Huffington Post* announced that the Trump campaign would be reported on in their entertainment section. Marquee journalists such as Jim Rutenberg of the *New York Times* and Christiane Amanpour of CNN claimed that they could no longer—and should no longer—stay mere neutral reporters, given their low opinion of Trump. Advocacy, not unbiased reporting of the White House, was now supposedly the only moral choice.

The point is *not* to whitewash Donald Trump's excesses or to denigrate his predecessors, but rather to suggest that many of his negative portrayals were a result of an ongoing feud with a media that in historical terms had never before offered as much negative coverage of a president. The asymmetrical coverage reached such a degree that in an April 2018 Monmouth University survey, 77 percent polled that the major media outlets offered "fake news." Had such bias in major network news coverage been true of Trump's predecessor, no one knows how an often thin-skinned Obama would have reacted, much less had he been the daily target of an ongoing special counsel investigation of IRS abuses or improper surveillance of US citizens.

How did the media and progressive critics reconcile a supposedly historically unhinged and dangerous president with a largely successful agenda that by mid-2018 was polling positive? And how exactly had such a flawed character as Trump made impressive cabinet appointments and restored economic vibrancy at home and deterrence abroad? Stranger still, Trump earned vitriol often for voicing positions shared by past progressive presidents and presidential candidates: skepticism over NAFTA and the Trans-Pacific Partnership trade agreements, slapping tariffs on Chinese companies for dumping, congratulating Vladimir Putin and General Abdel Fattah el-Sisi of Egypt for their "election" victories and Xi Jinping on his "extraordinary elevation," or issuing expansive executive orders as Obama had.

Finally, the anti-Trump progressives and Democrats, especially those in the media, did not fully appreciate that the more they voiced loudly their antipathy to Trump, and did so in escalating fashion, the more Trump was able to manipulate them as proof of how unhinged and excitable the alternative to himself was.

In one of the great paradoxes of our age, the media knew well that its approval ratings were at record lows (a 32 percent

positive approval rating in a Harvard-Harris spring 2017 poll).
It accepted that at least some of the loss of reputation was due
to its fixations with Donald Trump that were perceived as both
inordinate and unfair. And yet in the habit of an end-stage ad-
dict, the media simply could not stop its Trump fixations that
it knew were suicidal. Or perhaps Trump-obsessed reporters
considered themselves kamikazes whose own self-immolation
would at least incinerate Trump.

The small number of Never Trump conservatives, who
equally despised Trump, also felt his crudity was unlike any
other president's. But unlike progressives, they faced an additional dilemma: the presidential messenger was often successfully enacting an agenda that they not only had in the past
supported, but also, at least, privately admitted was empowered
by Trump himself. Nonetheless, their complaint was that Republicans stood for character. And Trump lacked it. Thus, the
short term utility of seeing a conservative agenda reified was
hardly worth the long-term damage to conservatism by earning
unneeded charges of hypocrisy or apostasy from prior moral
codes.

Many of my colleagues at *National Review* were especially
vocal in equating Trump's character with a betrayal of their conservative values. In April 2018, the essayist and music critic Jay
Nordlinger summed up the Never Trump disgust well:

> Trump likes to say "little" about those he wishes to disparage:
> "Little Marco," "Liddle Bob Corker," "Little Adam Schiff."
> Big men don't have to do this. In fact, it makes them little. I am
> told every day by the Right that populism is part of conserva-
> tism. And that Trump "tells it like it is" and "fights." I'm not
> sure he tells it like it is, frankly. And his fighting often seems
> like brattishness to me. In any event, good manners and de-
> cency are part of conservatism, for sure.

His colleague Jonah Goldberg likewise emphasized that Trump's character had seemed to nullify much of his otherwise conservative message:

> From his jawboning of Carrier (which failed, by the way) to the president's celebration of Sinclair Broadcasting and tirade against Amazon over the last forty-eight hours, the president has established a hard precedent that businesses and news organizations (and in some cases, foreign allies) must take into account the president's entirely personal preferences and psychological needs or potentially face dire consequences. The president's outbursts may not have the force of law or regulation, but they cannot be wholly separated from the world of "policy" either.

The Greek philosopher Heraclitus's enigmatic fragment *êthos anthrôpô daimôn* ("a man's character is his destiny") was often cited by Never Trumpers as support for their views. But such sanction was apparently based on their misreading of the Greek "*êthos*" as something akin to "good" or "bad" "character" in the modern sense of public behavior or moral bearing, rather than just innate traits.

Heraclitus, an obscure thinker whose work exists only in fragments, likely meant that who we intrinsically are will eventually determine how we end up. He did not necessarily argue that a supposedly good character led to a good destiny, or vice versa, but rather that our multifaceted destinies will be predicated on our prior diverse inborn traits.

A Trump supporter might argue that Trump's innate craftiness and intuition meant that he could ultimately advance conservative messages in a way a George H. W. Bush could not; a Trump critic might counter that Trump's signature loquaciousness and lack of discipline will mean that he will finally talk himself into endless melodramas and eventual irrelevance. Both are legitimate interpretations of the fragment.

Through the 2016 campaign and first two years of the Trump presidency, Never Trump conservatives fought over the degree to which Trump the messenger vitiated his mostly conservative message. Given their acknowledgment of a biased media, and given their inability to show that lying, exaggeration, and crudity were always singularly Trump's, it became hard for Never Trumpers to calibrate just how low Trump had gone—much less how low he had to go to cancel out superb judicial picks, inspired cabinet officers, or a robust economic turnaround from the Obama years.

Was there some framework or hierarchy of presidential sins that the Never Trumpers envisioned? Or were their views of Trump's crudity something akin to what the late Supreme Court justice Potter Stewart had in frustration scoffed about pornography: "I shall not today attempt further to define the kinds of material I understand to be embraced . . . But I know it when I see it"?

Never Trumpers may have felt that had Trump tweeted more judiciously and more sparingly in the manner of Obama or pruned his crude outbursts, he would have been largely exempt from such strident criticism. It was likely the frequency as well as the invective and earthiness that had apparently singularly tarred Trump as something unprecedentedly bad.

On matters of character, did Trump's tawdry trysts with women, often a decade before his presidency, mean that he lacked character and thus stained the conservative cause, in a way that the often promiscuous Roosevelt, Kennedy, and Clinton had not rendered their own liberal accomplishments null and void? When reports surfaced that George H. W. Bush, in his eighties and nineties, had serially groped a few women and embarrassed them with nasty jokes, did conservatives recalibrate his administration's record?

In fact, later media accounts appeared suggesting that Bush, the paragon of Republican manners and decency, may have *in the past* groped a bit while president in 1992. And when out of office in 2003, Bush had again purportedly grabbed an underage female. Had Americans known all that, and possibly more of his private life, would our views of the sober and judicious Bush have changed? Was he an ineffective president for in retirement groping a minor or because he offered a false "read my lips" promise not to raise taxes?

History could have offered Never Trump conservatives some guidance about this age-old philosophical dilemma that rearose so concretely with Trump. Dwight D. Eisenhower was a successful president in the manner that he had been an effective supreme allied commander. His administrative skills were demonstrable. Ike was fair minded. He was deferential without being weak. He was certainly practical and a consensus builder who got things done without the narcissism and egoism of most of his military and political rivals. Eisenhower's forbearance kept alive the often tense Anglo-American alliance, without which the D-Day invasion of June 1944 would have been impossible.

Yet under current Trump-era workplace protocols, Ike would likely never have been nominated, given his poorly hidden relationship with his divorced chauffeur Kay Summersby and his implausible outright denials of the affair (and efforts of his staff to hide the relationship and later to marginalize the publicity-seeking and book-touring Summersby) while he held the title of Supreme Commander of Allied Expeditionary Forces in Europe. Our current media and political climate would have judged the careful Eisenhower reckless, or indeed callously immoral, in his downtime with the loquacious Summersby while battle raged just miles away from his headquarters. Or would the media have contrasted his indiscretion with his wife Mamie's loyal support back home or with Kay's seemingly cuckolded fiancé, who was tragically killed in combat while she dallied with Ike?

Was Eisenhower, then, a bad man but a good president, or a good man and a good president who was mortal rather than divine? Was his apparent onetime dalliance (of uncertain dimensions) forgivable? If so, witness the quite different fate of General David Petraeus, whose own amorous transgression that destroyed his career may have been similar to Eisenhower's, if certainly more discreet than Ike's, in an insurgency war rather than an existential conflict.

Certainly, by today's standards, World War II icons like Generals Douglas MacArthur and George S. Patton, and especially Admiral Ernest King, would have been cashiered (or worse) for improper sexual relationships while in uniform. (MacArthur carried on an affair with an initially underage sixteen-year-old Filipino national, Isabel Rosario Cooper—who would later commit suicide—and was blackmailed by muckraker Drew Pearson.) How many men might have died in Operation Cartwheel, MacArthur's effort to recover the Philippines in dismantling the Japanese empire, or during the Third Army's dash to the Rhine had either MacArthur or Patton (who seduced his own step-niece) been sent home?

Gerald Ford and Jimmy Carter were both emblematic of flyover state, rock-solid values. They stayed married. They did not cash in while in their offices. They largely told the truth. Their administrations were mostly free of scandal, at least in comparison to those of the Clinton and Obama administrations. Their speech was rarely ad hominem. America certainly benefitted from their personal probity. They were, in other words, role models and ethical public servants.

But both Ford and Carter proved largely ineffective presidents. In terms of economic stagnation between 1974 and 1981, millions of lives were perhaps worse off for their tenures. Few can point to any lasting substantial achievements, apart from airline deregulation and the Arab-Israeli Camp David Accords in the aftermath of the Yom Kippur War. Ford's sad "Whip Inflation

Now" button campaign and Carter's serial disasters (stagflation, the appeasement of Ayatollah Khomeini's Iran, the rudderless foreign policy) are not arguments that good character does not matter, only that it is not necessarily always a guarantee of good governance.

Ronald Reagan was a fine person. He was clearly a successful president. Reagan is an argument that ethical character can enhance a good message to ensure a good presidency. Reagan was, of course, no saint. He was often criticized as an inattentive father. He could be intemperate and reckless in some of his private and public statements, whether joking on a hot mic about nuking the Soviet Union or earlier as California governor in 1969 threatening Berkeley protestors with violence: "If it takes a *bloodbath*, let's get it over with, no more appeasement."

Oddly, some conservative Never Trump Republicans claimed Trump had forsaken the high Reagan ground. Again, they forgot about the other Reagan, the hardcore 1964 Goldwater zealot who preferred that his party would lose purely in 1964 rather than reach out to moderates, who once swore he would never give back the Panama Canal, derided "welfare bums," promised to clean up the "mess" at Berkeley, and joked that he hoped the free food for poor communities leveraged by the Symbionese Liberation Army, a domestic terrorist organization, might be infected by botulism. Reagan, remember, was damned by his party's establishment as a nihilist disrupter for trying to storm Republican conventions in both 1968 and 1976 to win the nomination from supposedly far more stable and experienced Republicans—narcissistic gambits that were said to have undermined Republican unity and played into the hands of progressives.

Little more need be said of Bill Clinton. The general consensus still holds. Given his political sixth sense, he could be at times an effective president, at least in terms of finally balancing the budget, compromising with congressional Republicans, overseeing economic growth, bridging hard Right and hard Left politics, and using force to discredit Serbian president Slobodan Milosevic, who would eventually resign and be indicted for war crimes.

Yet, ethically, Clinton may rank as the least principled president in a century—impeached, disbarred, chronically lying, a sexual assaulter, callous with women to the point of being pathological, and scandal ridden without any sense at all of financial probity. In 2018, Clinton sought absolution from past charges of sexual coercion by chalking up his prior improper behavior simply to the libertine tenor of the times, and therefore rightfully only earned himself more odium. Ex-president Clinton may well soon be regarded as the most corrupt former president of the last hundred years, given the yet largely unexplored scandals surrounding the Clinton Foundation, his globalized quid pro quo honoraria, and sybaritic lifestyle on the private jet "Lolita Express," even as pundits now nostalgically rewrite his presidency as one without the rancor and nihilism of twenty-first-century politics and an example of how to partner with Congress to halt deficits and grow the economy.

All that said, Clinton is certainly said to have been a better president than was Carter—and a far worse man. George W. Bush and Barack Obama, despite the allegations of their political opponents, were good husbands and fathers. They were politically savvy, albeit hardball partisans. Neither was dishonest, at least in the manner of most politicians. Given today's political rancor, we do not know yet how historians will finally assess their presidencies, but each was unique in doubling the national debt. It can be said that no recent Republican president before Trump incurred such dislike from Democrats as did Bush, and no Democrat so alienated Republicans as did Obama.

In some sense, Donald Trump was replaying the role of the unpopular tenure of loudmouth Democrat Harry Truman (president, 1945–53). "Give 'em Hell" Harry came into office following the death of Franklin Roosevelt. He miraculously won the 1948 election against all expert opinion and polls. Truman left office in January 1953 widely hated. Indeed, his final approval ratings (32 percent) were the lowest of any departing president, except for those of Richard Nixon.

The outsider Truman had always been immersed in scandal, owing to his deep ties to the corrupt Kansas City political machine, and Truman's patron, the unsavory boss Tom Pendergast. When the novice Vice President Truman took office after Roosevelt's death in April 1945, he knew little about the grand strategy of World War II—and nothing about the ongoing atomic bomb project. For the next seven-plus years, Truman shocked—and successfully led—the country.

Over the objections of many in his cabinet, Truman ignored critics and ordered the dropping of two atomic bombs on Japan to end the war. Against the advice of most of the State Department, he recognized the new state of Israel. He offended Roosevelt holdovers by breaking with wartime ally the Soviet Union and chartering the foundations of Cold War communist containment. Many in the Pentagon opposed his racial integration of the armed forces. National security advisors counseled against sending troops to save South Korea.

Liberals opposed fellow Democrat Truman's creation of the Central Intelligence Agency. Truman was widely loathed for firing controversial five-star general and American hero Douglas MacArthur. There were often widespread calls in the press for Truman to resign. Impeachment was often mentioned. Truman, in short, did things other presidents had not dared to do.

Truman occasionally swore. He had nightly drinks. He played poker with cronies. And he shocked aides and the public with his vulgarity and crass attacks on political enemies. Truman cheaply compared 1948 presidential opponent Thomas Dewey to Hitler, and attacked him as a supposed pawn of bigots and war profiteers. Truman hyperbolically claimed a Republican victory in 1948 would threaten America's very liberty.

In the pre-Twitter age, Truman could never keep his mouth shut: "My choice early in life was either to be a piano-player in a whorehouse or a politician. And to tell the truth, there's hardly any difference." When a reviewer for the *Washington Post* trashed Truman's daughter's concert performance, Truman threatened him with physical violence. "It seems to me that you are a frustrated old man who wishes he could have been successful," Truman wrote in a letter to critic Paul Hume. "Someday I hope to meet you. When that happens, you'll need a new nose, a lot of beefsteak for black eyes, and perhaps a supporter below!" Such outbursts were Trumpian to the core.

Truman trashed national icons, in a way that often exceeded Trump's smears. He deprecated the military leaders who had just won World War II. He was childishly vulgar in his dismissal of MacArthur: "I didn't fire him because he was a dumb son of a bitch although he was, but that's not against the law for generals. If it was, half to three-quarters of them would be in jail." The latter was an astounding charge in an age of Bradley, Eisenhower, LeMay, Patton, and Ridgway, and admirals such as Halsey, King, Nimitz, and Spruance.

It took a half century for historians to concede that the mercurial and often adolescent Truman had solid accomplishments, especially in foreign affairs—in part because Truman conveyed a sense that he did not much care for staying in Washington, a city in which he was not invested, did not like, and would quickly leave at the end of his tenure. Even Truman's crassness eventually was appreciated as integral to his image of a "plain speaking" and "the Buck Stops Here" decisive leader.

Had Truman access to Twitter, or had he a Kansas City federal prosecutor to hound him for his checkered past, he could have self-destructed in a flurry of ad hominem electronic outbursts. Yet Truman proved largely successful because of what he did, and in spite of what he said.

In answer to our initial Trump inquiries, it is (perhaps regrettably) not evident that personal sins equate to failed presidencies. Character lapses are certainly not to be encouraged, but in the Machiavellian landscape of global politics they do not preclude wise leadership either.

Values are absolute and transcend time and place. But the notion of public versus personal, and private sin versus public guilt, changes constantly. In the past, pragmatism guided us about sin and politicians: a man's demons were his own unless they reached a point of impairing his public career or shaming his office in the eyes of the public. Two nightly martinis at home were okay. Four to five at a restaurant would inevitably become a matter of public concern.

"Damn" in public was tolerated within limits, the F-word never was. Visiting a mistress was regrettable. But, then, who knew the possible private incompatibility or unhappiness within anyone's marriage? In contrast, sexually cavorting in the Oval Office was inexcusable. Private adultery was a matter of guilt to be judged by God. Sex in the workplace was shameful and to be condemned by the living.

One of the great ironies of our age is that we have somehow managed to become far more sanctimonious than previous generations—and yet far more immoral by traditional standards as well. We can obsess over an unartful presidential comment, but snore through the systematic destruction of the manufacturing basis of an entire state or ignore warlike violence on the streets of Chicago.

Donald J. Trump's presidency is too brief to yet be judged absolutely. His personal foibles are too imbedded within current political and media hatred to be assessed dispassionately. Too many assessments too quickly have been made about Trump, without much historical context and usually with too much passion. Neither is it yet clear that Trump is a bad man or a good president, or vice versa, or neither or both. But if the past is sometimes a guide to the present, Trump in theory certainly could become a more effective president than would have been his likely more circumspect Republican primary rivals, while perhaps demonstrating that he is far more uncouth. The paradox again raises the question, When any one man can change the lives of 330 million, what exactly is presidential morality after all—private and personal sins, or the transgressions that affect millions of lives for the worse?

The Trump base had no such moral dilemmas over Trump the messenger as did the Never Trumpers. As we have seen, they believed that no other Republican or Democratic candidate could have been trusted to address illegal immigration, deindustrialization, and globalization, and to adopt pro-jobs economic and Jacksonian foreign policies. They could not have cared less that Trump had called the psychopath Kim Jong-un "Little Rocket Man," or had a sordid dalliance with Stormy Daniels a decade earlier.

The real obscenity in their view was appeasing such a lethal monster as Kim, and his father and grandfather for nearly the past seventy years. They appreciated that Trump ordered Mexico to stop a series of advancing "caravans" of Central Americans promising to crash the American border. The real villains, to the Trump base, were those who believed that noncitizens could dictate to a country not their own—along with those Americans who encouraged them to believe such heresy.

Trump supporters also had little problem with the president of the United States ad nauseam referring to "Crooked Hillary." Their sense of travesty was not that a president had "stooped" to voice such a blunt truth, but the Beltway indifference to the reality that a national figure had committed likely serial felonies, with exemption, and yet was still considered a judicious Washington fixture. In some sense, Trump was the deplorables' version of the rash and often destructive and coarse Alexander the Great, who slashed rather than wasted his time untying the Gordian knot, as if someone in a hurry to get things done that long ago should have to play by arcane rules designed to thwart outsiders.

Donald Trump inherited from his supposed betters an array of perennial crises when he was sworn in as president in 2017. Certainly, he did not possess the traditional diplomatic skills and temperament to deal in "normal" fashion with any of them. But was not his unfamiliarity with Washington why he was elected?

A lunatic North Korean regime purportedly had gained the ability to send nuclear-tipped missiles to the US West Coast. China had not only been violating trade agreements, but quite outrageously forcing US companies to hand over their technological know-how as the price of doing business in China. Iran had used its cash infusions from the so-called Iran deal to fund terrorism, intervene in Syria to support the genocidal Assad regime, and buy and build new missiles. NATO may have been born to protect the European mainland, but a distant United States was paying an increasingly greater percentage of the alliance's budget to maintain NATO than were its front-line partners (some of which were concluding lucrative trade deals with Vladimir Putin's Russia) and often was ankle-bitten by the beneficiaries of its largess.

Mexico kept sending its impoverished citizens to the United States, who usually entered illegally. That way, Mexico relieved its own social tensions, developed a pro-Mexico expatriate community in the United States, and gained an estimated $30 billion a year from undocumented immigrants—often on the assumed premise that American social service subsidies must free up immigrants' cash to send home.

Germany ran up an annual $65 billion trade surplus with the United States. It refused to meet its modest NATO requirements of investing 2 percent of its GDP on defense, although over thirty-five thousand American troops were still stationed in Germany to ensure its NATO-guaranteed security. Berlin warped international trade by piling up the world's second-largest annual trade surplus at over $285 billion, while Germans polled the most anti-American of all nations in the European Union. Yet somehow Germany thought Trump's criticism of its attitudes and practices was unprofessional and uncouth.

In the end, were euphemisms or crudity the real sin? How moral and ethical was it really to characterize the Fort Hood massacre as "workplace violence," or to rename deadly Islamic terrorism as a "man-caused disaster"? We forget that euphemisms can be more obscene than coarse obscenity.

In the past, traditional and accepted methods—the deep state's and establishment's normal way of doing things—had failed to deal with an array of existential challenges. Nice phrases such as "Agreed Framework," "six-party talks," and "strategic patience" essentially had offered North Korea cash to denuclearize and yet resulted in an arsenal that might well have threatened the major cities of the West Coast.

Trumpism, then, was the idea that there were no longer taboo subjects. *Everything was open for negotiation; nothing was sacred.* So, yes, the Trump base liked the enhanced effect of Trump the messenger. It was as if "their guy" finally told off the so-called elites of the country and the world on their behalf. Such tolerance of Trump's ungentlemanly behavior would last indefinitely, at least until either Trump reneged on his campaign promises or his nostrums sank the economy or his bluster and brinksmanship got the United States into a major war.

As we shall see in the next chapter, what made President Trump himself a force multiplier of his unorthodox message was the venom he brought out in his opponents. His supporters argued that compared to the hysterias of the media, the deep state, the Republican establishment, and the progressive identity politics movements, Trump was not so uncouth after all.

PART FOUR

THE ORDEAL, TRIUMPH—AND ORDEAL—OF PRESIDENT TRUMP

Why, man, he doth bestride the narrow world
Like a Colossus, and we petty men
Walk under his huge legs and peep about
To find ourselves dishonorable graves.
Men at some time are masters of their fates:
The fault, dear Brutus, is not in our stars,
But in ourselves, that we are underlings.
　　　　　—Shakespeare, *Julius Caesar*

Chapter Ten

END TRUMP!

*"F**k you. F**k you . . . Yes, I'm angry. Yes, I'm
outraged. Yes, I have thought an awful lot about
blowing up the White House."*
—Madonna, Women's March on Washington address,
Inauguration Day, 2017

Never in the history of the American presidency has there
been such an immediate and sustained effort by the opposition to remove an elected president before completing his
first term. The growing furor against Bill Clinton that sought
to impeach him came halfway in his second term. As we have
seen, the existential hatred for Trump was due to a variety of
reasons—the shock of Hillary Clinton blowing the 2016 election following the progressive eight years of Barack Obama, the
unpredictability and volatility of Trump, the breakneck speed
at which Trump sought to undo the Obama legacy, and the progressives' belief that noble ends excused any means to achieve
them. But whatever the cause and manifestations of Trump hatred, the efforts to delegitimize or even destroy him seemed to
have ushered in a veritable second American civil war.

Donald J. Trump was elected to the presidency on November 8, 2016. He lost the popular vote to Democratic candidate Hillary Clinton by a 48.2 percent to 46.1 percent margin, or by some 2.8 million votes. Yet Trump won decisively in the Electoral College with a vote of 304 to 227—the *fifth* time in American history that the winner received fewer popular votes than did the loser. Almost immediately, Trump-elect was met with intense and multifaceted protests. Much worse would come by Inauguration Day.

Four prior presidents who had similarly come into office without popular majorities also faced harsh opposition and charges of illegitimacy. George W. Bush was dogged until the terrorist attacks on September 11, 2001, by the accusation of "selected, not elected." John Quincy Adams, Benjamin Harrison, and Rutherford B. Hayes were all under suspicion of some sort of Electoral College "crooked bargain" that plagued them well into their presidencies.

Trump faced even greater public and government resistance, and much sooner, than past presidents who had not won the popular vote. He had campaigned against the Obama-Clinton progressive project, the Republican establishment, and the proverbial deep state. That left him orphaned from all the old Washington hands and all the traditional foci of political power. In defeat, the establishment's ensuing pushback was like nothing seen before against an incoming American president.

After the election, all of the theoretical ways of killing Donald Trump soon exhausted the imagination of celebrities, near celebrities, and fringe public figures. Assassination chic was uncoordinated and messy. But the collective effect was to help drive down Trump's popularity and further delegitimize his presidency, often before it had even started.

Decapitation? The comedian Kathy Griffin did a video holding up a bloody facsimile of Trump's head.

Knife work? A Free Shakespeare in the Park troupe in New York ritually stabbed a Julius Caesar–Donald Trump in each of their nightly productions of *Julius Caesar*.

Shooting? The multimillionaire rapper and exhibitionist Snoop Dogg (Calvin Cordozar Broadus Jr.) blasted away at a Trump likeness in one of his videos.

Classic presidential assassination? The actor Johnny Depp joked in an interview: "When was the last time an actor assassinated a president? . . . It has been a while, and maybe it is time." Imagining the death of a sitting president was not just confined to celebrities.

Mainstream Democratic officials got in on the act too. In April 2018, when California senator Kamala Harris was asked by talk show host Ellen DeGeneres, "If you had to be stuck in an elevator with either President Trump, Mike Pence, or Jeff Sessions, who would it be?" Harris screwed up her face and in turn asked back, "Does one of us have to come out alive?"

These examples from 2016 to 2018 of Trump kill chic could be expanded. A writer for the *Huffington Post* had demanded Trump's trial and execution. Near my home, at the California State University, Fresno campus, a history professor openly called for Trump to be hanged, while a colleague at the Hoover Institution had mused on German television that Trump could be removed by a murder in the White House. A Missouri state legislator had posted on her Facebook page: "I hope he is assassinated." Actress Rosie O'Donnell bragged that she had created an electronic game in which Donald Trump jumped off a cliff to his demise.

Such lethal dreams and near threats continue well into 2018 and will do so throughout the Trump first term. Given that four previous presidents had been assassinated and two wounded, there were lots of reasons why even joking about presidential assassination previously had been traditionally off-limits. But the idea of violently nullifying Trump seemed immune from the normal taboos. In April 2018, Hollywood director Joss Whedon tweeted: "Donald Trump is killing this country. Some of it quickly, some slowly, but he spoils and destroys everything he touches. He emboldens monsters, wielding guns, governmental power, or just smug doublespeak. Or Russia. My hate and sadness are exhausting. Die, Don. Just quietly die." At about the same time, on news reports of a mysterious and fatal fire in Trump Tower, the 1960s rocker David Crosby (of Crosby, Stills, Nash and Young) tweeted: "Oh boy . . . burn baby burn."

There were very few repercussions for talking about killing Trump. Snoop Dogg and Kathy Griffin assumed that there was zero chance of ever ending up on a no-fly list for a few weeks for normalizing the rhetoric of violence against the president. They also knew even better that there was an unspoken asymmetry in such dark humor or morbid speculation.

Had the presidents been reversed, and a Madonna or the Shakespeare in the Park players considered metaphorically or ritually blowing up or stabbing Barack Obama in anger over his "tea-baggers" crude sexual smear or his insensitive joke about the Special Olympics or his campaign advice "to get in their faces" or "take a gun to a knife fight," their careers likely would have been over. In contrast, in August 2013 conservative officials at the Missouri State Fair voted to ban for life a minor rodeo clown who dared to appear with an Obama mask on during a bull-riding contest. For all their supposedly edgy hipness and spontaneous cool, actors and celebrities calibrated carefully the politics of what they said and did.

Given that all through the campaign and transition, Trump remained loud and accusatory, his attackers justified their violent fits as tit-for-tat escalation in reaction to Trump's customary feuding. Actor Robert De Niro dreamed of punching out candidate Donald Trump ("He's an embarrassment to this country. It makes me so angry this country has gotten to this point that this fool, this bozo, has wound up where he has. He talks how he'd like to punch people in the face? . . . Well, I'd like to punch him in the face.").

But De Niro, who about every three months offered a new scenario about clobbering the president, claimed that his desire to bloody Trump was only retaliatory for Trump's on-the-stump loud warnings for someone to physically stop a rally intruder. At the 2018 Tony Awards, De Niro earned a standing ovation from fellow actors for simply uttering his first words, "F**k Trump!"

As Madonna demonstrated on Inauguration Day, shock and bewilderment also explained a lot of the venom. Almost all the polls had assured the country that Trump would not just lose the election, but he would surely go down to defeat in a landslide and destroy the Republican Party, as well as repudiating and ending for good his off-brand populist nationalism. When Trump won, polls, conventional wisdom, political science—accustomed reason itself—were discredited. The utter shock was reminiscent of the stunned and defeated British army band purportedly playing the "The World Turned Upside Down" ("Yet let's be content, and the times lament, you see the world turn'd upside down") after their utterly unexpected defeat at Yorktown, or more recently the shock of the Brexit vote among British elites.

The response, then, to Trump's win was collective furor at the sheer nonsense—and unfairness—of it all. Even comedians became unhinged at being forced to accept the surreal and resorted to violent imagery. Late-night host Stephen Colbert concocted a strange homophobic slur routine to give words and imagery to his own derangement:

Mr. President, you're not the POTUS, you're the "gloat-us." You're the glutton with the button. You're a regular "Gorge Washington." You're the "presi-dunce," but you're turning into a real "prick-tator." Sir, you attract more skinheads than free Rogaine. You have more people marching against you than cancer. You talk like a sign-language gorilla that got hit in the head. In fact, the only thing your mouth is good for is being Vladimir Putin's c**k holster.

Obscenity and scatology were routinely used to demonize Trump both by politicians and celebrities. Democratic players such as Democratic National Committee chairman Tom Perez, California senator Kamala Harris, and New York senator Kirsten Gillibrand routinely began using "f**k" and "sh*t" slurs in efforts to arouse their supporters against Trump. A *New Republic* author cheered the coarseness on, and demanded even more scatology from anti-Trump politicians.

CNN's Anderson Cooper on air smeared a Trump supporter by alleging that he would continue to slavishly defend Trump even if Trump deposited his feces on his desk. *Politico*'s Julia Joffe seemed to be suggesting that Trump had committed incest with his own daughter ("Either Trump is f**king his own daughter or he's shirking nepotism laws. Which is worse?"). Comedian Bill Maher, who would soon declare that he welcomed an economic recession if it would stop Trump's reelection bid, graphically joked that Trump and his daughter engaged in oral sex. The cruder the allusion, apparently the higher the standing of the slanderer in the eyes of the "Resistance." By creating a popular landscape in which the president was guilty of the worst sorts of crimes against nature, what then should he, or his family, logically deserve as punishment?

Actor Peter Fonda seemed to answer that question in summer 2018, during another immigration crisis at the border, when he tweeted a series of threats to the Trump family: "We should rip Barron Trump from his mother's arms and put him in a cage with pedophiles and see if mother will stand up against the giant asshole she is married to." It is impossible to imagine that any Hollywood actor would have dared to say something similar about any prior president's family, or having any sort of career had he or she voiced such sick hatred. In some sense, the United States was entering a climate of hatred analogous to that of 1860 or 1968.

Well before Trump, and given the liberal tilt in popular entertainment, the arts, and media and two Electoral College bombshells within twenty years, it had become increasingly tolerable to talk of violence against a conservative president. In 2012, the chopped-off head of George W. Bush turned up on a pike in HBO's *Game of Thrones* ("by accident"). In the midst of the 2004 election, Nicholson Baker published *Checkpoint*. The novel was mostly a tiring dialogue of characters dreaming about how to assassinate President Bush. (It has now been "updated" in 2017 with the title *To Kill the President*, by British writer Jonathan Freedland [a.k.a. Sam Bourne], a supposed melodrama about assassinating a Trump-like president.)

Also, during the hotly contested election of 2004, long before Johnny Depp's John Wilkes Booth rant about Trump, *Guardian* guest columnist Charles Brooker lamented in an op-ed that there was no presidential assassin around to kill Bush: "John Wilkes Booth, Lee Harvey Oswald, John Hinckley Jr.—where are you now that we need you?" All such venom thankfully had mostly quieted in the eight years following 2008 and the election of Barack Obama.

But now with the end of the Obama administration the progressive hysteria resumed, intensified, and occasionally spun off into real violence, as when self-described Bernie Sanders supporter James Hodgkinson shot at prominent Republican politicians practicing for a charity baseball game. He gravely wounded Republican House Whip Steve Scalise before being stopped by Capitol police, who aborted his planned efforts to shoot more assembled conservatives. More recently, in September 2018, at a festival in Castro Valley, California, one Farzad Fazeli tried to

stab Republican congressional candidate Rudy Peters, after going on a long shouting tirade about President Trump.

In just one week, in mid-June 2018, the media reported the
following events: Actor Peter Fonda had tweeted a call for exposing the names and addresses of Immigration and Customs
Enforcement agents so that their children could be harassed at
school (e.g., "Find out what schools their children go to and
surround the schools . . . Need to make their children worry
now"). Department of Homeland Security secretary Kirstjen
Nielsen, while dining at a New York eatery, was confronted
by a mob of Democratic Socialists of America protesters and
physically driven out of the restaurant. At the same time, the
US Marshals were searching for a Pennsylvania man who had
threatened President Trump on social media with a promise to
"put a bullet in the head of President Trump."

Congresswoman Maxine Waters (D-CA) summed up the
week's general strategy of "resistance" to Donald Trump by
calling for 24/7 physical and vocal confrontations: "If you see
anybody from that cabinet in a restaurant, in a department store,
at a gasoline station, you get out and you create a crowd, and
you push back on them, and you tell them they're not welcome
anymore, anywhere."

Again, the common theme was to normalize the unlikely or
unthinkable effort to delegitimize a controversial president by
taking these efforts to such a degree that it would become the natural and indeed laudable or even necessary thing to do. Rarely
did his fervent opponents offer a point-by-point, issue-by-issue
refutation of Trump's agenda, much less a constructive alternative to sway Trump voters to their own progressive programs.

In May 2017, eight months after her defeat, Hillary Clinton
announced: "I'm now back to being an activist citizen and part
of the Resistance."

What exactly did Clinton mean by "Resistance," a psychodramatic borrowing of the Maquis French guerilla fighters in

World War II (*La Résistance*) organized to sabotage and kill oc-cupying Nazi forces? Did Hillary assume that Trump was anal-ogous to an occupying *Obergruppenführer* and she, with a beret and Sten submachine gun in arm, was ambushing his minions in the highlands?

In fact, Clinton was a Johnny-come-lately to the movement. Formal efforts to stop the Trump presidency had begun im-mediately following the election. According to a *Rolling Stone* encomium published a week before Inauguration Day, the Re-sistance had five, if mostly incoherent and vague, strategies to emasculate Trump: (1) "leverage" Trump's unpopularity, (2) "bleed" his political capital, (3) outright political resistance in the blue states, (4) go on the offense, and (5) sue.

Right after the election, the media and Democratic Party critics had leveled charges that pro-Trump Russians had sought to shut down power grids in Vermont. The *Washing-ton Post* blared out the accusations and had them fueled by de-nouncements such as those of Senator Patrick J. Leahy (D-VT), who thundered: "This is beyond hackers having electronic joy rides—this is now about trying to access utilities to potentially manipulate the grid and shut it down in the middle of winter."

The subtext of the *Post* hit was that the sort of obvious Rus-sian collusion with Trump during the campaign had now been reified by existential dangers to the people of Vermont before Trump had even taken office: "President-elect Donald Trump has repeatedly questioned the veracity of U.S. intelligence pointing to Russia's responsibility for hacks in the run-up to the Nov. 8 election. He also has spoken highly of Russian President Vladimir Putin, despite President Obama's suggestion that the approval for hacking came from the highest levels of the Krem-lin." The *Post* failed to note that Obama had known of Rus-sian hacking and interference since at least 2014, done nothing about it, and, on the eve of a certain Hillary Clinton victory, had ridiculed the notion that anyone—apparently Vladimir Putin included—had any power to warp decentralized, state-control of a US election.

However, within two weeks of the Clinton defeat, Hillary's aides and democratic activists, especially those led by third-party candidate Jill Stein, charged that voting machines in Wisconsin, Michigan, and Pennsylvania had been hacked—again, presumably by pro-Russian, pro-Trump operatives. No real evidence was adduced. The suits were eventually all dismissed. But the point again was not veracity, but instead to create such a vast corpus of alleged Trump felonies that it might reach a critical mass and thereby destroy the president's ability to govern.

More dramatic was a comprehensive, well-organized—and anti-constitutional—attempt to warp the Electoral College vote so that it would not represent the tallies of individual states. Ultimately, it was another desperate effort that went nowhere. Hollywood celebrities ran ads beseeching Trump electors not to follow their constitutional directives and either vote against Trump or abstain from voting. Five million signed an online petition requesting the same. Liberal political action committees entreated: "They're [celebrities] not asking you to vote for Hillary. 37 Electors can be American heroes by voting their conscience for a real leader. Find local vigils and support rallies."

The Resistance organized both popular demonstrations on Inauguration Day along with congressional boycotts of the swearing-in ceremony. Over fifty House members refused to attend. Later, a small group of progressive congressional representatives introduced five articles of impeachment in November 2017. All of them died on the floor.

By December, a federal judge had dismissed lawsuits alleging that a supposedly profiteering Trump could be removed by violations of the emoluments clause of the Constitution, a theme the media had fueled with lurid reports of Trump hotels and concessions abroad enjoying a surge of post-inauguration business. In fact, by autumn 2018 *Forbes* and NBC were suddenly reporting that Trump had lost an estimated $1 billion in net worth since being elected president. Without a second of reflection, the media flipped. It went from once alleging that Trump in unconstitutional fashion was unduly profiting from his presidency to gloating that his now higher profile had only eroded his brand appeal, and thus was de facto evidence of his general unpopularity.

As early as the 2016 campaign, Democrats had envisioned going after Trump for supposed violations of the Logan Act, a 1799 law that prohibited American citizens from freelancing in matters of foreign policy. The statute had only been enforced on two occasions—the last 166 years ago. More recently, no Logan Act investigation was mounted against former president Jimmy Carter's unauthorized trips to North Korea that enraged the Clinton administration, nor against Barack Obama's own back-channel contacts with Iranians during his 2008 presidential run, nor against John Kerry, who in 2018 met several times in secret with Iranian operatives, purportedly in hopes of saving the doomed Iran deal by undermining his government's current policies toward Iran.

Sally Yates, an Obama holdover and temporary head of the Trump Justice Department, after just four days of Trump in office, sent her investigators into the White House to interrogate Michael Flynn. She had hopes that Obama officials might have a case against him under the Logan Act before they were transitioned out and a new team arrived. Soon, however, the Resistance, as in the case of the emoluments clause, dropped the futile Logan Act gambit—and for good reason, given that many former Obama appointees, such as former secretary of state John Kerry, were reassuring foreign officials that Trump's efforts were ephemeral and not to be taken seriously.

Still, there were other avenues for aborting the Trump presidency to be explored. Later, one Dr. Bandy X. Lee, a Yale University psychiatry professor, testified before Congress about

Trump's purported mental impairment. After a series of private meetings with congressional members, Lee warned: "He's going to unravel, and we are seeing the signs." By January 2018, the Resistance was talking of redress through the Twenty-fifth Amendment to seek Trump's removal on grounds that he was mentally impaired and unfit to continue as president. In one sense, Lee was right: if insanity was defined as attempting to reverse the entire Obama agenda, then perhaps Trump really was unhinged.

Dr. Lee had never met, much less examined, Trump. Nonetheless, in probable violation of professional canons, she wondered whether Trump might have to be physically restrained and forced to undergo examination. Ostensibly, Lee was advocating a virtual coup d'état, if not also channeling the old Soviet remedy of smearing political undesirables as mentally unbalanced and in need of hospitalization.

In the end, the White House physician, Rear Admiral Dr. Ronny Jackson, held a press conference to report on his physical examinations, especially highlighting that Trump scored a thirty out of thirty on a screening exam for dementia, known as the Montreal Cognitive Assessment. To a room of sorely disappointed Washington reporters, Jackson announced that "I can reliably say, and I think that the folks in the mental health [field] would back me up on the fact that if he had some kind of mental, cognitive issue, that this test is sensitive enough, it would have picked up on it. He would not have got 30 out of 30."

At no time did politicians, celebrities, and elites of the Resistance ever ask why their sequential efforts to subvert the Trump presidency continually failed. Much less did they imagine what their own reactions might have been had Trump partisans employed the same sort of subversions in response to the November 2008 election of Barack Obama, channeling their fantasies (shared and spread by Trump himself) about Obama's supposed non-US birth, about talk of possible payoffs to silence Reverend Jeremiah Wright, the firebrand anti-Semitic former pastor of Barack Obama, and about rumors of Obama's personal life into organized efforts to create some sort of popular conservative movement to remove him from office.

The Resistance eventually learned that even liberal justices routinely found their suits without merit, that the people did not marshal behind them to remove Trump, and that their charges were usually not based on demonstrable actionable evidence. Nonetheless, their continuance of such resistance was envisioned as imperceptible taps to a fragile shell. The supposedly ineffective blows were, in truth, all inflicting silent but cumulative stress fractures that at some point might suddenly implode the Trump edifice with just one lighter knock—perhaps a 2019 effort of impeachment in the House of Representatives after the midterm elections of 2018. Even if the bashers did not crush the Trump presidency, anti-Trump activists and Never Trump conservatives found their furor a sort of way of venting, or rather signaling, their own virtue to one another. Certainly, celebrities, journalists, op-ed writers, and politicians all sought to outdo each other in showcasing brilliantly expressed or unmatched hostility to Trump.

More ominously, a number of leftover Obama appointees— well aside from the deeply embedded holdovers in the new Trump administration—began to organize resistance to Trump in a way not characteristic of past emeriti officials. In February 2017, Loretta Lynch, former attorney general (and still under a cloud of suspicion for allegedly improper behavior during the Clinton email investigations of 2015–16), issued a video calling for resistance to the Trump presidency, in overly melodramatic language:

> I know it's a time of concern for people who see our rights being assailed, being trampled on, and even being rolled back. I know that this is difficult, but I remind you that this has never been easy. We have always had to work to move this country

forward to achieve the great ideals of our Founding Fathers. It
has been people, individuals who have banded together, ordinary people who simply saw what needed to be done and
came together and supported those ideals who have made
the difference. They've marched, *they've bled and yes, some of
them died.* [italics added]. This is hard. Every good thing is.
We have done this before. We can do this again.

Was Lynch suggesting that freedom from Trump might require
the same bloodletting that had won Americans their freedom?

Lynch's predecessor, former attorney general Eric Holder,
remained in war readiness throughout the Trump transition
and presidency. Following the election, a bitter Holder advocated abolishing the Electoral College. He derided Trump as
"an orange man" and a veritable advocate of neo-Nazis. Soon
he went to work for the State of California to nullify Trump
administration executive orders, and barnstormed the country
for the Resistance, channeling his former boss's "gun to a knife
fight" braggadocio: "We have to be ready to, you know, not do
anything inappropriate, not do anything improper, certainly not
do anything unlawful. But to the extent that they want to have a
fight, let's do it. You want to rumble, let's rumble. You want to
have a knife fight, we're gonna do it." In spring 2018, he toyed
with the idea of running against Trump in 2020. Senator Corey
Booker, like Holder, also took up the earlier Obama campaign
tough talk of 2008. During the Brett Kavanaugh Supreme Court
nomination hearings, he rechanneled the erstwhile Obama call
"to get in their faces": "Before I end, that's my call to action
here. Please don't just come here today and then go home. Go
to the Hill today. Get up and please get up in the face of some
congresspeople."

Later, on the eve of the 2018 midterms, former attorney
general Holder renewed his extremist braggadocio: "Michelle
[Obama] always says, you know, 'When they go low, we go high.'

No. When they go low, we kick them. That's what this new Democratic Party is about." Hillary Clinton rallied to the new calls for incivility, adding: "You cannot be civil with a political party that wants to destroy what you stand for, what you care about. That's why I believe, if we are fortunate enough to win back the House and or the Senate, that's when civility can start again."

Holder, like so many of the Resistance, had little humility and entertained less self-reflection, especially in his use of knife-fight imagery that channeled his former boss Barack Obama's unfortunate 2008 paraphrasing of a line from the film *The Untouchables* ("If they bring a knife to the fight, we bring a gun"). Holder was the first cabinet secretary in US history to have been held in contempt of Congress. He had ordered data collection on Associated Press reporters. And in tawdry fashion, he had used a government luxury Gulfstream jet and security guards to fly to the Belmont Stakes horse races for a day's outing with family and friends.

All through autumn 2018, the political back-and-forth seemed to escalate through a series of violent incidents. They ranged from a massive rock being tossed through the window of the Bakersfield, California, headquarters of House majority leader Kevin McCarthy and a threatening letter claiming to be laced with the nerve agent ricin, sent to Senator Susan Collins, to a series of inert bombs delivered to Democratic critics of Trump by unhinged Trump partisan Cesar Sayoc.

Conservatives claimed that nonstop progressive hate rhetoric had prompted such incidents of violence, along with the earlier shooting of Representative Steve Scalise by Bernie Sanders backer James Hodgkinson. Progressives retorted that the bombs arriving at the offices of Trump critics were a direct result of Trump's own over-the-top rhetoric at his rallies. No one, however, had defined the exact relationship, if any, between edgy speech and violent behavior in order to provide some uniform standard of civility applicable to all political figures.

Meanwhile, former Obama administration deputy national security advisor Ben Rhodes and former White House deputy assistant Jake Sullivan (policy advisors to Hillary Clinton's 2016 campaign) had formed a new anti-Trump foreign policy action network. "We're committed to organizing an effective, strategic, relentless, and national response to this administration's dangerous approach to national security," Sullivan said in a news release. "Our role is to help shape the public debate on foreign policy and national security, holding Trump accountable and lifting up an alternative, affirmative vision."

Sullivan declared that the group was "advancing a progressive vision of American global leadership and opposing the Trump administration's reckless foreign policy." In other words, Rhodes and Sullivan thought they were forming some sort of British-style shadow government, as if we operated under a parliamentary system rather than one of constitutionally defined presidential tenures.

Breaking past protocol, in April 2018 even former First Lady Michelle Obama blasted Trump. In puerile terms, she compared her husband's presidency to a proper adult parent, and Trump's to the very opposite: "I think what we see is what happens when we take things for granted. For the eight years Barack was president, it was like having the 'good parent' at home. The responsible parent, the one who told you to eat your carrots and go to bed on time. And now we have the other parent. We thought it'd feel fun; maybe it feels fun for now because we can eat candy all day and stay up late, and not follow the rules," she said, loosely referring to Trump's freewheeling style of governance.

For much of 2017 and 2018, Michelle Obama ("I can be standing here as your forever First Lady") barnstormed the country—and the world. She reminded Americans how foolish they had been to elect Donald Trump (e.g., "Any woman who voted against Hillary Clinton voted against their own voice." "If we're not comfortable with the notion that a woman could be our president, compared to *what?*").

Soon, the mostly frustrated Resistance began to regroup and transmogrify into a more organized state, often to nullify federal law. In one of the strangest political transformations in memory, blue states became states-rights, would-be nullifiers of federal law. Since the Civil War, liberals had insisted on the primacy of more reliably progressive federal jurisdiction—in everything from gun and environmental regulation to past crises of desegregation and busing. But now they began declaring themselves exempt from federal immigration enforcement. California announced itself a sanctuary state, along with some five hundred other local and state jurisdictions. It declared that some of Washington's laws did not apply, in the antebellum fashion of secessionist South Carolina. Its California Values Act insisted that all its cities were now part of a holistic refuge in which federal Immigration and Customs Enforcement agents had lost jurisdictional rights of extradition over illegal aliens currently held in state and local jails.

Nor were California citizens and businesses under proposed new laws allowed to cooperate in the detention and deportation of illegal aliens. Governor Jerry Brown justified defiance of the US government by even evoking God to impugn Trump's religiosity: "I don't think—President Trump has a fear of the Lord, the fear of the wrath of God, which leads one to more humility." Soon, Brown was touring abroad as a quasi-state commander in chief, urging foreign leaders to deal with California as a near-autonomous country. When secularists invoke "the wrath of God" and liberal states mimic the rejectionist methodologies of George Wallace's 1960s Alabama, the world indeed has turned upside down in the age of Trump.

After the election, one-third of California residents polled in favor of Calexit, or a "peaceful" withdrawal from the United States. Most were ignorant that such declarations had been some of the triggers to the Civil War. Nor did they seem to appreciate that the federal government owned vast national parks, military bases, and federal facilities inside the state's borders that were not subject to state secession much less confiscation—without a dangerous pushback.

In response to new Trump-sponsored 2018 federal tax statutes that limited state income and local tax deductions to $10,000, California officials also began contemplating ways to nullify federal tax law. Among the remedies under review was the idea of redefining California's income taxes as "charitable contributions" in order to reinstate their mostly lost federal tax deductibility. Legislators apparently did not realize that any other state could do the same and thereby sabotage the entire federal tax system that hinged on honest individual reporting. Nor did they understand the optics: liberal supporters of steep taxes were now trying to find loopholes to help the wealthiest state residents evade their federal tax liabilities.

Even wackier, there was no legal consistency in California's defiance. Indeed, during the Obama administration, the state of Arizona had been sued successfully by the federal government for its too zealous help in enforcing immigration law. But states were now arguing the very opposite in the era of Trump. They suddenly had the right *not* to assist in immigration enforcement. The only common denominator was Trump. Whatever he was for, the Resistance was against—and made the necessary adjustments in logic and consistency to empower such opposition. No anti-Trumper imagined or cared that he had set a precedent: in the future, anyone willing to use any means necessary to nullify the results of a US election could simply point to the model of 2016.

Most of the assassination chic and the efforts of the Resistance were the work of progressives, some bitter enders of the Clinton campaign, as well as state governments worried that the once sympathetic federal government had gone from hard progressive to hard conservative.

But not all who fought Trump, both during the campaign and his presidency, were left-wing.

Many Republican establishmentarians, neoconservatives, and some on the religious right early on had loathed Trump. But when his nomination seemed certain by spring 2016, a variety of groups swung into more formal action to abort his candidacy, and soon his presidency. Dubbed by many as "Never Trumpers," a derivative perhaps inspired by a special February 2016 *National Review* issue titled "Conservatives Against Trump," their nickname was somewhat misleading because many would eventually support the Republican nominee. A better label might have been "Against Trump—at Least for Now."

Nonetheless, their practical opposition to an outsider candidate without political and military experience was at first understandable. Their ideological opposition to a Republican candidate formerly liberal was plausible. Their moral opposition to a controversial candidate with a checkered personal and professional past and an often outrageous present was explicable.

Yet the venom for Trump among Never Trump conservatives seemed fueled by a less overt cultural resistance. His most vehement establishment conservative critics assumed that sober Republican public officials were to have met certain prerequisites—defined in terms of credentials, degrees, careers, service, and résumés. Comportment was certainly a key to performance. Or rather, the latter was assumed impossible without the former.

Circumspect politicians calibrated their views and campaign strategies not in absolutes, but in relation to other politicians' views. Temporizing and judicious contextualization were always preferable to blunt, much less coarse, bombast. These traits were tempered in high government, especially diplomatic service, and in academia. They were entirely absent in Trump's past landscapes of reality television, real estate deals, professional wrestling, beauty pageants, casino development, and brand-name merchandising.

At one time or another over the 2016 campaign, Never Trumpers included past establishment conservative luminaries like author William Bennett, former CIA director and secretary of defense Robert Gates, former national security advisor and secretary of state Colin Powell, and George Shultz, who had headed four cabinets under Republican presidents. Ex-governors and -senators joined too, such as John Huntsman Jr., Tim Pawlenty, and Arnold Schwarzenegger. Current senators like Susan Collins, Jeff Flake, Mike Lee, John McCain, and Ben Sasse were especially vocal anti-Trumpers both during the primary and, in some cases, the general election and on through much of the Trump presidency.

As a precursor of the later Resistance's efforts to undermine the Electoral College, some Never Trumpers met in March 2016 at the Army and Navy Club in Washington, DC, as the primaries waned. They mused how to derail the steamrolling Trump at the convention. Could they forge a Ted Cruz and John Kasich unity ticket? Could they contest the convention rules, or peel off pledged Trump delegates under some sort of new "conscience clause"? Surely party stalwarts must have envisioned firewalls for sudden conflagrations like Donald Trump that might engulf and incinerate Republicans?

For a while, conservative "Free the Delegates" efforts were welcomed in the liberal press that otherwise enjoyed the blood sport of Republican civil war. When all those efforts failed, Republican Never Trumpers symbolically rallied around 2012 standard-bearer Mitt Romney (who had successfully solicited Trump's support for his presidential bid, and who would soon interview for a position as President Trump's secretary of state).

Romney soon exhausted the vocabulary of sin as he blasted the Trump creed as "racism, misogyny, bigotry, xenophobia, vulgarity and, most recently, threats and violence." Romney added: "Here's what I know: Donald Trump is a phony, a fraud. His promises are as worthless as a degree from Trump

University. He's playing members of the American public for suckers: He gets a free ride to the White House, and all we get is a lousy hat?'"

Trump more ceremoniously retorted of Romney's 2012 loss, "That was a race, I have to say, folks, that should have been won. I don't know what happened to him. He disappeared. He disappeared. And I wasn't happy about it, I'll be honest, because I am not a fan of Barack Obama, because I backed Mitt Romney. I backed Mitt Romney. You can see how loyal he is." Yet by summer 2018 when Romney eyed a run for a Utah Senate seat, he was acknowledging Trump's successful record on the economy and foreign policy.

Republicans in the Senate and House, especially Speaker Paul Ryan and Senate majority leader Mitch McConnell, were in a quandary. They and most of the party leadership had not supported Trump in the primaries. Given their druthers, they did not wish to do so either in the 2016 general election. But to oppose the Republican nominee would implode the party's unity and might give the Democrats back the House and Senate.

On the other hand, to embrace the volatile Trump might couple the demure congressional leadership to the supposed Trump train wreck. The leadership might incur blame when the Democratic landslide threw a generation of Republicans out of office, destroying majorities in the Congress and ceding the Supreme Court to progressives for a generation. In the end, the majority of rank-and-file Republicans and their leaders adopted Speaker of the House Paul Ryan's pragmatic approach of supporting Trump by focusing on the worse alternative of Hillary Clinton, while disassociating themselves periodically from Trump's politically incorrect bombast and reappearing scandals from his past. Later Senate majority leader McConnell had so mastered Senate rules of judicial confirmation that he almost single-handedly ushered through confirmation of a near-record number of Trump nominated federal judges.

After Trump's nomination, more desperate efforts ensued as the Never Trump ranks both thinned and became more out-spoken and desperate. Groups like "Our Principles PAC" and "Never Trump PAC" sought to find a supposedly conservative third-party presidential alternative. All Republican officehold-ers turned down such offers. So did former officials such as Condoleezza Rice and retired generals like Stanley McChrys-tal. Self-appointed presidential nominator William Kristol of the *Weekly Standard* finally ran out of potential candidates. He at one time considered a run by *National Review* writer David French, before settling on the obscure Evan McMullin.

McMullin's selection was instructive of the movement's naiveté and the desperate loathing that Trump incurred. While Trump was already aiming at populist swing states to win a purple swath that no Republican had pulled off since 1988, Never Trumpers thought his antidote was to be found in an uncharismatic former CIA operative and Goldman Sachs banker with zero name recog-nition, but with a propensity to sound smug and self-righteous. (By mid-2018, McMullin was hounded by campaign creditors al-leging that he still owed them $670,000 in unpaid bills.)

The rationale was apparently that Utahan and Mormon Mc-Mullin might at least win his home state. That unlikely victory supposedly would then throw a hoped for and nearly even pop-ular vote—and thus likely deadlocked Electoral College—into the House of Representatives. Once the election rested there, thoughtful Republicans could step forward to save the country by caucusing to select a properly presidential establishment fig-ure such as Ted Cruz, John Kasich, or Marco Rubio, who had all just lost the nomination to Trump.

As Trump began to unite the party and realistic alternatives faded, the Never Trump movement gradually began to break up during the 2016 campaign into various smaller factions. Some, of course, would sit out the election.

Some would vote for third-party candidate, libertarian, and former New Mexico governor Gary Johnson. A few would switch to Hillary Clinton. As soon as Trump seemed destined to win the nomination, for example, *Wall Street Journal* conservative op-ed writer Bret Stephens announced his preference for Clinton: "I will never vote for Donald Trump. I have a very, very hard time voting for Mrs. Clinton. I think that for the United States, Hillary Clinton, as awful as I find her, is a survivable event. I'm not so sure about Donald Trump."

Perhaps a third of the original small group of Never Trump Republicans would hold their nose and vote for Donald Trump. Or as the astute essayist Norman Podhoretz put it in September 2016: "Many of the younger—they're not so young anymore—neoconservatives have gone over to the Never Trump movement. But I describe myself as anti-anti-Trump. While I have no great admiration for him, to put it mildly, I think she's worse. Between the two, he's the lesser evil."

Still, it was astonishing that for all its scenarios and media attention, the Never Trump movement had almost *no* practical effect on Election Day. Trump was estimated to have won the same roughly 90 percent or so of Republican voters as had McCain and Romney respectively in 2008 and 2012—and a slightly higher margin of Republicans than Hillary Clinton's estimated 89 percent vote of Democrats. That effect served as a sort of earthquake in conservative circles. Sober punditocracy and opinion journalists exercised almost no electoral influence on their own readers or voters at large. As an example, conservative talk radio host Glenn Beck in May 2016 had exclaimed: "I don't want my children to look at that man and say, 'Yeah, he's my President.' I won't have that. I will not endorse it, I will not tolerate it." But by 2017, Beck was emblematic of the crumbling Never Trump establishment and soon would be on radio defending much of President Trump's agenda.

A few of the small group of Never Trump conservative die-hards had stayed obdurate. Unlike former officials and sitting governors and senators, they never recanted their opposition, and throughout Trump's first year doubled down on their opposition. Especially outraged at the idea of a president Trump were opinion journalists Max Boot, David Brooks, Mona Charen, Eliot Cohen, David Frum, Robert Kagan, Jennifer Rubin, Bret Stephens, George Will, and many of the senior editors of *Commentary*, *National Review*, the *Weekly Standard*, and a few of the columnists of the *Wall Street Journal*.

In May 2018, for example, George Will, the doyen of conservative pundits, blasted any Republican who would supposedly debase himself by working with a president Trump. Will, who would later advise voters to vote Democratic in the November 2018 midterm elections to derail the Trump presidency, focused his wrath on Vice President Mike Pence:

> The oleaginous Mike Pence, with his talent for toadyism and appetite for obsequiousness, could, Trump knew, become America's most repulsive public figure. And Pence, who has reached this pinnacle by dethroning his benefactor, is augmenting the public stock of useful knowledge. Because his is the authentic voice of today's lickspittle Republican Party, he clarifies this year's elections: Vote Republican to ratify groveling as governing.

When Trump's raucous presidency proved neither liberal nor ineffectual, the remnant Never Trumpers often found new avenues to express their contempt. A tiny cadre, or the so-called Meeting of the Concerned, became more vocal about the threat posed by the Trump administration to Robert Mueller's special counsel investigation of alleged Trump-Russian collusion.

Most of the time, Trump's Republican critics, however, simply sought to outrival one another in splenetic invective. Historian Max Boot's assessment of Trump's first year suggested that president Trump was even more distasteful to Never Trumpers than had been either candidate Trump or transition Trump:

> In many ways, the damage he's doing at home is even worse, where he's undermining the rule of law. He's obstructing justice. He's lending the support of the presidency to monsters like Roy Moore [the former judge and failed Republican senate nominee in Alabama]. He is exacerbating race relations. He is engaging in the most blatant xenophobia, racism and general bigotry that we have seen from the White House.

Harvard law professor and former George W. Bush Department of Justice official Jack Goldsmith summed up the Never Trump contempt in the *Atlantic* with the favored word "never":

> We have never had a president so ill-informed about the nature of his office, so openly mendacious, so self-destructive, or so brazen in his abusive attacks on the courts, the press, Congress (including members of his own party), and even senior officials within his own administration. Trump is a Frankenstein's monster of past presidents' worst attributes.

The Never Trump movement by early 2018 had turned into a waiting game on the assumption that Trump might still fail. Then adults like themselves would be called in to repair the mess of the *enfant terrible*. "At some point, the Trump train's going to come to a glorious wreck," promised a confident David Jolly, a defeated two-term congressman from Florida. "Who's going to be there to pick up the pieces? I don't think it'll be the people who enabled him."

In late October 2017, outgoing senator Jeff Flake (R-AZ), whose political future ended with his Never Trump invective, seemed to make Republican support for the president a test of conservative morality in an address to the US Senate: "When the next generation asks us, why didn't you do something? Why didn't you speak up? What are we going to say? . . . I rise today to say, enough. We must dedicate ourselves to making sure that the anomalous never becomes the norm."

The venom often appeared in regrettable fora. In August 2018, the funeral of Senator John McCain turned into a veritable Trump hate fest. Of course, McCain and President Trump had hardly been friends. During the 2016 election, Trump in crude fashion had impugned McCain's stellar military service, which included a horrific five and a half years as a prisoner of war in a dank North Vietnamese prison. For his part, McCain had earlier cruelly called Trump supporters "crazies." Later McCain had helped to bring the largely discredited anti-Trump Fusion GPS dossier to the attention of federal authorities in a rather desperate effort to destroy Trump. Out of spite, McCain had flipped on his earlier support of Obamacare just to cast the deciding vote that defeated Trump's effort to repeal and replace it.

During the funeral service itself, in not so veiled allusions, daughter Megan McCain received loud applause for blasting Trump, as if she had delivered a partisan campaign speech: "We gather here to mourn the passing of American greatness, the real thing, not cheap rhetoric from men who will never come near the sacrifice he gave so willingly, nor the opportunistic appropriation of those who live lives of comfort and privilege while he suffered and served."

Indeed, the atmosphere soon resembled that of a campaign rally, analogous to the funeral fiasco sixteen years earlier of Senator Paul Wellstone (D-MN), who had tragically died in a plane accident. Wellstone's Minnesota funeral was meant to be a commemoration of the life of a public servant well lived. But the funeral service was soon hijacked by partisan speakers and ended up a loud and often offensive political pep rally that turned off the nation.

Former president Barack Obama used his televised moment to reference Trump, with similar not so subtle attacks: "Much of our politics can seem small and mean and petty. Trafficking in bombast and insult, phony controversies and manufactured outrage." Likewise, former president George W. Bush, also no friend of Trump and who had taken an oath during the Obama administration not to attack a sitting president, nevertheless took a swipe as well. He contrasted McCain with Trump's policies on illegal immigration and the summit with Vladimir Putin: "He [McCain] respected the dignity inherent in every life, a dignity that does not stop at borders and cannot be erased by dictators."

Megan McCain, Obama, and Bush were apparently all unaware of their self-created paradoxes of calling for greater tolerance while using a funeral occasion to score political points against a sitting president. Once funeral solemnity is sacrificed, it then becomes legitimate to remember that Bush himself had once infamously looked into the eyes of Putin and said he saw a soul "straightforward" and "trustworthy," a characterization mocked by John McCain.

Obama had waged an often brutal 2008 campaign against McCain that saw constant insinuations leveled at McCain as too old and at times near senile. Bush was accused by McCain in 2000 of running a dirty primary battle, including robotic calls alleging McCain had fathered an out of wedlock child. In other words, both Obama and Bush found themselves in an Orwellian position of calling for greater civility at a funeral by uncivil references to a president whom they felt had been too harsh with John McCain—a deceased onetime bitter political rival who had criticized both presidents in the past for undermining him in savage fashion.

In the end, what marginalized conservative Never Trumpers was their inability to raise, much less answer, questions that weighed heavily on the vast majority of Republican voters. Was not voting for Trump, de facto, in essence a vote for Hillary Clinton, and, with it, surety of at least a twelve-year Obama-Clinton project that would virtually ensure an activist Supreme Court and continuance of the Obama progressive fundamental transformation of the country?

The Never Trumpers rarely self-reflected about *why* their party had not won the popular vote in five out of the six last elections, or why the last Republican president had left office with near historic unpopularity, doubled the debt during two terms, and passed arguably progressive legislation such as No Child Left Behind, Common Core, and an unfunded Medicare prescription drug benefit. Nor did the Never Trumpers advance agendas and strategies that might in the future once again win the Midwest swing states in 2020, which moderates and centrists like McCain and Romney had in the past failed to do.

Like the Resistance, the Never Trumpers failed in all their political aims at removing or delegitimizing Donald Trump. Never Trump *New York Times* columnist David Brooks in April 2017 summed up the anguish of the movement: "A lot of us never-Trumpers assumed momentum would be on our side as his scandals and incompetences mounted. It hasn't turned out that way. I almost never meet a Trump supporter who has become disillusioned. I often meet Republicans who were once ambivalent but who have now joined the Trump train."

From posts at mostly influential media, universities, and think tanks, an echo chamber of outrage hammered Trump daily. Sometimes the collective megaphone opposed the very positions that Never Trumpers had supported for their entire lives as now stained by association with Trump. Orphaned from the Republican Party, wrong about the Trump nomination and election, mistaken that Trump's record would be insubstantial or liberal, and convinced that more invective would bolster their predictions, throughout 2017 and 2018 they continued nonetheless in the belief that they too might imperceptibly delegitimize

Trump and help to abort his presidency—and thereby purport-edly save the country.

The Never Trumpers could encourage the Mueller investi-gation. They could work on swinging Republican moderates to join Democrats should congressional writs of impeachment follow the 2018 midterm elections. Or by appearing nonstop in liberal media such as CNN, MSNBC, and NPR, they could give credence and "conservative" authenticity to progressive efforts to discredit Trump.

By 2018, Never Trumper conservatives had been hired by marquee progressive newspapers and magazines like the *New York Times*, the *Washington Post, Salon,* and the *Atlantic* on the expectation that, at least for the duration of the Trump presi-dency, their singular venom would continue unmatched (as fer-vor so often is with apostates). And, in fact, they would become the loudest, if not most impotent, of all Trump's critics.

National Review author Charles Cooke noted of Never Trump critic Jennifer Rubin that almost any position that Trump embraced, she opposed—including most of those that she once had enthusiastically supported: "Contrary to popular myth, she is not in fact writing from a 'conservative perspective,' but as just one more voice among a host of Trump-obsessed zealots who add nothing to our discourse. In so doing, she does conservatism a sincere disservice."

Thousands of essays and investigative reports have been published about special counsel Robert Mueller's probe of al-leged Trump collusion with Russian interests to warp the elec-tion and ensure the defeat of Hillary Clinton. Little more need be said about such a complex labyrinth of rumor, conspiracies, and self-serving testimonies, since the ultimate outcome of the Mueller investigation is not yet known.

Since May 2017, Robert Mueller has investigated Russian in-terference in the 2016 election. So far he has not indicted anyone for colluding with the Russians to warp an election, his originally mandated aim. A few Trump officials—former national security advisor Michael Flynn, former campaign chairman Paul Manafort, minor campaign operatives like Rick Gates and George Papadopoulos—were indicted on or pled guilty to charges of providing false statements, fraud, and money laundering.

But, again, no one has yet been indicted on the foundational collusion allegations that had prompted Mueller's investigation and supposedly guided his inquiries. In that sense, the Mueller inquiry resembled past special counsel and special prosecutor efforts, especially those of Patrick Fitzgerald to indict former vice-presidential aide Lewis Libby (pardoned by Trump in April 2018) or the expansion of Kenneth Starr's Whitewater probe to investigate the sexual antics of, and cover-up of them by, President Bill Clinton. Struggling with difficulty to find wrongdoing elsewhere serves as recompense for not finding it anywhere one was supposed to find it easily.

By spring 2018, the Mueller investigation was by report (through leaks to sympathetic media) looking into Trump's personal life, his taxes, and his business practices. By April, Mueller had outsourced his focus on Michael Cohen, Trump's personal attorney, to the US Attorney's Office for the Southern District of New York. Agents of the federal attorney then raided the office of Cohen, who had sought to profit in the private sector by his supposed ties with the incoming president—and who secretly had taped his telephone calls with client Trump. Mueller's attorneys had been initially interested in any communications of Cohen dealing with the Trump–Stormy Daniels affair of a decade prior, and the circumstances around nondisclosure payments with others, such as a former Playboy Playmate, to keep long ago sexual liaisons private. Cohen later would plead guilty to a number of charges involving financial impropriety and allegedly cooperated with the federal attorney to provide any information deemed relevant to the Mueller investigation.

If the past were any guide, anytime a special counsel radically departed from his original mandate—in this case Trump-Russian collusion—it was a worrisome indication that it had become a political rather than legal inquiry. Consequently, the ego and reputation of the special counsel became invested in any sort of indictment, and welcomed an unwise reactive pushback from his targets, as a way of tapping new avenues of media-generated hysteria.

The never-ending investigation certainly served the aims of the Resistance and the Never Trump movement. It contributed somewhat to keeping Trump's polls mostly below 50 percent through constant leaks that some sort of bombshell indictment of Trump or his family was always just over the horizon. For most of 2017–18, daily news blared that an indicted Michael Flynn would incriminate Trump, that Carter Page, an energy consultant and erstwhile low-level Trump campaign official, would be indicted and spill the proverbial beans of collusion, that new evidence would corroborate the Steele document, that Trump's son or son-in-law would face charges, or that Trump attorney Michael Cohen would soon release taped phone calls confirming Trump's illegal behavior. The daily stream of gossip was never reified, but again served the larger purposes of distraction and delegitimization.

Yet there were existential contradictions that made the entire effort near nonsensical. While Mueller was investigating Trump, an entire generation of FBI and Obama Department of Justice officials insidiously either were fired, resigned, or were reassigned by agency overseers. Most allegedly had acted unethically, improperly, or perhaps illegally in conducting investigations of Donald Trump. Most were either knee-deep in opposition research efforts funded by the 2016 Clinton campaign against the Trump candidacy or involved in past investigations of Hillary Clinton herself.

In sum, as the official collusion investigation sputtered, officials were losing their jobs over their involvement in real collusion that as of yet lacked a special investigator or counsel. Apart from the Trump firing of FBI director James Comey, the cast of those who turned up in emails, texts, and the media in connection with either investigations of Hillary Clinton or Trump, or were involved with Clinton opposition research efforts against Trump, and who left their posts without Trump's direct involvement were demoted, resigned, or retired, were legion. They included officials from both the FBI and DOJ such as James Baker, Peter Kazdik, Michael Kortan, David Laufman, Andrew McCabe, Bruce Ohr, Lisa Page, James Rybicki, Peter Strzok, and Sally Yates.

Scurrilous rumors about Trump's supposed collaborations with Russians were leaked by likely government and Clinton campaign sources in the closing days of the 2016 campaign. They originated out of the so-called Fusion GPS dossier compiled by British subject and ex-covert operative Christopher Steele—albeit with help from a number of as yet not clearly defined foreign sources. Marc E. Elias, a lawyer with the Washington law firm of Perkins Coie, who was hired by both the Clinton campaign and the Democratic National Committee, had retained Fusion GPS as a firewall intermediary designed to mask any Clinton fingerprints on the Steele dossier.

Steele's ensuing anti-Trump dossier was a product of partisan political efforts and unconfirmed and often absurd purchased Russian smears. Incredibly, it was soon used by members of the FBI and Obama Justice Department to obtain FISA court warrants to surveil or supposedly incidentally sweep up American citizens allegedly colluding with Russians. The court warrants were a result of massaged requests that failed to apprise the FISA justices explicitly that the Clinton campaign had funded the dossier, that the FBI had neither verified its contents nor was confident in the veracity of Christopher Steele's testimony, that the FBI had in fact severed relations with Steele on grounds that he had violated past FBI agreements, and that supposedly corroborating news sources were themselves, in circular fashion, derivative of the dossier for their information.

Stranger still, after over two years of supposed media investigations, it was disclosed in May 2018, two years after the fact, that in 2016 the FBI had hired at least one informant, Stefan Halper, to be inserted into the 2016 Trump campaign. Ostensibly the Cambridge professor, with prior connections to both the CIA and FBI, was tasked with pursuing rumors of Russian collusion. In actuality, at best he seems to have fanned rumors raised by the mostly fallacious so-called Steele dossier, commissioned by the Clinton campaign. At worst, Halper sought to entrap, then embarrass Trump functionaries.

Amid subsidiary scandals about the use of Hillary Clinton's private email server to conduct State Department official business, of efforts of the Russians to gain ownership of sizable amounts of American uranium, and of the unlawful surveillance and leaking of names of American citizens, two additional paradoxes arose that continued to plague the entire Mueller investigation.

One, there would be neither scandals nor a Mueller investigation if Hillary Clinton *had just won the election*—as all involved in likely illegal or unethical behavior had probably assumed. Neither the FBI nor the Justice Department would in a Clinton administration have disclosed the existence of the Clinton oppositional research dossier and its progenitors, much less the details of FISA-ordered surveillance or FBI informants implanted into presidential campaigns.

Many of those on the Obama national security team, the FBI, or the Justice Department who were deeply involved in the sourcing or dissemination of the Steele dossier would have perhaps been privately congratulated by the incoming Clinton administration. Current scandals would not have been scandals.

Second, once more "projection," or the defense mechanism of imputing one's own improper behaviors and motives to someone else as a way to excuse or at least rationalize them, played a role. There was real Russian collusion. Yet such collaboration was likely between Christopher Steele, Fusion GPS, and the Hillary Clinton campaign to thwart the Trump campaign in the waning days of the 2016 election—with timely help from James Comey's FBI and shadow support from John Brennan at the CIA. Before the Trump victory, the very idea of anyone swinging the election had been written off as patently absurd by President Obama (who was likely privy, even if secondhand, to the Steele dossier's contents):

> There is no serious person out there who would suggest that you could even rig America's elections, in part because they are so decentralized. There is no evidence that that has happened in the past, or that there are instances that that could happen this time . . . I have never seen in my lifetime or in modern political history, any presidential candidate trying to discredit the elections and the election process before votes have even taken place. It is unprecedented. It happens to be based on no fact. Every expert regardless of political party . . . who has ever examined these issues in a serious way will tell you that instances of significant voter fraud are not to be found.

Of course, Obama had good reason to anticipate a whiny, petulant, and bothersome post-election defeated Trump in exile. He was forewarning the country not to listen to such a likely bitter ender. Again, the charge of Russian collusion arose mostly because Hillary Clinton had through intermediaries hired a British former spy to compile dirt on Donald Trump as a sort of insurance policy to weaken his candidacy in the campaign. When Clinton lost, the dossier (*inter alia*) was reified as an excuse for her own inept campaign. Eventually, it became a last-ditch mechanism by which to organize resistance to both the transition and presidency of Donald Trump.

In other words, special counsel Robert Mueller's targeting of Trump for collusion was a strange sort of distraction that blinded him, willfully or not, to the likely Fusion GPS–Russian connection. Worse, each day that Mueller's investigation wore on, it became ever more likely that the Russians did in fact interfere in the 2016 election, mostly by feeding various narratives to the Clinton-hired Fusion GPS efforts, and therefore to the press to damage the Republican nominee or at least sow general chaos amid the 2016 election.

Most Orwellian was the realization that had Clinton won the election, as almost everyone thought she would, only *one* interest would have likely released information to the public concerning the Clinton effort to buy Steele's smears and dirt on her losing opponent, Donald Trump: operatives of the Russian government. They alone would have likely been able to leverage their own involvement at an opportune time. Russians might well have argued that they had helped elect a US president by fabricating and passing on information to Christopher Steele and his associates—and now wanted their quid pro quo recompense. Steele, remember, had been on the FBI payroll.

Again, despite the undeniable policy successes in Trump's initial two years, his polls rarely until summer 2018 topped 50 percent. Much of his relative unpopularity was due to the formidable forces arrayed against him—the Resistance, the Never Trump movement, the Mueller investigation, and the media. But not all the opposition to Trump was from without.

What may have initially prevented Trump from capitalizing on the often unhinged hatred of his enemies and the dramatic upswing in the US economy was his own thin skin—or perhaps more charitably, his understandable frustration and exhaustion at being a victim of Russian collusion at the very time he was being accused of it.

Chapter Eleven

TRUMP, THE TRAGIC HERO?

*No man is an island, entire of itself; every man is
a piece of the continent, a part of the main . . . and
therefore, never send to know for whom the bell
tolls; it tolls for thee.*
 —John Donne, *Devotions Upon Emergent Occasions*

The very idea that Donald Trump could, even in a perverse
way, be heroic may appall half the country. Nonetheless,
one way of squaring both Trump's personal excesses and his accomplishments is that his traditionally nonpresidential behavior may have been valuable in bringing long-overdue changes in
foreign and domestic policy.

Tragic heroes, as they have been portrayed from Homer's
Iliad and Sophocles's plays (e.g., *Ajax, Antigone, Oedipus Rex,
Philoctetes*) to the modern western film, are not intrinsically noble. Much less are they likeable. They can often be obnoxious
and petty, if not dangerous, especially to those around them.
These mercurial sorts rarely end up well, and on occasion neither do those in their vicinity. Oedipus was rudely narcissistic. In the film *Hombre*, antihero John Russell (Paul Newman)
proved arrogant and off-putting.

Tragic heroes are often unstable loners. They are aloof by preference and due to society's understandable unease with them. Sophocles's Ajax's soliloquies about a rigged system and the lack of recognition accorded his undeniable accomplishments is Trumpian to the core. They are akin to the sensational rumors that late at night Trump is holed up alone, brooding, eating fast food, apart from his wife, and watching Fox News shows.

The tragic hero Achilles in Homer's *Iliad* is an outlier from Thessaly. He is self-absorbed and pouts that his service is never rewarded commensurately by the Greek's deep-state leaders, the mediocre Menelaus and his brother the overrated careerist King Agamemnon. At a late April 2018 rally in Michigan, Trump complained to his supporters that the "fake news" establishment would never give him any credit for thawing relations with North Korea: "What do you think President Trump had to do with it? I'll tell you what. Like how about everything?"

Achilles is tribal like all tragic heroes. His foremost loyalty is to his clan and friends, more so than to the larger Greek commonwealth. Tragic heroes cannot fit in with their times, even at the acme of their success, because they are pre-civilizational. They are more worried about their band or tribe than about the city-state. Personal loyalty, not civic duty, is their creed. They are keenly aware that a world of contemporary nuanced values has left them far behind. One builds a polis with men like Odysseus, not with a tribal chieftain such as an uncouth Achilles. The Magnificent Seven are not the stuff of school boards and city hall. You would not want an Ajax permanently in the modern State Department, given that his forte is not discourse but action and disruption, the more Manichean the better.

Loyalty's twin, honor, is all important to tragic heroes. They rage when it is not won fairly and squarely. The subtext of many of Trump's tweets is either the disrespect shown him or the desire for respect commensurate with his perceived accomplishments. Read of Achilles whining about the lack of booty that comes his way, or Ajax brooding that the lesser man like the fixer Odysseus wins the prized armor of Achilles, and Trump leaps out on the pages—bitter over "fake news" and "rigged" polls that do not give him credit for his economic and foreign policy successes.

Outlaw leader Pike Bishop (William Holden), in director Sam Peckinpah's *The Wild Bunch*, is an unapologetic killer. Yet his final gory sacrifice results in the slaughter of the toxic General Mapache and his corrupt local Federales (with whom Bishop for a time was willing to do business). A foreboding Ethan Edwards (John Wayne), of John Ford's classic 1956 film *The Searchers*, alone can track down his kidnapped niece. But Edwards's methods and his recent murky past as a Confederate renegade make him suspect and largely unfit for a civilizing frontier after the expiration of his transitory usefulness. At times, we do not quite know what the racist firebrand Edwards will do to his long ago kidnapped and now adult niece when he finds her—kill or maim her? These characters are not the sorts that we would associate with the more predictable and reliable Bob Dole, Paul Ryan, or Mitt Romney.

The tragic hero's change of fortune—as Aristotle reminds us, always from good to bad—is due to an innate flaw (*hamartia*). Nonetheless, at least in some cases, this intrinsic and usually uncivilized trait can be of service to the community, albeit usually expressed fully only at the expense of the hero's own fortune. The problem for civilization is that the creation of those skill sets often brings with it past baggage of lawlessness and intolerable comfortability with violence.

The threatened establishment almost seems embarrassed that it had to stoop to find salvation in such anti-establishment methods—especially if they serve as reminders of its own feral and now happily forgotten past, and, far worse, its present inability to deal with the very world it created.

Trump's cunning and mercurialness—honed in Manhattan real estate, global salesmanship, reality TV, and wheeler-dealer investments—may have earned him ostracism from polite Washington society. But these talents also may for a time be suited to dealing with many of the outlaws of the global frontier, such as the Iranian theocracy or North Korea's Kim Jong-un. And those outlaws are many and they are formidable. Of course, Trump lives in the real world—not that of cinema and the Athenian stage—in which the pressures on a polarizing outsider like himself are nearly unimaginable to most Americans.

At rare times, a General George S. Patton ("Give me an army of West Point graduates and I'll win a battle. Give me a handful of Texas Aggies and I'll win a war.") could be harnessed to serve the country in an existential war. Yet as a later out of place American proconsul in post-war Bavaria, Patton could not cease his boisterousness. He soon earned a forced reassignment. Apparently, without an SS Division with Tiger and Panther tanks facing American GIs, Patton was now expendable. After the war, a circumspect—and far less militarily talented—General Omar Bradley grew on us in peace, even if he could hardly have done what Patton had in battle.

General Curtis LeMay, architect of the low-level B-29 fire raids over Japan, also did what others could not—and would not: "I suppose if I had lost the war, I would have been tried as a war criminal. . . . Every soldier thinks something of the moral aspects of what he is doing. But all war is immoral and if you let that bother you, you're not a good soldier."

Later, the public exposure given to the mentalities and behaviors of such controversial figures would only ensure that they would likely be estranged from or even caricatured by their peers—but only after they were no longer needed by those whom they had benefitted. When one is willing to burn down with napalm 75 percent of the industrial core of an often genocidal wartime Japan, and thereby help bring a vicious war to an end, then one looks for sorts like the off-putting, cigar-chewing Curtis LeMay and his thunderous B-29s.

In the later calm of peace, comfortable and safe Americans are often shocked that America ever had been so desperate. Stanley Kubrick's classic 1964 film *Dr. Strangelove* drew on Curtis LeMay for two of its delusional and trigger-happy generals: the cigar-smoking General Jack D. Ripper (Sterling Hayden) and General Buck Turgidson (George C. Scott). In truth, LeMay was one of the most careful, sober, and courageous American air force generals in history, beloved as a war hero by 1945, cruelly caricatured as a Cold War relic in 1964.

What makes such men and women both tragic and heroic is their knowledge that the natural expression of their personas can lead only to their own destruction or ostracism from an advancing civilization that they seek to protect. And yet they willingly accept the challenge to be of service. That is the element of tragedy: no solution, no out in a world of bad and worse choices.

Yet for a variety of reasons, both personal and civic, their characters not only should not be altered, but could not be, even if the tragic hero wished to change, given his megalomania and absolutist views of the human experience. In the classical tragic sense, Trump likely will end in one of two fashions, both not particularly good: either spectacular but unacknowledged accomplishments followed by ostracism when he is out of office and no longer useful, or, less likely, a single term due to the eventual embarrassment of his beneficiaries, as if his utility is no longer worth the wages of his perceived crudity.

Clint Eastwood's Inspector "Dirty" Harry Callahan cannot serve as the official face of the San Francisco Police Department any more than Donald Trump could appear presidential in the fashion of a Barack Obama. But Dirty Harry has the skills and ruthlessness to ensure that the mass murderer Scorpio will never harm the innocent again. In the finale, he taunts and then shoots the psychopathic Scorpio, ending both their careers, and walks off after throwing his inspector's badge into the water.

Marshal Will Kane (Gary Cooper) of *High Noon* did about the same thing with his tin star, but only after gunning down (with the help of his wife) four killers whom the law-abiding but temporizing elders of Hadleyville proved utterly incapable of stopping. The embarrassed town's elites are grateful to Kane, but privately they are gladder that he, now with blood on his hands, realizes that he must leave town.

The out of place Ajax in Sophocles's tragedy of the same name cannot function apart from the battlefield. Unlike the duplicitous and smooth-talking Odysseus, old Ajax lacks the tact and fluidity to succeed in a new world of nuanced civic rules. So he would rather "live nobly, or nobly die," "nobly" meaning according to an obsolete black-and-white code that is no longer compatible with the ascendant polis.

In George Stevens's classic 1953 western, *Shane*, even the reforming and soft-spoken gunslinger Shane (Alan Ladd) understands his own dilemma all too well. He alone possesses the violent skills necessary to free the homesteaders from the insidious threats of hired guns and murderous cattle barons (but how he got those skills—as in the case of Trump—especially worries those he plans to help). Yet by the time of his final resort to lethal violence, Shane has sacrificed all prior chances of reform and claims on reentering the civilized world of the stable "sodbuster" community. As Shane tells young Joey after gunning down the three villains of the film and thus saving the small farming community: "Can't break the mold. I tried it, and it didn't work for me. . . . Joey, there's no living with a killing. There's no going back from one. Right or wrong, it's a brand, a brand that sticks. There's no going back."

Trump could not cease entirely his tweeting, not cease his rallies, not cease his feuding, and not cease his nonstop motion and unbridled and often vicious speech, even his fast and loose relationship with the truth, if he wished to. Right or wrong, it is his brand that sticks to him. Such overbearing made Trump, for good or evil, what he is. His raucousness can be managed, perhaps mitigated for a time—thus the effective tenure of his sober cabinet choices and his chief of staff, the ex–marine general, no-nonsense John Kelly—but not eliminated. His blunt views cannot really thrive, and indeed can scarcely survive, in the nuance, complexity, and ambiguity of Washington.

Tragic heroes do not necessarily intend to be heroic. Sometimes their motives for confronting dangers or solving crises can just as easily be self-centered or arise from a desire for personal vengeance or fantasies of self-redemption or just an endless need for adulation. Again, they care for their reputations and their sidekicks more than they do the law.

Will Kane, for a while, thought he could get out of Hadleyville with his bride, ahead of the arriving gunslingers on the noon train, and only on second thought realized escape was not a practicable alternative—killing killers in the streets was his own only salvation. Shane would have preferred for a while longer to vainly try to readjust to his new life as a stationary farm hand, had events not forced his hand. Trump himself may have had all sorts of reasons to run for president, many of them self-centered and narcissistic. But the various circumstances in which tragic heroes appear on the scene, inadvertently or by design, are not so important as the fact that they sometimes do.

Moving on, sometimes fatally so, is the tragic hero's operative exit. Antigone certainly makes her point about the absurdity of small men's sexism and moral emptiness in such an uncompromising way that her own doom is assured. Tom Doniphon (John Wayne), in John Ford's *The Man Who Shot Liberty Valance*, unheroically kills the thuggish Liberty Valance to advance the cause of civilized progress despite violating his own heroic protocols of a fair fight. He births the career of Ranse Stoddard and his marriage to Doniphon's girlfriend, and thereby ensures civilization is Shinbone's frontier future. His service done, Doniphon burns down his house and degenerates from feared rancher to alcoholic outcast.

Critics mostly disliked director Tony Scott's inspired *Man on Fire*, in some sense a post-modern replay of *The Searchers*. In the judgment of reviewers, Scott had turned the hired killer and bodyguard John Creasy (Denzel Washington) into what they deplored as an unsympathetic and merciless vigilante. In truth, Creasy was a social misfit and tragic hero who chose the path to a violent demise because he knew that he alone had the frightening abilities to deal with lethal cartel kidnappers, and was not especially worried about dying in the effort. As his friend Paul Rayburn says of Creasy's looming vendetta: "A man can be an artist . . . in anything, food, whatever. It depends on how good he is at it. Creasy's art is death. He's about to paint his masterpiece." Trump is no killer like Tom Doniphon or John Creasy. But he has useful skills and a single-minded temperament. Thereby, he understands why his polls stay relatively low. And, certainly, he is perceptive enough to suspect by now that he is good at effecting overdue change. Yet, for that success, he may increasingly grasp that he will not end up all that well.

At the end of *The Magnificent Seven*, the village's old man bids farewell to what is left of the Seven: "The fighting is over. Your work is done. For them, each season has its tasks. If there were a season for gratitude, they'd show it more." The surviving gunslingers would no longer be magnificent had they stayed on in the village ("They won't be sorry to see us go, either"), settled down to age, and endlessly rehashed the morality and utility of slaughtering the outlaw Calvera and his banditos. As Chris rides out, he sums up to Vin their dilemma: "The old man was right. Only the farmers won. We lost. We always lose." I doubt that president emeritus Trump will attend many future solemn ceremonial assemblages of ex-presidents.

Chris knows that few appreciate that the tragic heroes in their midst are either tragic or heroic, until they are safely gone and what they have done in time can be attributed to someone else. Worse, he knows that such gunslingers have by their violent beneficence given up any claims on the nourishing networks and affirmation of the peasant's agrarian life. But they can for a while save civilization by their very uncivilized behavior.

John Ford's most moving scene in his best film, *The Searchers*, is Ethan Edwards's final exit from a house of shadows, swinging open the door and walking alone into sunlit oblivion, the community he has saved symbolically closing the door on him. If he is lucky, Trump may well experience the same self-inflicted fate. By his very excesses, Trump has already lost, but in his losing he might alone be able to end some things that long ago should have been ended.

As President Trump's second year of governance began, a Quinnipiac poll reported that only 34 percent of its respondents thought that he was honest (63 percent did not). About 38 percent believed that he cared about average Americans, and even fewer (32 percent) thought that he shared their values. Only 28 percent considered him "level headed." Some 59 percent denied Trump possessed good leadership skills. Yet by summer 2018, Trump was some days polling near 50 percent in many surveys, as his popularity spiked on good economic news and progress abroad.

No one can still quite calibrate whether Trump's combativeness and take-no-prisoners management style always hurts him as president, or is a necessary continuum of his persona that ensured his unlikely election and early political effectiveness as president. And no one quite knows either whether Trump's inexplicable outbursts are sometimes planned by design to unnerve his critics and the media, or are instead spontaneous expressions of indiscipline and crudity. Conventional wisdom squares these circles by concluding that Trump's ferocity shores up his base, but his base is not large enough to give him a reliable 51 percent popularity rating among voters. Most also have concluded that Trump's unorthodox style, speech, and comportment likewise are designed to advance his agendas, but are usually overtaken by his fury. The result is one step forward due to cunning, one backward due to sloppy speech.

Trump, in unorthodox fashion, certainly won praise for his against-the-odds boldness—demanding a comprehensive tax bill not seen since Reagan's administration, destroying ISIS, exposing the media as abjectly biased, pulling out from the Paris climate accord, moving the US embassy to Jerusalem, renouncing the Iran deal, declaring that after seventy years the Palestinians were no longer refugees (in the manner that Jews cleansed from the Middle East or Prussians sent back into Germany were not either), taking on the entire NFL and revealing, if crudely so ("sons of bitches"), the paradoxes of multimillionaires posing as such victims of American unfairness that they cannot stand for the national anthem.

Yet on the cusp of success, Trump also seems to erode his own real achievements with raging Twitter outbursts against nonentities, or a needless slap at one of his own appointees, or a sudden firing, or mutually incompatible stories about a long-ago liaison of some sort with an adult film star, or a thin-skinned rally boast that he was really right after all as he recounted yet again the glories of the increasingly distant 2016 campaign.

When Trump entered office, he was immediately faced with a self-created contradiction. He had won the key midwestern and purple swing states on promises of "draining the swamp." That refrain was taken by his base to mean both dismantling the permanent deep state and staffing his administration with unorthodox appointments that would lessen the opportunities for corruption.

Yet Trump clearly needed tried old hands who knew the deep state and yet were not part of it. But how many such loyal fellow iconoclasts were there? Was a Stephen Bannon or Jared Kushner up to fighting with the likes of veterans Nancy Pelosi, Charles Schumer, John Brennan, or Robert Mueller? How many General Michael Flynns existed, and how savvy about Washington were they really?

Added to Trump's conundrum were two other challenges. One was certainly political. Trump's agendas that had won him the presidency were deeply antithetical to those of most of the bipartisan Washington hierarchy. In terms of economic policy, Trumpism, at least in theory, did not appeal to Republicans with prior government service, blue-chip academic billets, and directorships of major companies and corporations. The usual Republicans eager for high office were precisely those most likely to oppose Trump's promises to leave Afghanistan, avoid most overseas interventions, level tariffs, or build a border wall.

Secretary of State Rex Tillerson (previously CEO of Exxon) and chief economic advisor Gary Cohn (formerly CEO of Goldman Sachs) were appointed on the basis of their business success and net worth that superficially appealed to Trump as proof of their assured future excellence in government. But as internationalists, globalists, and corporate magnates with unlimited powers, it was inevitable that such proud men would clash both with an even prouder Trump and with Trump's nationalist agendas—and eventually both be forced out of the administration.

Trump forged a management style foreign from almost all prior presidents, born from Manhattan real estate brokerage, reality television, and entrepreneurial salesmanship. Drama, even chaos, was considered "energy," even creativity. Loyalty and compatibility above all were prized, even over competence. Looks and fashion mattered, on the principle that both drove up ratings. How something was said and who said it were as important as what was said.

Hiring and firing for Trump were also organic processes. Trump consulted outsiders in the private sector almost as frequently as he did his own team. Turnover was a necessary means of finding those with "talent" whose personalities jibed with Trump's own mercurial moods. CIA director Mike Pompeo might be more of an interventionist than was Secretary of State Rex Tillerson, and thus less in sync with Trump's opposition to optional military expeditions, but he certainly was both skilled and as the new secretary of state would be far more in tune with Trump's personal wavelength.

In prior administrations, "stability" and "continuity" were more prized. Difficult or even unimpressive figures who should have been promptly fired often were not, on the principle that their abrupt departures might signal poor presidential judgment or incur crises of confidence at the center of the global order, or, more mundanely, earn a spate of incriminating, get-even, tell-all memoirs.

Susan Rice, Barack Obama's UN ambassador and national security advisor, repeatedly and publicly flat-out lied (on Benghazi, the Bergdahl swap, nerve agents in Syria, and FISA warrant surveillance and unmasking), and did so without worry about losing her job. Eric Holder assumed that being held in contempt by Congress did not threaten his job security. When top advisors and cabinet secretaries left other administrations— such as George W. Bush's secretary of defense Donald Rumsfeld or Kathleen Sebelius, Barack Obama's secretary of health and human services—the departures were announced as normal retirements or transitioning to the lucrative private sector, and not necessarily due to feuding with the president.

Trump was not ideologically driven. He did not fire subordinates for political apostasy. A Trump sin was not so much straying from party lines as leaking, causing needless public relations problems, or bad-mouthing Trump himself. In some sense, Ronald Reagan was similar. Until Trump, Reagan was the best known "firing" president of the post-war age, who had no patience with big egos, braggarts, and freelancers. The common themes of the Al Haig (secretary of state), Don Regan (chief of staff), and David Stockman (director of the Office of Management and Budget) firings or forced resignations were not political, but rather perceived arrogance, indiscretion, and disloyalty—or getting on the wrong side of Nancy Reagan.

Critics charged that Trump often selected some appointees on the basis of their cable-news screen presence. After watching hours of Fox News, he supposedly hired national security officials and legal advisors such as K. C. McFarland, Sebastian Gorka, and Jay Sekulow on the basis of their demonstrable screen skills in repartee and impromptu commentary, the more pro-Trump, the better. Media analysts harped that Trump cared nothing for proper academic or government credentials. Instead, they charged, he rarely even read résumés. He did not adjudicate academic degrees or ask "experts" about the general reputations of those he appointed. (Few in the media fathomed that their being such unorthodox figures might have been the reason that the unorthodox Trump, and his unorthodox supporters, were fond of them.)

Historians gleefully noted that during Trump's first year an astounding 34 percent of his "senior" (variously defined) employees resigned, were reassigned, or were fired. By the end of his first sixteen months in office, that percentage had supposedly grown to over 40 percent—a new record of turnover for the first two years of any presidential administration.

Among the departed were some of Trump's closest and most loyal 2016 campaign associates—national security advisor Michael Flynn (25 days in office), press secretary Sean Spicer (182 days), chief of staff Reince Priebus (189 days), and chief strategist Stephen Bannon (211 days). Others who resigned or were fired either had not supported Trump in the election or were considered well-regarded establishmentarian centrists such as top economic advisor Gary Cohn, secretary of state Rex Tillerson, and Trump's second national security advisor, H. R. McMaster.

Especially transitory were employees attached to Trump's chief of staff, the Office of Communications, the Press Office, and the National Security Council. According to media reports, in the first fifteen months in office, twenty-eight workers of sixty-five had been reassigned or changed jobs. Among the most controversial were Michael Dubke (communications director), Anthony Scaramucci (communications director), Hope Hicks (communications director), Omarosa Onee Manigault Newman (Office of Public Liaison), and Rob Porter (White House staff secretary).

What were the reported reasons for these brief tenures? Traceable leaks, foolish on-the-record interviews, alleged disloyalty, or purported personal scandals prompted most departures. The most likely common denominator, however, was simply inexperience with Washington, especially its media, and the naïve assumption that working for Donald Trump, president of the United States, somehow provided one with exemptions rather than nullified them.

Even those not in Washington's swamp were often reluctant to work for Trump. In part, they feared that they might be fired or worried about the ostracism that might ensue from working for such an unpopular president, at least as his polls rested in his first five hundred days. Would they be castigated as "sell-outs" for working for the controversial Trump, or praised as patriotic Americans who saw as it their duty to right the ship of state during Trump's stormy voyage? Or become endless targets of the media and Robert Mueller's prosecutors?

Washington Never Trump pundit David Frum outlined the establishment career risks of working for Trump, concluding with: "If the Trump administration were as convinced as you are that you would do the right thing—would they have asked you in the first place?"

But Michael Caputo, a minor Trump campaign aide who was never charged, but nearly bankrupted by special counsel Robert Mueller's inquisition, put it quite differently:

I think they want to destroy the president, they want to destroy his family. They want to destroy his businesses. They want to destroy his friends so that no billionaire in let's say fifty years wakes up and tells his wife, "You know this country is broken and only I can fix it." His wife will say, "Are you crazy? Did you see what happened to Donald Trump and everybody around him?" That's what this is about . . . I certainly didn't sign up for this when I went to work for the Trump campaign. And I will never, ever, work on another Republican campaign for as long as I live.

Did the apparent bedlam bother Trump?

Not particularly. Trump may have worn out his staff, exhausted his appointees, and institutionalized chaos that sent even his aides into despair. But he was tasked by voters with "draining the swamp," a task that meant that the splashed and soiled drainer would become nearly as stained as what was drained. After the March 2018 departure of National Security Advisor McMaster, Trump tweeted: "The new Fake News narrative is that there is CHAOS in the White House. Wrong! People will always come & go, and I want strong dialogue before making a final decision. I still have some people that I want to change (always seeking perfection). There is no Chaos, only great Energy!" Note Trump's style: after unceremoniously firing his secretary of state and forcing the resignation of national icon and military hero General H. R. McMaster, Trump was not only *not* disturbed about accusations that he had created chaos, but rather promised even more "energy," and thereby apparently more forced dismissals.

Amid the disruptions, lost was the fact that in terms of process, Trump met the press frequently. He was far more candid and accessible than had been Barack Obama. His inner team was as diverse in terms of race, sex, class, and prior political leanings as most prior administrations. His tweets held back nothing. And yet that accessibility and informality were mostly lost on the press. Or such familiarity with Trump only bred more media contempt.

Forgotten was Trump's occasional magnanimity. After a brutal primary campaign in which Trump smeared and was smeared, he ended up welcoming a few of his once archrivals into his cabinet such as Secretary of Housing and Urban Development Ben Carson and Energy Secretary Rick Perry. No one in the press praised him for his "team of rivals" magnanimity. He mended fences with former opponents like Senators Ted Cruz ("He's not Lyin' Ted any more. He's Beautiful Ted. I call him Texas Ted.") and Rand Paul. Fierce critic John Huntsman became ambassador to Russia. Trump had hired both Democrats and centrists such as Gary Cohn. When the smoke of firing had cleared, by mid-2018 Trump had nevertheless ended up with a stellar array of superb national security professionals: National Security Advisor John Bolton, UN ambassador Nikki Haley, Defense Secretary James Mattis, and Secretary of State Michael Pompeo.

Did the constant hiring and firing, arrivals and departures hurt Trump? No doubt, at least in his initial eighteen months. The charge of a nonstop White House revolving door also contributed to the Trump paradox of solid achievement not earning commensurate public support. Or as a diehard Trump supporter remarked to me in spring 2018 following the Tillerson and McMaster firings: "I like everything Trump is doing, but I'm getting sick of the drama."

Drama was not always bad—in measure. If after an initial acculturation, Trump finally found those he felt comfortable with and who reflected his views, and the length of their ensuing tenures increased, then the turnovers were well worth it. But if the personalities proved secondary reflections of Trump's innate volatility, then the swamp was not so much drained by the president as it had flooded into the White House.

Some weeks or days Trump welcomed controversy upon controversy to the extent that the frenzied media dropped its usual charge of "chaos" and came up with the replacement compound phrase "hyper chaos." During the third week of March 2018, the following events occurred all nearly simultaneously: Trump asked for the resignations of, or had them submitted from, National Security Advisor H. R. McMaster and the head of his legal team, John Dowd. In their places, he named the controversial John Bolton and the take-no-prisoners Washington former prosecutor Joseph diGenova, himself soon to bow out for reasons of possible conflicts of legal interests. Veterans Affairs secretary David Shulkin was out, Ronny Jackson was in as his replacement—and then was forced out as his nomination earned a firestorm of resistance.

At the same time, Trump was warring with both his base and the Republican establishment: with the former over his concessionary signing of a huge $1.3 trillion budget bill to the delight of progressives and to the furor of his old Tea Party and "Make America Great Again" base. They had no patience with Trump's mea culpa that only by signing the bill would he get record defense increases. Due to a fractured Republican Party in the House and a razor-thin majority in the Senate, Trump had had no choice but to sign the bill or shut down the government with a veto. Conservative talk-radio went wild with threats of sitting out the 2018 midterm elections. Meanwhile, the US Chamber of Commerce and think-tank Republicans damned Trump's targeted tariffs on about $60 billion worth of Chinese imported goods, more concerned with Trump's ideological heresy and threats of stiff countertariffs than with the data on Chinese serial cheating in matters of trade, copyrights, and patents. Farmers, a Trump constituency, complained that the president's tariffs had already diminished their exports to China.

On the domestic front, Trump's lawyers were once again dueling with alleged past paramours who had claimed that they had engaged in consensual relations over a decade earlier with private citizen Donald Trump, and who had now popped up in search of celebrity and money, goaded on by Trump's enemies. For days on end, they gave lurid interviews to CBS, CNN, and MSNBC about their former sexual antics with Trump and their supposed pay-offs.

Tell-all porn star Stormy Daniels and Karen McDougal, an ex–Playboy Bunny, were also being threatened with lawsuits by Trump for their violations of past nondisclosure agreements. They answered questions from a crazed media over whether the president had "used protection" or had disclosed whether he had judged their sexual performance on a comparative basis. To the extent the media and Democratic operatives goaded them on, such sensationalism was seen as a tactic of pressuring Trump's evangelical base, which increasingly supposedly could be embarrassed into renouncing its support on the basis that Trump was not just on occasion morally suspect, but rather an inveterate sinner.

Nonetheless, numerous polls in March 2018 portrayed a yawning general public: what Donald Trump had done in his own private life more than a decade prior to his presidency was apparently his own business.

No paramour had come forth claiming that she was having sexual relations with Trump while he was president, while she worked for him, or while he was physically in the White House. The press and popular culture long ago had so lowered the bar for presidential conduct during the Bill Clinton–Monica Lewinsky interlude that its present feigned outrage convinced few that Trump's past behavior was national news rather than something better kept private. Indeed, *Newsweek* in early April 2017 reported that following charges by porn star Daniels that she and Trump conducted an affair in 2006 (his wife Melania had just given birth to son Barron), Trump's positive ratings among male voters in the Harvard CAPS/Harris Poll rose from 50 to 53 percent compared to the prior month.

Trump meanwhile was busy himself. He was engaged in a Twitter spat with former vice president Joe Biden. On two occasions, Biden, in Robert De Niro fashion, had all but threatened to physically clobber the president of the United States. In March 2017, Biden foolishly bragged: "They asked me would I like to debate this gentleman, and I said no. I said, 'If we were in high school, I'd take him behind the gym and beat the hell out of him.' . . . I've been in a lot of locker rooms my whole life. I'm a pretty damn good athlete. Any guy that talked that way was usually the fattest, ugliest S.O.B in the room." Biden's threat was his second, an expansion on his early 2016 boast that "I wish we were in high school—I could take him behind the gym. That's what I wish."

Most targeted presidents would have let the sloppy Biden have yet another moment of his characteristic braggadocio and not responded in kind. Not Trump. He immediately attacked (in his textbook "don't tread on me" retaliatory style): "Crazy Joe Biden is trying to act like a tough guy. Actually, he is weak, both mentally and physically, and yet he threatens me, for the second time, with physical assault. He doesn't know me, but he would go down fast and hard, crying all the way. Don't threaten people Joe!"

Suddenly, the uncouth Trump saw an opening both to display his deterrent take-no-prisoners style while soberly calling on Biden, a possible 2020 Democratic presidential candidate, not to "threaten people." Again, the net result of Trump's customary pushback was that a supposed iconic establishmentarian like Biden had ended up starting a puerile name-calling match with the supposedly adolescent Trump—and lost as the more immature foe and thus backed off.

In early March 2017, in reaction to some of the above-noted supposed chaos and its apparent inability to tank Trump's polls, a somewhat frustrated *Washington Post* columnist Max Boot summed up the Republican Never Trump anger and perplexity:

"This administration was born in chaos and will die in chaos because Trump has a chaotic mind and a compulsion to inflict his mental disorder on the wider world. This is how the American era will end—not with a bang but with buffoonery." Yet the American "era" was not ending, but at that time enjoying the strongest GDP growth, job reports, energy production, business and consumer confidence, and foreign policy successes in fifteen years.

As far as the nation's soul was concerned, America's elites— academic, journalistic, and political—were revealing to the American people the sort of crude put-downs, stereotyping, and biases about Trump supporters that questioned the value of their cultural advantages, higher education, and privilege, given that they had proved so unsteady, profane, and unhinged. No establishmentarian quite figured out that any success that Trump enjoyed was often seen as a de facto negative referendum on the past performance of the status quo—and by extension themselves.

It was hard to see how US relations with key allies or deterrent stances against enemies were not improved since the years of the Obama administration, at least in the sense that there was no more naïve Russian reset. China was on notice that its trade cheating was no longer tolerable. The asymmetrical Iran deal was over. And the United States was slowly squeezing with sanctions a nuclear North Korea. Was chaos or predictability the more dangerous message in dealing with thuggish regimes?

An "adults in the room" anti-Trump narrative was hyped through deliberate media massaging. "Anonymous" senior officials winked and nodded on "background" to reporters that, if had it not been for their own sober stewardship, the entire Trump administration would have imploded. Here the *locus classicus* was the tabloid "insider" story of the Trump White House, Michael Wolff's *Fire and Fury: Inside the Trump White House*. While much of his lurid exposé was demonstrably false (e.g., Trump was certainly not having an ongoing affair with UN ambassador Nikki Haley), some of Wolff's explosive stories came from interviews with senior White House advisor Stephen Bannon, which led to his forced resignation. Why any White House would invite in a disreputable author like Wolff was iconic of Trump's undisciplined and naïve staff.

After Trump made his March 2018 controversial congratulatory call to Vladimir Putin following his rigged election, someone on the National Security Council leaked to the press their team's supposed talking-point warnings that were given to Trump before calling Putin. The cautionary prompt read in capital letters: "DO NOT CONGRATULATE." The pathetic leak seemed aimed to suggest that Trump's wise and circumspect staffers had given their president the tools to handle Putin, but the headstrong and nearly illiterate Trump had not even taken the time to read them. No matter—a few months later Trump himself announced that the exiled Vladimir Putin belonged back in the G-7, without much worry as to why Russia had been expelled in the first place.

As a general rule, any call Trump made to a foreign leader, any private conversation he had with staffers, or any meeting he had with Congress could within forty-eight hours find itself in the news. The September 5, 2018, op-ed by "Anonymous" had claimed that such "resistance" was the work of patriotic Republicans deeply embedded within the Trump administration who felt it their constitutional duty as "adults in the room" to undermine and subvert supposedly dangerous Trump directives, and leak all they could to the media.

The firings of both McMaster and Tillerson were preannounced by journalists, as were the appointments of their successors. No one could be trusted: not James Comey to keep his notes of a private one-on-one presidential meeting confidential, not Stephen Bannon to be careful about what he told arsonist journalist Michael Wolff, and not Chuck Schumer to respect the privacy of his chats with Trump about immigration from the developing world.

Why did White House staffers, as well as high officials connected with the FBI, CIA, and Justice Department, leak in a manner not quite seen before in prior administrations?

A variety of reasons come to mind:

(1) Carelessness and inexperience meant that Trump naïvely assumed loyalty when there was none.

(2) The outlier Trump had never fully cleaned out the Obama administration holdovers at the Department of Justice, the National Security Council, and the various cabinet departments. As part of the Resistance and deep state they blabbed all they knew, both to discredit Trump and to magnify their own importance. If fired, they figured that they would be martyred and find lucrative billets, rather than become disgraced and unemployed.

(3) Given that Trump's polls by mid- and late-2018 were not yet consistently hitting 50 percent, and at times were closer to 40 percent, many leakers in the first two years of his administration thought Trump was done for, and were already looking ahead to post-Trump Washington careers by establishing their fides as chronic, but, as of yet, closet anti-Trumpers.

(4) Many leaks either came from special counsel Robert Mueller's investigatory team or at least those in Congress sympathetic to it, and were designed as a way of deterring any Trump effort to shut down the special counsel's investigations.

(5) Finally, the media remained overwhelmingly anti-Trump. Any potential leaker knew that his identity would be protected and his "bombshell" hyped, in a fashion opposite from the Obama administration, when journalists had no overarching desire to peddle incessantly gossip about their favorite president, and, if they did, could well be surveilled as in the case of Associated Press journalists.

Whatever the causes, the leaks continued. Remedies from firings to threatened prosecutions did little. Instead, the public learned immediately about everything from CIA covert assistance to Syrian rebels to Trump's furor at an unfavorable Obamaera immigration deal in a phone call with the Australian prime minister.

Trump also drove himself into endless cul-de-sac fights with celebrities and politicians. Again, he believed that he was reestablishing deterrence (hit back three times as hard to discourage future critics from gratuitously attacking him). And perhaps he was. But Trump was also wasting precious moments evening scores with nonentities and furthering a media narrative that he was isolated, petulant, puerile, and erratic. When the often opportunistic junior New York senator Kirsten Gillibrand attacked Trump, he responded immediately with "Lightweight Senator Kirsten Gillibrand, a total flunky for Chuck Schumer and someone who would come to my office 'begging' for campaign contributions not so long ago (and would do anything for them), is now in the ring fighting against Trump. Very disloyal to Bill & Crooked—USED!"

When Stephen Bannon was identified as the source of many of the disastrous leaks to author Michael Wolff, Trump fired him, but still fumed: "Steve Bannon has nothing to do with me or my Presidency. When he was fired, he not only lost his job, he lost his mind." As the public read these news accounts and were supposed to become further irate at Trump's immaturity, they may have just often laughed out loud at his outrageousness.

Where Trump usually got in the most trouble was when he sounded uncouth on taboo subjects, such as Senator John McCain's military service, the ethnic heritage of a judge assigned to a civil suit against a Trump company, and Pakistani American Gold Star parents, or on solemn occasions such as state funerals, the anniversaries of 9/11, and natural disasters such as the hurricanes in Puerto Rico and North Carolina, to continue to get even with his critics—all losing propositions that were usually followed by a drop in the polls.

As the media splashed lurid stories about Trump's supposed derangement, following in the wake of Secretary of State Tillerson's supposed off-the-cuff slur that Trump was a "moron," Trump protested too much about his singular sanity: "Throughout my life, my two greatest assets have been mental stability and being, like, really smart. Crooked Hillary Clinton also played these cards very hard and, as everyone knows, went down in flames. I went from VERY successful businessman, to top T.V. Star . . . to President of the United States (on my first try). I think that would qualify as not smart, but genius. . . . and a very stable genius at that." Critics were left to decipher whether Trump was an egotist, a prevaricator, a clever ironist, a lampoonist, a child, a naïf, or a brilliant rhetorician—or all or none of that and more.

Even when Trump set his sights at bigger targets, he stunned the press with his hyperbole and invective. When Kim Jong-un threatened the United States, Trump sought to appear more volatile than Kim: "North Korean Leader Kim Jong Un just stated that the 'Nuclear Button is on his desk at all times.' Will someone from his depleted and food starved regime please inform him that I too have a Nuclear Button, but it is a much bigger & more powerful one than his, and my Button works!"

Did such hyper chaos tank the Trump presidency? At least not immediately. Trump's polls by late March 2018 either were unchanged or went up—and by early summer Trump's handling of the North Korean crisis and the economy was reflected for a while in near 50 percent approval ratings in a few polls. Indeed, Trump by mid-June was polling about like Barack Obama had at an identical point in his presidency. His popularity would soon dip again as the midterm elections neared, and after the force-multiplying effects of the September 5 "Anonymous" *New York Times* op-ed, the Bob Woodward tell-all *Fear*, and the wild Brett Kavanaugh Supreme Court nomination hearings.

But for his own part, Trump does not seem to care whether he is acting "presidential." As we saw earlier, the very adjective, as he admits, is foreign to him. He does not worry over the effect on others or the public from his furious tweets. He seems not to care too much whether his revolving-door firing and hiring and his rally counterpunches reveal a lack of stature or are becoming an embarrassing window into his own insecurities and apprehensions. Meanwhile, the Beltway media world closes in upon him in the manner that the trapped western hero felt the shrinking landscape was increasingly without options in the new twentieth century, and the time was nearing to move on or go out in a blaze of glory.

The best and brightest résumés of the Bush and Obama administrations had doubled the national debt—twice. Three prior presidents had helped to empower North Korea, now with nuclear-tipped missiles pointing at the West Coast. Reread all the sophisticated foreign policy journals of the establishment apparat—*Foreign Affairs*, *Foreign Policy*, *National Interest*, and so on—and North Korea was rendered as an intractable problem, so complex, so layered with fourth- and fifth-level counterfactual speculations that such overthinking academics and nuanced ex-diplomats end up sounding like academics at acrimonious department meetings stymied over allotting $500 of travel reimbursements.

Refined and sophisticated diplomats of the last quarter century, who would never utter the taunt "Little Rocket Man," nonetheless had gone through a series of failed engagements with North Korea. Three administrations had given Pyongyang quite massive aid to behave, and either not to proliferate or at least to denuclearize. And it was all a failure, and a nuclear and deadly one at that.

How smart was thirty years of stale diplomatic conventional wisdom that appeasing Chinese serial trade cheating would eventually lure a prosperous Beijing into the family of Western and law-abiding democracies? How brilliant was tilting away from Israel and the moderate Gulf monarchies, Egypt, and

Jordan to cut a deal with an anti-American and revolutionary theocratic Iran in hopes that such deference might convince an ascendant revolutionary Tehran that the West sympathized with Iran's frustrations with not being appreciated for its power and history?

For all of Barack Obama's sophisticated discourse about "shar[ing] the wealth" and "you didn't build that," vast expansions of the money supply, zero-interest rates, massive new regulations, the stimulus, much of health care nationalized, and shovel-ready government-inspired jobs, he could not achieve 3 percent annualized economic growth, and so his economists declared that to do so was no longer structurally possible.

Half the country, the more desperate half, believed that the remedy for a government in which the IRS, the FBI, the DOJ, and the NSA were weaponized by elites with impressive dossiers and blue-chip degrees, often in partisan fashion and without worry about the civil liberties of American citizens, was not more temporizing technicians. They were desperate enough to welcome any pariah who cleaned house and moved on.

Certainly, Obama was not willing to have a showdown with the Chinese over their widely acknowledged coerced expropriation of US technology. He whined but otherwise shied away from confronting the NATO allies over their chronic welching on prior defense commitments. He preferred to remain blind to the North Korean capability of hitting US West Coast cities. He had no desire to lock horns with Mexico over its deliberate policy of exporting human capital in exchange for $30 billion sent home in remittances, or with the European Union over its mostly empty climate change accords. Massive trade deficits with China, Mexico, and Germany did not much bother Obama.

The real moral question is not whether the gunslinger Trump could or should become civilized (again defined in our context as becoming normalized as "presidential"). Rather, the key is whether he could be of service at the opportune time and right place for his country, crude as he is. After all, despite their decency, in extremis did the frontier farmers have an orthodox solution without Shane? Mexican peasants did not enjoy a realistic alternative to the Magnificent Seven, and the town elders of Hadleyville had no viable plan without Marshal Will Kane in the streets. Even Agamemnon's ego did not convince him that he would ever have had any chance of killing "man-slaughtering Hector" without a petulant and dangerous Achilles.

Trump's dilemma was always that at some likely point his successes on the economy and in foreign policy might create a sense of calm prosperity—and thereby, in counterintuitive fashion, allow voters the luxury of reexamining the messenger more so than the message. In other words, if crudity got results, then the results might appear no longer to hinge on further crudity. Every tragic hero realizes that he can be driven out of town, not just after the original threat is ended, but when it first appears that soon the danger will be neutralized. For civilized society, the perceived coarseness of the tragic hero always remains nearly as repugnant as the threat that brought in its deliverer in the first place.

In sum, the nation may believe that it could not withstand the fire and smoke of a series of Trump presidencies. But given the direction of the country over the last sixteen years, half the country, the proverbial townspeople of the western, wanted some outsider, even with a dubious past, to ride in and do things that most normal politicians not only would not, but could not do—before exiting stage left or riding wounded off into the sunset, to the relief of most and the regret of a few.

With the constant shouting against candidate and then president Trump, and Trump's monotonous Twitter and campaign-rally pushback against the "fake news" media, the new left-wing Democratic Party, the Never Trump establishment, and the progressive cultural world, Trump's actual record of governance was often drowned out. Yet what he accomplished in his first twenty months in office was undeniably impressive. As we shall see in the next chapter, Trump has enriched the country, and, far from ruining the post-war order, he has restored much of the power and influence of the United States abroad.

Chapter Twelve

MR. TRUMP GOES TO
WASHINGTON

*Fortunately for the country, flawed as Trump is
by aberrant personality defects—overweening
self-centeredness, an inadequate attention span,
and an inability to deal with criticism except in
the angriest terms—not everything hinges on the
president, even if, at age seventy-eight, assuming
he had won a second term, he did somehow
decide he wanted a third.*
       —Michael Nelson, *Trump's First Year*

Donald Trump's initial two-year record, like most presidencies, can be evaluated by lots of different criteria: from economic performance at home to statecraft abroad; as well as his legislative record, presidential executive orders and cabinet policies; judicial, economic, and political appointments; party losses or gains; a general sense of national purpose or lack of same—and his polls. Former advisor Stephen Bannon purportedly had a whiteboard in his office with one column showing promises made in the campaign, the other how many of them had been fulfilled.

By late 2018, two questions arose about the state of the United States. One, were things seen as better or worse than in 2016? Two, to what degree was President Trump responsible for the change?

The first question is answered below. The second is made easy by the stark antitheses between Trump and Obama. Just as Obama was not a centrist Bill Clinton, so too Trump was not an establishmentarian President Bush. In fact, the Trump and Obama agendas were polar opposites. What Obama did, Trump methodically sought to undo, from the Affordable Care Act to the Iran deal.

For every Obama executive order, there arose a Trump antithetical executive order. And for every mellifluous Obama put-down of an opponent, there was a cruder and sharper Trump riposte. Obama sought to manage the economy; Trump to free it. The former believed in the therapeutic view of human nature; the latter the tragic—and acted accordingly with both friends and enemies. In other words, Trump framed his presidency in antithesis to 2009–17, in hopes that the country could judge for itself under which of the two administrations it was better off.

Economically, the verdict was mostly unambiguous. Indicators by summer 2018 were continually getting better, and seen so by the public as improving in a fashion not seen in decades. The economy over eighteen months had grown faster than at any comparable period from 2009 to 2016. Business investment in the first quarter of 2018 had increased by almost 40 percent. At the end of the first five hundred days of Trump's tenure, both critics and supporters agreed that the economy was performing at a level not yet seen in the twenty-first century.

The gross domestic product continued to expand at an annualized rate well over 3 percent, progress never reached over a year during the Obama administration. During the second quarter of 2018, GDP growth hit an astonishing 4.1 percent. Unemployment was not just lower, but by December 2017 had neared record peacetime levels at 4.1 percent—and the lowest in ten years. By May 2018, unemployment had dipped even lower to 3.9 percent—a record for the twenty-first century—and would soon dive to 3.8 percent.

Over a dozen states were reporting some of the lowest unemployment rates (2–3 percent) in their history. California had never before reached its current 4.1 percent unemployment rate since it began collecting such data. Trump's critics now flipped, no longer warning of stagnation but of a wild inflationary boom that could only lead to bust.

The labor participation rate was up to 63 percent. That was the highest in fifteen years. By March 2018, weekly applications for unemployment benefits were the lowest in forty-eight years. Two million fewer Americans were on food stamps. Trump, in his first two years, had achieved somewhat of an economic miracle, one that was rarely reported in the network news.

But Americans saw anecdotally, and firsthand, the accuracy of such statistical data. There was certainly more traffic on the roads. Stores were more crowded, labor scarcer. Omnipresent new construction and flurries of business activity spawned worries about inflation rather than recession. Even in the deindustrialized Midwest, "Now Hiring" and "Help Wanted" signs began popping up in previously stagnant small towns.

Polls showed that the good economic news had somewhat eroded political opposition from the Democratic Party against the Trump economic agenda. The scenario in theory might have resembled something like the beginning of the startling political transformation in the country between November 1983 and November 1984. Then most agreed that the economic upsurge of a 7 percent annualized growth in GDP had transformed the Reagan presidency from a supposed "trickle-down" failure to "Morning in America."

A roller-coaster stock market, always rattled by Trump's rhetoric, but usually reassured by his action, had climbed at least 30 percent since January 2017 to record highs. The ascendance was contrary to predictions such as those by *New York Times* columnist and Nobel Prize–winner Paul Krugman, who proved the epitome of anti-Trump pessimism on the economy. He had infamously predicted right after the election that the market would never recover. Indeed, the economy itself was all but doomed. And Krugman cited the person of Donald Trump as responsible for it: "If the question is when markets will recover, *a first-pass answer is never* . . . [emphasis added]. So we are very probably looking at a global recession, with no end in sight. I suppose we could get lucky somehow. But on economics, as on everything else, a terrible thing has just happened." Esteemed economist Larry Summers similarly had charged that Trump's boast that he would achieve 3 percent economic growth was the stuff of those who believe in "tooth fairies and ludicrous supply-side economics."

Yet, again, to what extent was Donald Trump really responsible for the remarkable economic surge? Former president Barack Obama in September 2018 reemerged from his retirement to campaign against Trump in the final weeks before the midterm elections. Oddly, Obama's stump strategy was not to deny Trump's economic success, but instead to take credit for it, on the new theory that a president's record in his first two years, at least if wildly successful, is actually attributable to his successor.

In truth, Trump's boosterism and salesmanship had released the proverbial animal spirits suppressed during the Obama administration's anemic recovery. Trump had surely sent a message to small businesses, investors, entrepreneurs, and corporations that from 2017 to 2020 at least, it was far more likely that taxes would decline than rise. Regulations would more likely taper off than increase. The US government would prefer to encourage profitability as a sign of nationalist recovery for all than to see profit making as a sort of selfishness to be regulated, taxed, and redistributed. And Trump himself would be as wild in his praise for companies that brought jobs home as he would be wildly furious at businesses that moved them abroad.

Impressions and zeitgeist no doubt mattered. By late spring 2018, the National Federation of Independent Businesses' Small Business Optimism Index had found sixteen consecutive months of near record highs. In a general sense, Trump in both economic and foreign policy seemed to convey the image that anything was now possible. Old deadlocks and debates were no longer impasses. Status quo wisdom was no longer either wisdom or status quo—as defined by opening up the Arctic National Wildlife Refuge for drilling, repealing the Obamacare mandate, renegotiating trade with China, and slashing capital gains and corporate income taxes, and who knew what next?

But the changes were not just psychological. Trump also fostered economic growth through legislation, by executive orders, and by cabinet appointees, at least to the extent any president could in his first two years. Trump's executive-order deregulations (said by the end of his first year to have numbered sixty-seven major deregulatory acts, and by mid-2018 over eight hundred in total), his opening up of more sites for oil, gas, and coal production, his cabinet secretaries' slash-and-burn attacks against bureaucratic red tape by the Interior Department and at the Environmental Protection Agency all helped to streamline the economy and had a force-multiplying effect of promoting economic growth. Trump's critics saw his zealous deregulation as an existential threat to the environment and a driver of inequality. His supporters wanted good jobs now, and would worry about carbon emissions and too many multimillionaires and billionaires later.

The Republican Congress passed the Tax Cuts and Jobs Act of 2017. The reduction and restructuring of the tax code enraged liberal think tanks, university economics departments, and Democratic politicians. They all variously charged that the new law would explode the deficit, expire in 2025 without effect, contribute to inequality, and do nothing about spurring economic growth. They may well have been right on a few of their complaints, but abjectly wrong that the tax cuts did not foster economic growth—the chief aim of Trump's entire economic agenda.

Almost all tax brackets were lowered. The standard deduction doubled for married couples. The child care tax credit also doubled, from $1,000 to $2,000. Most workers got to keep more money. Employers enjoyed accelerated depreciation tables and corporate and capital gains tax breaks. Corporations began returning off-shored capital to take advantage of lower tax rates.

The big losers (apparently by design) were high-income salaried professionals in blue high-tax states, who in 2018 could no longer write off most of their state income and local taxes as federal tax deductions. The result was that residents of states like California, Connecticut, Illinois, Massachusetts, and New York faced substantial tax increases on their 2018 returns.

Yet many of them had little moral authority to complain. In the past, well-off blue-state liberals had voiced loud ideological support for higher taxes in general, and in particular redistribution by taxing the affluent and spreading the wealth through government entitlements. Trump cynically gave them their wish, albeit with an unspoken assumption that most of such vulnerable high-tax states were permanently blue.

American gas, oil, and coal production in aggregate reached historic highs, making the United States the largest producer of fossil fuels in the world—at a time when a growing global economy and production shortages had sent oil prices to over $70 a barrel. But, unlike the past when such cartel spikes hit the US economy, this time around the United States, as both the world's largest consumer *and* its largest oil and gas producer, was not just a casualty but, in a collective sense, a beneficiary as well of high prices.

On the foreign policy front, the verdict by mid-2018 was still out. Trump was finding that overseas engagement was antithetical to his campaign promises of ending optional strikes and interventions. Yet hitting back was also necessary from time to time to restore US deterrence in line with his Jacksonian promises of muscularity. Bombing in Syria and new rules of engagement in Afghanistan decimated ISIS and made inroads against the Taliban.

But a persistent ground force in either country was contrary to Trump's campaign pledges of not sending, or sometimes even keeping, troops around the world to intervene in civil wars, justified either by humanitarian grounds or US long-term strategic interests—or both. For now, Trump bent to the will of his generals and kept American troops in Afghanistan and as peacekeepers in Syria after the rout of ISIS.

Trump's madman act with North Korea—posing as unhinged in rhetoric as "Little Rocket Man" Kim Jong-un was frequently in deed—may have unsettled both China and North Korea, at least enough to bring them to the point of talking about negotiating away North Korea's nuclear arsenal. Beefed-up sanctions were slowly strangling Pyongyang. In return for denuclearization, America would likely promise not to invade, bomb, or to encourage reunification under South Korean auspices, or perhaps even to offer diplomatic recognition.

China was willing to intervene with the North Koreans to discourage their nuclear brinksmanship, given that, for the first time in memory, the United States talked credibly about reexamining the entire asymmetrical trade relationship between Washington and Beijing. In addition, Trump, more overtly than past presidents, raised the specter of nuclear proliferation on China's borders. In the next cycle of proliferation, it was likely a matter of democratic Japan, Taiwan, South Korea, and other US allies obtaining nuclear status, and their fleets of nuclear-tipped missiles would be pointed in a very different direction—at China and North Korea. In the end, Trump sought to remind China that its delight with the status quo that the new American president had inherited—a rabid nuclear North Korean pit bull occasionally let off its Chinese chain to consume US attention and resources—was untenable and could not continue.

Yet Trump's first two years were also marked by a number of setbacks. He did not usher through enough funding for the construction of a border wall, much less make Mexico pay for it. Radical reductions in illegal migration were predicated on his initial bombast and administrative orders to energize immigration enforcements, but those steps had a brief shelf life. If no concrete border wall was to be approved by Congress, Trump would suffer considerable political damage with his base by not delivering on his signature campaign issue, especially if he relented on guest worker and DACA issues involving allowing youths brought illegally into the country by their parents to avoid deportation by proof of good works.

Trump had seemingly forgotten that borders were open not just because of Democratic demographic strategy and the identity-politics industry. The Republican Congress was in large part beholden to corporate interests that demanded access to cheap labor, subsidized by the state's social welfare apparatus. Left and Right were terrified of a wall, given that such fences and barriers abroad and throughout history had a good record of securing borders. And yet without a wall, it proved difficult to turn back serial caravans of illegal aliens from Central America—given unimpeded transit through Mexico and the bad optics of using military force to break up huge columns surging over the border.

In one of the strangest political developments in recent memory, a Republican House and Senate could not dismantle the once widely unpopular Affordable Care Act, although almost all Republicans had for years vigorously campaigned on instant repeal the moment they captured the presidency and retained majorities in the Congress. The late John McCain's personal animus for Trump perhaps explains why his "no" vote on repeal derailed, by a single vote, the Trump health care reform/repeal effort.

While the individual mandate for health insurance was eliminated in the new tax law, and other elements of Obamacare eroded by cabinet-level directives, Trump was unable to do much about the reality that Americans had suffered huge increases over the last few years in their health insurance premiums, deductibles, and co-pays—often to the point of despairing whether their plans could be defined as insurance at all.

No one could predict the size of the 2018 budget deficit. Some estimates suggested that even with 3 percent per annum growth, it could reach somewhere between $500 billion and $1 trillion. Slashing taxes, increasing defense spending, and ignoring preset spiraling entitlement costs were traditionally considered unsustainable in a nation burdened with $21 trillion in existing debt and a huge cohort of baby boomers retiring at an approximate rate of ten thousand a day.

The last two two-term presidents had doubled the debt over their respective eight-year tenures. It was unclear whether the nation could endure a third such presidency—at least without massive cuts in entitlement expenditures, discretionary spending, and near permanent low-interest rates to allow the huge debt to be serviced without warping the budget. Part of the uncertainty involved the effect of massive growth of the economy providing record revenues, and whether such largess in and of itself would drive down the deficit without massive cuts in domestic spending. In Trump's case, as the economy heated up, the Treasury announced record receipts of monthly revenues, but without much change overall in the budget deficit, given the failure to deal with expanding Social Security, Medicare, and

Medicaid entitlements, as well as increases in defense and domestic spending.

What accounted for Trump's occasional legislative failures?

His past feuding with primary election rivals and his present attacks on an anemic Republican congressional leadership (in early 2018, House Speaker Paul Ryan announced his intention to retire from Congress) vitiated any chance that Trump could count on 100 percent support from his Republican congressional contingent. Yet such near absolute fealty was necessary to pass legislation, given Trump's own failure in his first eighteen months to have achieved, for any sustained period, a 50 percent popularity rating. The relatively thin Republican margins he enjoyed in the House and Senate were plagued by apostates and a few holdover anti-Trump representatives and senators. Standing up to Trump "on principle" by voting against a presidential initiative or appointee—especially in the cases of Senators Corker, Flake, McCain, and Paul—was always an enticement for Republican congressional establishmentarians, at least as long as Trump did not have a majority approval rating and struggled with such a thin Republican majority in the Senate.

As mentioned, some of Trump's dismal poll ratings were due to 90 percent negative media coverage. But the remedies for rectifying such bias were limited. To gain enough clout to keep the Congress Republican in the 2018 midterm elections, or to ensure the president could work with the congressional leadership to herd members to unify and thus pass legislation by narrow margins, meant that Trump himself would have to either defer more to individual congressional members, prune his more outrageous tweeting, radically jack up his polls to over 50 percent, or create such momentum with economic and foreign policy successes that opposing him would prove politically foolish.

One of the great disconnects in the Trump presidency was the charge that he was both unfit for the presidency and yet had recruited rare talents as advisors and cabinet secretaries, particularly in matters of national security. Or put simplistically, Trump managed to find insider outsiders who distrusted, and were often distrusted by, the establishment, but enjoyed strong pedigrees that meant they could not be written off as cranks.

Defense secretary James Mattis had been previously let go by Barack Obama as the head of Central Command—without a phone call. Yet at retirement in 2013, he was generally considered America's foremost four-star general. Trump's third national security advisor, John Bolton, had never been able to win Senate confirmation for his 2005 recess appointment as George W. Bush's ambassador to the UN. Bolton might have been despised by Democrats, but not on grounds that he was either unknowledgeable or incapable.

Outspoken ambassador Nikki Haley, who announced her retirement effective at the end of 2018, replayed the role that Jean Kirkpatrick had once crafted at the UN. But if she lacked Kirkpatrick's intellectual heft, she more than compensated by being younger, a canny former two-term governor of South Carolina, and as quick as Kirkpatrick in repartee and toughness. Trump's second secretary of state, Mike Pompeo, was confirmed with the votes of only seven Democratic senators, given his outspoken opposition to the Iran deal as well as his unapologetic Christian evangelicalism. Yet Pompeo's background was nearly surreal in its breadth: top in his class at West Point, US Army captain, Harvard Law School graduate, independent entrepreneur, four times elected to Congress, and CIA director.

Trump had eventually discovered that there were all kinds of talented conservatives with vast experience who had not been fully appreciated by prior Republican administrations. One thing all four of his replacement foreign policy team members shared was an outspokenness and candor that had gotten all of them in prior trouble—and thus in Trump's own good graces.

After nearly two years in office Trump had also destroyed a number of Washington assumptions and diminished status quo protocols (the Palestinians were "refugees," the International Criminal Court was worth cooperating with, supporting the Paris climate accord was critical), from the trivial to the existential, and gotten himself into controversies beyond those of most prior presidents. Trumpism, remember, was never billed as a change in presidential administration or as marking a Republican renaissance. Rather, it was sold as an assault on the entire bipartisan culture of the elite "swamp" establishment by someone who had no prior investments in anything to do with the cultural landscape of Washington politics. In that sense, media and cultural elites were certainly warranted in fearing Trump and what he represented. He marked not so much a conservative reformation, much less a renaissance, as a wrecking ball that would leave to others to rebuild what he had felt long deserved to be dismantled.

After Trump's election, rumors grew that celebrities and millionaires, from Oprah Winfrey to Mark Cuban, were being mentioned as possible presidential candidates for 2020. Mayors like Michael Bloomberg (who poured his riches into defeating Republican candidates in the 2018 midterms) were pondering runs. Critics would say that Trump's loutishness so enraged the public that now almost anyone thought they could do a better job as president. Supporters would counter that Trump proved no worse than deep-state careerist politicians and had helped the country's return to the lost idea of citizen amateur public servants. For all the talk of a Barack Obama or Hillary Clinton smashing racial and gender barriers, no one had ever contemplated breaking the strongest impediment of them all: an absence of *all* prior military service and/or political office holding.

The old *cursus honorum* to the presidency—congressional representative, senator, or governor—was shattered. Trump proved, in defeating the most seasoned, well-funded, and connected Democratic candidate in a generation, that any celebrity in theory could be elected without prior military and political office. Washington found that frightening. Half the country saw it as liberating.

Many of Washington's cultural and political institutions popular during past administrations were nearly diminished in Trump's wild first two years of tweeting and *ex tempore* editorializing. The popularity of Hollywood, the universities, the National Football League, and the public's polled trust in the media only further declined—the more rapidly members of these groups seemed to be completely obsessed with Trump.

For a minor example of such psychodramas, consider again Trump's ongoing boycotts of the 104-year-old White House Correspondents' Dinner, an annual event at which the president joshed with often hostile White House correspondents. But Trump understood that most of his White House press coverage was now not just negative but hysterical. The event had long ago degenerated into a celebrity schmooze fest between actors, athletes, star-struck journalists, and politicos. And not much remained of the hallowed tradition except a media- and entertainment-driven comedic bashing of conservatives.

Trump skipped both the 2017 and 2018 dinners, and leveraged the absences to his advantage. While elite journalists made vulgar jokes, trashed the appearance of conservatives, and signaled their politically correct virtue to one another, Trump went into the heartland, socializing with his preferred company of deplorables, and bashed the correspondents' self-indulgences: "I was invited to another event tonight, the White House Correspondents' Dinner. But I'd much rather be at Washington, Michigan, than in Washington, D.C., right now—that I can tell you."

Trump brought nontraditional bloggers and hinterland reporters into the White House briefings. He skipped regular press conferences, only to appear suddenly at strange places amid reporters to conduct his own ad hoc question and answer sessions. In fireside-chat style, Trump tweeted daily to the public and answered almost any question a reporter screamed at him while entering and exiting the White House. He scripted and filmed his own cabinet meetings, as if they were episodes of *The Apprentice*. Trump knew that, in the age of reality television, Americans no longer could easily distinguish between reality and canned representations of reality.

All presidents have held election-cycle rallies. But, uniquely, Trump never ceased his, making appearances well beyond 2016. They continued as choreographed populist love fests in purple swing states, where Trump reminded the nation that those who won him the election were still as ecstatic over his victory as the elites whom he encountered in Washington remained irate.

Trump blasted "fake news" daily. But when nine out of ten stories that were reported on the White House were negative, the president had some reason to become suspicious, if not embittered. Oddly, Trump began to claim support for his defiance from a number of unexpected, if not outright weird, developments. The number of FBI and DOJ officials who were reassigned, quit, or retired in connection with suspicious conduct during the 2016 election cycle grew. In addition, a few federal judges at times began to question the ethics of the Mueller investigation in matters of the Manafort and Flynn indictments and confessions, respectively.

While there was no clear cause and effect relationship, the careers of a number of luminaries in the New York and Washington media abruptly imploded. And whereas Trump was still standing after unprecedented media criticism, many members of the press, as well as celebrity and legal powerhouses, were not. Many had voiced their utter disgust, or at least dislike, of Trump. Yet by 2018 they themselves were facing ostracism or disgrace, mostly on charges of sexual harassment or outright assault. Among the many who lost their jobs or were tarred with feminist vituperation, both conservative and liberal, were the once unquestioned media progressive establishmentarians Tom Brokaw, Chris Cillizza, Matt Lauer, Ryan Lizza, Charlie Rose,

and Tavis Smiley, as well as conservatives such as Fox News luminaries Bill O'Reilly and Eric Bolling. Former Fox anchorwoman
and Trump critic Megyn Kelly was fired from NBC for clumsily
referencing Halloween costumes. The fierce anti-Trump cru-
sader New York attorney general Eric Schneiderman resigned
after being accused of sexual assault by a number of women.
Hollywood celebrities who obsessed over Trump and voiced
an elemental hatred of him—such as Jim Carrey, Lena Dunham,
Samuel L. Jackson, Madonna, Rosie O'Donnell, and Robert De
Niro—on occasion found their own popularity waning.

Meanwhile, Trump found support from unlikely progressive
quarters, such as former liberal and soon to be disgraced actress Roseanne Barr, marquee rapper Kanye West, and newly
minted conservative and black activist Candace Owens. What
most scared Trump's Democratic opponents was his potential
appeal along class rather than racial lines. By recalibrating illegal immigration as unfair to the job aspirations of inner-city
blacks and second-generation Mexican Americans, by selling
his deregulation and tax cuts as efforts to create jobs and higher
incomes for the stubbornly unemployed, and by reminding
America that Trump liked to build things and to hire workers
and buy American products, Trump, in theory, at some future
date thought that he could capture 20 percent of the black vote
and perhaps 40 percent of the Latino electorate. Polls showing
increased minority support for Trump suggested that Trump in
2020 might well siphon off traditional Democratic minority voters. Yet given the hemorrhaging of the white working class from
the Democratic Party, progressives could not afford *any* defec-
tions from their monolithic rainbow coalition. But Trump's
"Make America Great Again" became subversive if it were to be
translated among the poor as something akin to "Make the Poor
Wealthy Too."

Trump also openly bashed both his own party leadership
and inexplicably even his own cabinet officers. Even-handed

invective left observers perplexed as to whether his apparently suicidal behavior explained why his aggregate polls remained in the low forties after occasionally nearing 50 percent, or whether such fickleness kept his team guessing and eager to avoid publicly leaking confidential information or crossing their boss. At various times, House Speaker Paul Ryan, Senate Majority Leader Mitch McConnell, Attorney General Jeff Sessions, and cabinet secretaries like former secretary of state Rex Tillerson were directly attacked by Trump for supposed lethargic displays of loyalty, often in cruel and adolescent fashion. The Republican weariness with such internecine invective might explain in part the dismal record of the Republican Congress that in 2017–18 squandered its majorities and ended up only with tax reform and little other major legislation.

More substantively, Trump blew up the Israeli-Palestinian deadlock. Once he unilaterally announced transfer of the American embassy to Jerusalem, a number of other countries expressed their intention of following suit. He periodically threatened to cut off all US aid to the Palestinians and eventually trimmed most of it. He recalibrated alliances with the Gulf monarchies and both Egypt and Jordan on the subtext that they agreed that Iran was the common existential enemy of both Arabs and Jews. In that regard, Trump argued that the Palestinians, recipients of millions in US aid, should worry less about Israel and fret more about their own economic development and their occasional dangerous flirtations with Iranian interests.

Trump walked away from the Paris climate accord. When critics sought to damn him for such heterodoxy, they were left defending a mostly empty agreement that did nothing concrete to reduce carbon emissions. A prior treaty that, in fact, had more muscularly addressed human-induced global warming was the so-called 1997 Kyoto accord. Yet the US Senate, including *every* Democratic member, had voted 95-0 in favor of the so-called Byrd-Hagel Resolution that voiced disapproval of the accord,

ensuring that the United States became the only signatory that
had not ratified the agreement.

Meanwhile, thanks to American frackers, American oil and
natural gas supplies soared, and with them far cleaner electri-
cal generation. No wonder that in the most recent year of re-
cording (2016–17), the United States had reduced its carbon
dioxide emissions by 2 percent (due largely to increased natural gas availability and a reduction in coal-fired generation
plants), while the European Union's greenhouse gas emissions
increased by 1.6 percent.

Most experts had known that the Obama-led Iran deal was
unworkable and thus unsustainable, given that it was passed off
as a nontreaty to bypass the need for Senate ratification. It certainly did not allow open and snap inspections of all Iranian
nuclear sites. It did nothing about Iran's growing ballistic missile program. It did not deter Iranian terrorism and regional aggression.

Once Trump crashed the deal, new disturbing disclosures
arose about the Iran deal's cash for hostages. In addition, it was
learned that the Obama administration had sought to undermine US banking laws to facilitate the transference of released
Iranian funds into Western currencies. And newly embittered
and spiteful Iranians claimed that Iran had, in fact, empowered
the al-Qaeda terrorists who murdered three thousand Americans on September 11, 2001.

Yet conventional diplomatic wisdom demanded that the
accords, arranged by Obama's presidential fiat, be honored.
Renewed scrutiny of its accords followed that led most to be
reminded why the deal was flawed—well aside from its flagrant
bypassing of Senate ratification, and the *ex post facto* boasts of
some of its architects that they had created an "echo chamber"
among "know nothing" reporters to advance their untenable
pro-deal narratives. Trump suggested that the fear of a likely Iranian bomb would have to be met in the future either with regime

change, a preemptive strike, or, as most wished, by reinstitution of sanctions leading to the slow collapse of the revolutionary theocracy.

Trump further argued that the agreement had sent billions of dollars in cash into Iranian coffers, which explained why Hezbollah, the Assad government in Syria, and Shiite militias in Yemen were all at war and ascendant. In truth, it was likely that Iran would *not* have obtained a nuclear weapon anyway in the ensuing ten years without the deal *if* sanctions had just been continued and tightened, which had already led to increasing civil unrest and diplomatic ostracism of Iran.

In fact, Iran had always likely assumed from its one-sided agreement that, once freed from sanctions, it could build up cash reserves during its decade of nonproliferation compliance, use its newfound income to advance its ballistic and cruise missile programs, subsidize terrorism and insurrections, build a Shia crescent through Syria and Lebanon, and all the while accelerate nuclear research and technology. And then, after a decade of prosperity amid technological advances, the Iranians could develop a weapon quite quickly.

When a president of the United States publicly dusts off dandruff from the coat of a visiting French president or reminds a North Korean madcap dictator that he has a bigger nuclear button than what is found in Pyongyang, then chaos reigns. The result is either a managed chaos that brings dividends of confusing and keeping off guard rivals and enemies of the United States, or a destructive chaos that eventually leads to more disorder and dangerous misdirection. The first year at times brought both.

In sum, the Trump foreign policy and domestic doctrines, if such formal things existed, were simple.

What Trump inherited abroad as "normal"—the Iranian deal, the Palestinians as key to Middle East calm, a nuclear North Korea with missiles pointed at the United States, a mercantilist China cheating on trade and bullying its neighbors, outreach to Cuba, Nicaragua, and Venezuela, adoration of the European Union, an empowered Russia appeased by past reset diplomacy, acceptance of the European shortfall on contractual military obligations—was abnormal. The credentialed experts who crafted or accepted these realities as normal were themselves not so expert, and practiced a sort of chaos of their own.

At home, the old consensus—peacetime unemployment would not dip below 4 percent, the gross domestic product could not exceed 3 percent growth per annum, structural impediments prevented minority unemployment from dipping below 6 percent—was just as flawed. Academics, politicians, think-tank scholars, and insider marquee journalists had created an echo chamber, driven by near-obsessive collective hatred of Trump. Groupthink was still groupthink, no matter how mellifluous and degreed its practitioners.

When Trump threw his sledgehammer into the fragile establishment glass screen of conventional wisdom, it did not mean that his own innate cunning was necessarily superior wisdom. After all, it is easier to wield a crude weapon than to build elegant technology. Rather, as an insurrectionist, Trump was arguing that the old order was calcified and not worthy of the esteem and reputation that it demanded, given the questionable results it had achieved.

Whether Trump can construct something superior to what he has discredited will be the story of his presidency. By his second year in office, politically not much had changed. Half the country abhorred the idea that on any given day President Donald Trump could say and do almost anything anywhere. Half the nation was liberated, if not exhilarated, by that reality.

It would be left to his actual record of governance to heal or widen the sharp divide between two increasingly geographically and economically distinct Americas.

PART FIVE
EPILOGUE

TRUMP TRUDGES ON

The 2018 Midterms and Beyond

As 2018 ended, the country remained as bitterly divided as when Trump entered office in January 2017. The general fault lines remained unchanged. A mostly upscale and coastal urban professional and educated elite was politically aligned with minorities and the poor. They were usually opposed by suburban conservatives and a rural and small-town middle class in the nation's interior.

Trump had neither expanded his appeal to include more independents or suburban women, nor had he lost a scintilla of his rock-hard base. Consequently, the 2018 post-election red-blue schema of congressional districts more or less resembled the Electoral College map of 2016: a sea of red in the interior of America was more than matched in population size by the far smaller blue geography of the two coastal corridors.

Throughout the summer and early autumn of 2018, election experts had often predicted a massive blue wave of radical progressive pushback against Trump in the 2018 midterms: the long-awaited negative referendum on both his agenda and behavior, and thus at last an overdue reckoning for his entire Twitter-fueled presidency.

The Democratic tsunami against the incumbent president was promised to be analogous to the wipeout suffered by President Bill Clinton after his first two years (fifty-three House, eight Senate seats), or Barack Obama's even more disastrous 2010 loss (sixty-three House, six Senate seats). The nonstop media attacks on Trump, still consistent with the 90 percent negative news coverage of his first few months in office, had certainly seemed to energize Democrats.

Indeed, by election eve, Democrats, in the preponderant manner of the 2016 campaign, had raised a record $1 billion for state, House, and Senate midterm races, with hundreds of millions more garnered by the progressive political action committees. Turnout in some states set records for any president's first midterm election.

Eleven days before the election, on Saturday, October 27, a vicious shooting rampage by an unhinged alt-right and anti-Semitic terrorist (and Trump opponent) inside a Pittsburgh synagogue left eleven worshippers dead. Four days earlier, a series of inert bombs delivered to liberal politicians and celebrities (by an unbalanced professed Trump supporter) was still being portrayed in the media as the logical result of Trump's bitter war with journalists and the Left. These last-minute tragic episodes tended to overshadow the prior conservative outrage over progressives' harsh treatment of Supreme Court nominee Brett Kavanaugh. In sum, the blue wave was thought by progressives still to be cresting on election day.

Yet, for all their premature self-congratulation, record campaign spending, and media blitz, the Democrats in strictly statistical terms had done historically not all that much better than most opposition parties in a president's first term.

The usual midterm congressional losses for a first-term president since 1934 have averaged about twenty-five House and two Senate seats. Trump lost thirty House seats (the number will likely increase when recounts are finished) and with them control of the House itself. But he picked up two Senate seats, one of the more respectable Senate gains by an incumbent president in his first midterm since Franklin Roosevelt's nine-seat pickup during the 1934 referendum on the New Deal.

By historical standards, Trump's wins and losses meant that he had performed better in his first midterm election than had Bill Clinton and Barack Obama. Both former presidents had gone on to win handily their reelections.

Trump's favorability polls, while gyrating widely, were roughly equivalent to those of his Democratic predecessors at a similar time in their presidencies. Trump likely lost control of the House for the generic reasons that all presidents in their first terms on average lose twenty-five seats in the House: supporters grow complacent in victory, while in defeat overzealous opponents become more eager for a rematch.

The Republican Congress, thanks in part to a late spoiler vote by the late Senator John McCain, had failed to repeal and replace the Affordable Care Act, as once monotonously and simplistically promised. The result was that in 2018 there was no chance that unpopular soaring premiums, deductibles, and co-payments would become cheaper through more competition and a diversity of plans among private insurers, but a greater likelihood that talk of ending Obamacare without a replacement could be used to frighten voters that at least expensive Obamacare was better than no care at all.

By losing the House, Trump also faced the possibility of successful impeachment proceedings. In terms of partisan advantage, he perhaps hoped the optics of such a future event would reveal another Brett Kavanaugh–like progressive circus. Trump in 2019 certainly would no longer be able to pass any legislation akin to his tax reform act, and would have to increasingly rule by executive order or pickup support from Democratic representatives by compromises likely unpalatable to his base. New Democratic majority chairs of key House committees promised to reboot their past efforts to refocus investigations on Trump himself and jam the administration with endless subpoenas and requests for documents.

On the other hand, by slightly increasing his lead in the Senate with new, more conservative senators-elect, Trump had also marginalized somewhat the prior leverage of moderate Republican senators who had won concessions by threatening to oppose the administration's agenda. Trump's ability to conduct treaties overseas and confirm judges in the Senate was strengthened by the midterms. And he now clearly would never be convicted in the Senate and removed from office if impeached by the House.

So what had happened to the Democrats' predicted blue wave that supposedly would rack up huge House majorities and win back the entire Congress? And why did not $1 billion in campaign spending and a 13-1 negative to positive ratio of NBC/MSNBC and CNN media coverage of the presidency neuter Trump or his party after two years of governance?

The answers to those questions were thematic throughout this book. Aside from popular anguish over the way Democratic senators had savaged Supreme Court nominee Brett Kavanaugh, and worries over another larger immigration caravan of asylum seekers inching toward the southern border, voters in November 2018 were still uncomfortable with progressive politics and happy with the Trump economic boom. In statewide races, almost all hard progressive gubernatorial and senatorial candidates, from Florida to Texas, lost, if often narrowly so.

First, Trump's economic and foreign policy initiatives since 2017, if examined dispassionately, had been largely those centrist conservative agendas that had worked in the past, and continued to do so in the present. Unlike other past flash-in-the-pan mavericks, like former California governor Arnold Schwarzenegger or Minnesota's recent governor Jesse Ventura, Trump adopted traditional conservative issues and learned, if belatedly, to work with the Republican Congress to enact them. In counterintuitive fashion, the provocative and often off-putting Trump proved to be a far more effective uniter of his party than had any prior elected populist maverick.

Second, Americans continued to defy pollsters and pundits, at least at the local and state levels. Even without Trump on the ballot, Americans still were far more likely to voice their anti-Trump sympathies than their pro-Trump affinities—a lesson from 2016 that the media continued to ignore or perhaps to dream could not possibly occur twice in succession, despite their own habit of demonizing those who supported Trump and sanctifying those who despised him. As a result, many of the state and local pre-election polls in the key senatorial and gubernatorial races in Florida, Georgia, Indiana, and Missouri proved inaccurate.

Finally, the public weariness with political correctness, the desire for pushback against the administrative state, and the turnoff from progressives' 24/7 venom had not yet peaked. True, most of the country continued to see Trump as near-toxic chemotherapy, but half the nation also felt that such strong medicine was still necessary to deal with lethal tumors of the status quo.

As 2018 ended, the only mystery was whether the Democratic Party, after its failed rage of 2016 and its mixed midterm record of 2018, would learn from its errors. Many centrist Democratic House candidates, lots of them with military records, did well in the midterms, while solidifying the allegiances of minority and educated suburban women voters. In contrast, most blinkered Democrats in swing states, who as radical progressives doubled down on abolishing Immigration and Customs Enforcement, promoting Medicare for all, cancelling student debt, and impeaching Trump, faltered.

Nonetheless, it was uncertain whether the Democrats in 2020 would nominate another George McGovern–like leftist rather than correct toward the center with a candidate akin to Jimmy Carter or Bill Clinton, who had regained them the presidency for a collective three terms. Old-hand Democrats thought they knew how they could retake political power as their victory in the House suggested, but that pragmatic remedy for the new party base was felt to be worse than the disease of seeing Trump continue to dominate his opponents.

In terms of actual Trump governance, since the final draft of this manuscript was finished in September 2018, nothing much had changed by the time of the 2018 midterm elections. The third-quarter 2018 economic and monthly employment reports continued to set near records. The economy grew between July and September 2018 at a 3.5 percent clip, the first time in a decade that it had exceeded 3 percent growth over a consecutive twelve-month period.

In October alone, the economy added a quarter million new jobs, including *one thousand manufacturing jobs a day*. Unemployment still held steady at 3.7 percent, the lowest peacetime jobless rate in a half century. There were more unfilled jobs than the number of those unemployed. Wages grew 3.1 percent in 2018. Such an increase had not been seen since a temporary spike in the immediate 2009 aftermath of the financial crisis.

Most interesting, the number of Americans collecting unemployment benefits fell to just 1.63 million, *the lowest since 1973 when there were 120 million fewer Americans!* The public may not have become "tired of winning" as Trump had once promised, but growing economic tranquility and prosperity in an ironic sense were increasingly taken for granted by voters. Oddly, that sense of well-being allowed them to refocus on other social and cultural issues, and not always to Trump's advantage. Rarely had a president proved so successful in policy and yet so disliked in person, and so unable to translate far better times into far more votes. None of his supporters had figured out how Trump could curb his invective while still battling the "swamp" and energizing his base, much less whether Trump would even if he could.

Abroad, monthly incidents of Iranian hazing of US forces in the Persian Gulf remained nonexistent. North Korea had kept its moratorium on missile launches. China began to talk of trade negotiations after steadily increasing US tariffs and global worries of a destructive trade war. Mexico and Canada agreed to finish the NAFTA reset. Due to systematic Russian cheating and chronic violations, Trump also cancelled the 1987 Intermediate-Range Nuclear Forces Treaty that had prevented the United States and Russia from deploying ground-launched cruise missiles with ranges of 300 to 3,400 miles. By the end of 2018, Trump's hard-nose policies toward Moscow had completely replaced the Obama-era reset with Vladimir Putin—ironic when Trump at the same time was still being accused of appeasing Putin.

In its seventy-sixth week of investigation, the Mueller probe of alleged Russian-Trump collusion in the 2016 election continued—and continued to energize progressives, after the Democratic victory in the House, with the normal fare of daily leaked disclosures, and likely future indictments, despite no new discoveries concerning Russian election collaboration with Donald Trump to defeat Hillary Clinton, the original mandate of the special counsel investigation. The Mueller final report was promised by year's end, and few knew whether it would fuel or stymie impeachment proceedings.

Of course, the good economic and foreign policy news had not always been the theme of the 2018 elections, due to the hysterias of Trump critics and Trump's own furious don't-tread-on-me retaliatory salvos. Trump himself continued his tweet storms—and continued his anomaly of earning positive polls on his job performance and serial negative polls on his likeability. He persisted in near-daily Twitter duels with celebrities, Democratic politicos, and former Obama and Bush administration intelligence officials like John Brennan, James Clapper, and Michael Hayden, who variously called him near treasonous and, in the case of Hayden, Nazi-like.

Indeed, in the final days before the elections, former vice president Joe Biden once again talked of violence to Trump or his supporters. The new face of the Democratic Party, socialist Alexandria Ocasio-Cortez, attacked Trump and his congressional Republican allies as "cold-hearted monsters." Former president Barack Obama was still busy on the campaign trail, and continued to call Trump a shameless and serial liar, even as he claimed credit for the Trump economic miracle more than twenty-one months after leaving office and failing for eight years to achieve a single comparable twelve-month period of 3 percent GDP growth. The major Democratic senatorial and gubernatorial candidates in Florida and Georgia for whom Obama stumped the hardest lost their election bids. Through it all, Trump saw his popularity remain steady in the mid-forties— even as he alienated more suburban centrist voters. In the RealClearPolitics.com aggregate of early November, Trump earned a 44 percent positive rating; the Rasmussen Reports daily tracking poll had Trump at a 51 percent approval rating.

What then was next? Impeachment was promised in 2019. The establishment once again believed that an uncouth Trump was done for, even as he seemed to have grown ever stronger by weathering ever more attacks. In sum, the Trump paradox remained as much a mystery to his progressive critics as it always had—and perhaps always will.

INDEX

ABOUT THE AUTHOR

Victor Davis Hanson is the Martin and Illie Anderson senior fellow in classics and military history at the Hoover Institution, Stanford University, and a professor emeritus of classics at California State University, Fresno. He is the author of more than two dozen books, ranging in topics from ancient Greece to modern America, most recently *The Second World Wars: How the First Global Conflict Was Fought and Won*. He lives in Selma, California.